ANTIQUES
ROADSHOW

ANTIQUES
ROADSHOW

YOUR GUIDE TO ANTIQUES BY
THE BBC TEAM OF EXPERTS

BBC

A Marshall Edition

Published by BBC Books, a division of
BBC Enterprises Ltd,
Woodlands, 80 Wood Lane
London W12 OTT

First published 1992
ISBN 0 563 36752 0

Edited and designed by
Marshall Editions
170 Piccadilly
London W1V 9DD

Editor	Mary Devine
Consultant Editor	Mike Crossman
Art Editors	Helen James
	Roger Kohn
DTP Editor	Mary Pickles
Design assistant	Micky Pledge
Illustrator	Coral Mula
Production	Barry Baker
	Nikki Ingram
	Janice Storr
Photography	Norman Brand
	Clive Corless
Indexer	Anne Yelland

Originated by Scantrans Pte Limited,
Singapore
Type file by Dorchester Typesetting
Group
Printed and bound by Mohndruck
Graphische Betriebe GmbH

Valuation is an imprecise art and prices
vary for many reasons. The valuations
given are estimated auction prices from
1992. Since auctions take place in the
public arena, this is considered to be
the fairest method of valuation.

The *Antiques Roadshow* book is based
on The Antiques Roadshow Collection:
conceived by Wallington, Irving,
Jackson Ltd; edited and designed by
Marshall Editions Developments Ltd,
and published for BBC Enterprises by
Eaglemoss Publications Ltd.

Antiques Roadshow is a trademark of the
British Broadcasting Corporation and is
used under licence.

CONTENTS

FOREWORD 6
HUGH SCULLY

INTRODUCTION 7
CHRISTOPHER LEWIS

ROADSHOW GALLERY 10

A selection of favourite paintings and
illustrations from the 1992 Roadshows,
including Pre-Raphaelite portraits, animal
paintings, works by modern British and
Canadian artists, paintings of ships, works
by Helen Allingham and sisters Maud and
Alice West, and a poignant Christmas card
painted by Rex Whistler.

FURNITURE 16
JOHN BLY

FOREWORD
HUGH SCULLY
PRESENTER

In May 1977 a group of antiques experts, with little knowledge of broadcasting, met a group of professional broadcasters, with even less knowledge of antiques, in Hereford Town Hall. They were all there to make a television programme, but neither the experts nor the broadcasters were quite sure what was going to happen next. Many of the essential ingredients of television production were missing, not least a script. In other circumstances, this in itself would have been courting disaster. A script is like a route map. It tells everyone in the cast and crew where they are going.

The programme they were to record that day was what is known in broadcasting as a 'pilot', and it was given the working title 'Antiques Roadshow'. Dozens of pilot programmes are commissioned that never see the light of day. However promising an idea might look on paper, it may not translate successfully on to the small screen. But by some alchemy, the simple formula of experts talking to owners about their treasured possessions became an overnight success, and unusually, that first pilot edition of *Antiques Roadshow* was transmitted to a receptive and appreciative audience. It has not looked back since and, with an average audience of 13 million people each week, it has joined the ranks of Britain's most favourite programmes.

I am often asked to explain why the programme is such a runaway success and I always give the same reply. It is a programme that is as much about people as it is about antiques, and it is their charm and humour that makes it so very watchable. I often describe the programme as a conversation between two people with 13 million eavesdroppers.

There are other elements too, not least the valuations. In the second series there were fewer valuations than there had been before, and postbags full of complaints were received from viewers who thought that the valuations, and the looks of astonishment, or barely supressed disappointment, on the faces of the owners, were an essential ingredient in the Roadshow's rich and popular mix. Values are important because they give people a yardstick by which to judge an object. If a painting or a piece of porcelain is said to be worth a great deal of money, most of us want to know why. Our interest is aroused, and we listen to the experts with a keener ear.

In this lavishly illustrated book, with the superb photography of Clive Corless and Norman Brand, you will also find your attention drawn to the values and, like me, you will no doubt reproach yourself for not having taken the opportunity to buy some of these beautiful things when they were cheap. But you will at least have the satisfaction of knowing that, in buying this unique record of the many hidden treasures we have uncovered on the *Antiques Roadshow*, you have made a sound investment that will provide many hours of interest and enjoyment.

INTRODUCTION
CHRISTOPHER LEWIS
EXECUTIVE PRODUCER

After a visit to the show one of our many friendly 'customers' wrote: 'Please suppress my bit if it looks as if I am just flirting with the expert!' She needn't have worried. If she was flirting it didn't show. She simply appeared as excited as the expert concerned when he examined her fine 18th century silver rat-tail spoon.

A small proportion of the day's interesting finds at an *Antiques Roadshow* do not, sadly, survive the concentrated editing process that follows the recording day. We record slightly more than we can fit into the programme for a variety of reasons, the most obvious being that the treasures people bring to the show don't always arrive in the right order – we record one thing, then suddenly along comes a better one. Another reason for recording extra items is the balance of the programme. Each edition must have a range of objects to suit all tastes. In mentioning this, I am lamenting limitations imposed within a programme lasting a mere 44 minutes and 15 seconds. I am delighted that this book includes some of the wonderful objects that never quite made it on to the screen for no other reason than the shape of the programme on that particular day.

Recent audience research suggests that the programme has the balance about right, though some people want more militaria, others more furniture, and still others want to see Hilary Kay no matter what object she's describing. John Bly, too, has a particularly strong following, while David Battie's clear explanations and directness of style make him a television 'natural'.

The most common request from viewers is for more 'miscellaneous items', the things you and I own which we've never quite brought ourselves to throw away, which pass through a period of obsolescence in attics and garages to re-emerge as 'interesting' objects 20 years on. This book includes many such items, and I'm grateful for

◁ **MEADOWS TANKARD** *This inscribed wager tankard, given by the King of Denmark to Sir Philip Meadows in 1662, was brought to the Roadshow by a descendant of the recipient. It was valued at £20,000 – £25,000.*

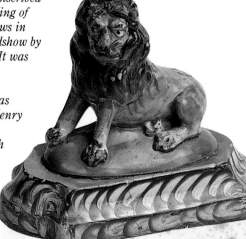

▷ **ENGLISH LION** *This lion was left over after a jumble sale. Henry Sandon declared him English, dated around 1870, and worth an astonishing £800.*

▷ **VOLCANO** *The owner of this Jules Tavernier painting of a Hawaiian volcano was astonished and delighted when it was valued at £10,000.*

▽ **LAMP** *Probably Italian, certainly made in the '20s, this wonderful lamp represents, in moulded glass, a lemon tree. It was valued at £200 – £300.*

◁ **PEMBROKE TABLE** *An 18th century Pembroke table inlaid with shells and flower heads in satinwood (view of top below), with the unusual feature of a baize-lined writing or brushing slide. It was valued at £15,000 – £20,000.*

its guidance when perusing local car boot sales.

One of the special features of the Roadshow is the way seemingly worthless objects suddenly hit the jackpot – like 'Ozzie the Owl', an undiscovered 17th century slipware owl jug which sold for £20,000 a few years ago. This year at the Roadshow a couple of primitive early English pieces turned up, both of them fragile pottery, and as such, miracles of survival. A late 18th century Elephant & Castle money box was worth far more than it could possibly contain, and a valuable creamware lion of similar age, remaindered at a jumble sale for just 25p, cheerfully attracted Henry Sandon's knowledgeable eye – even without its tail! Early English pottery, although often crude and rustic, is one field of collecting in which – had I Henry's knowledge – I would surely indulge. But collectors should beware, there are fakes about.

Fakes seldom turn up at the Roadshow, except for those very attractive Samson of Paris copies of 18th century Sèvres, Meissen and Chelsea Gold Anchor. Most of these were in fact merely reproductions, not attempts to deceive, and today they are collectable in their own right.

Our pictures experts saw several photographs which had been coloured over in oil paints, sometimes even stuck down on to canvas, resulting in paintings so realistic-looking that I found it almost impossible to spot that they were not genuine. Other items that didn't ring quite true included numerous Stradivarius violins, though it

△ **GOLD PLAQUE** *Without fail every series turns up an astounding object – like this 16th century Italian plaque in chased gold relief by the artist Guilliemo della Porta. Its value? At least £30,000.*

▽ **THE COLLAR OF A KNIGHT GRAND CROSS OF THE ORDER OF ST MICHAEL AND ST GEORGE** *Since 1948 all such collars have been required to be returned on the death of the recipient. (It was valued at £3,000.)*

must be said that many of those instruments were very playable and by no means valueless, and their misleading labels 'Stradivari fecit Cremona' were more a celebration of Stradivarius' genius than a serious attempt at deception.

Every year a few of our recordings stand out in my memory. A lady in Farnham brought us two pieces of painted furniture, one a 19th century revival, the other an 18th century original. Her joy at John Bly's enthusiastic explanation of the differences between the two pieces was only exceeded by her curiosity about the bronze figure she had also brought, which seemed to baffle our experts. Sebastian Pearson spent much time agonizing over the quality of the bronze. He thought it might be very good, but couldn't be sure. Six months later, the bronze, identified as 17th century and with its pair in the possession of a relative of the owner, is to be sold at auction with an estimate of £20,000 to £25,000. I'm proud that this difficult and fascinating object did not quite elude us. Our experts have the essential 'nose' to spot such rare objects.

The items pictured here show the extraordinary diversity of items that are brought to the Roadshow each series.

Christopher Lewis

GALLERY

▷ *'Anna Maria Gaigl' by Johann Delfer (below are details of family coat-of arms, the sitter's name and age, the artist's signature and date). 1797. 32in x 44in.* **£2,500 – £3,500**

Agreat many pictures, some very valuable, others less so, were brought to the picture table at the *Antiques Roadshow* as it travelled the length and breadth of Great Britain. A selection of the Roadshow pictures, notable either because they were singled out for special attention by an expert or because their appearance caused something of a stir, are featured in this chapter.

Among the most memorable portraits were those in the style of the Pre-Raphaelites. A striking example was the oil painting of an elderly Swiss lady, Anna Maria Gaigl, which was brought to the Cleethorpes Roadshow. It was painted by Johann Delfer of Zurich, who is considered by some to be a rather unsophisticated artist. Part of this particular painting's charm, however, lies in its naivety, the element of simplicity working distinctly in its favour. The detail of the costume here is so beautifully rendered that it temporarily distracts the

△ *'The Expectant' by Charles Rossiter. 1854; 22in x 19in.* **£15,000**

▽ *'Charles Edward Perugini' by Frederick, Lord Leighton. 1850; 22in x 21in.* **£15,000 – £20,000**

▽ *'Spring' by Charles Edward Perugini. 1880s; 19in x 17in.* **£3,000 – £5,000**

△ *'The Butcher's Daughter' by Corbould. 1851.* **£3,000 – £5,000**

viewer from the face of the subject.

Another sombre yet moving portrait, this time at Alexandra Palace, was 'The Expectant', painted in oils in 1854 by Charles Rossiter. As well as being an artist, Rossiter was art master at Uppingham School. Taking as its theme the eternal poverty trap of working women in the 19th century, the picture shows a wistful young seamstress sitting by a window. Painted with careful attention to detail in the figuration of the wood panelling and in the food and flowers, the palette is similar to that of the old masters and the early Dutch masters.

Images of animals have proved perennially popular with Roadshow visitors and experts alike, and a splendid selection of pictures with animals as their theme was seen during the '92 series. When presented with artist Sam Spode's painting of the Duke of Wellington's famous charger, 'Copenhagen', expert Stephen Somerville couldn't decide whether the creature's open-eyed stare was that of a frightened or a frightening horse!

A charming oil painting of two donkeys in a coastal landscape by Belgian artist Edmond Joseph de Pratere, one of the 19th century's most highly regarded animal painters, was brought along to the Queensferry Roadshow. Although the sentimental tone of the painting is typically Victorian, the atmospheric rendering of the landscape is almost certainly influenced by the Hague school of painting.

The romanticization of rural life is again evident in Belgian artist Louis Verboeckhoven's farmyard scene of hens and ducks, and in this painting too the colour and composition are greatly influenced by Dutch landscape painting.

Landscapes by modern painters proved plentiful in 1992, and a particularly charming example was the evocative Provencal scene by Scottish artist John Maclaughlan Milne who lived in France in the 1920s and whose work is much admired today. The Orkney show turned up another fine modern landscape painting, this time by a Canadian painter, Alexander Young Jackson. Although the artist visited Europe frequently to paint, the

△ 'Copenhagen' by Sam Spode. Late 18th century; 14in x 17in. **£700 – £800**

◁ Donkeys in coastal scene by Edmond Joseph de Pratere. 1880; 35in x 48in. **£3,000 – £4,000**

▽ Farmyard scene with hens and ducks by Louis Verboeckhoven. 1866; 17in x 24in. **£3,000 – £4,000**

example of his work shown here is of a Canadian landscape. The experts at Orkney were hoping to see works by native artists, and they were delighted by one of Orcadian artist Stanley Cursiter's paintings. Influenced by both Post Impressionism and Modernism, Cursiter painted 'Beached Boats and a Hut at Yesnaby' when he was 18 years old.

'Gwain, Maid of Milford', seen at the Farnham show, is a typical example of a picture that would have been commissioned by a ship's master. Painted by the Neapolitan artist Niccolo Funni in gouache on paper, this charmingly naive work shows the Bay of Naples with Mount Vesuvius in the background.

Pictures of marine subjects are highly prized even when – as here – little is known about the artist. A

△ *Provencal scene by John Maclaughlan Milne. 1910; 16in x 23in.* **£2,000**

more dramatic depiction of a ship at sea was brought to the Queensferry show. The 'Miles Barton' was almost certainly painted by Joseph Heard, an artist renowned for his distinctive rendering of storm-tossed waves.

Although Scottish painter James Drummond is best known for historical paintings, watercolours that take the sea as their theme number among his finest works. A delicate watercolour by Drummond of a coastal scene with two young girls whose faces are particularly well drawn, charmed the experts at Stratford-upon-Avon.

Two paintings with a fascinating connection were brought to Roadshows in different locations. The first, at the Cleethorpes show, was a charming painting by Charles Edward Perugini; entitled 'Spring', it shows a young woman with lilac blossom. The other, brought to York, was a portrait of Perugini painted by Frederick, Lord Leighton, a fellow student of the artist and in later years a president of the Royal Academy. The latter picture had been painted after the two young friends had returned somewhat the worse for wear from a costumed ball. Like

Leighton, Perugini belonged to a group of neo-classical artists known as the 'Olympians' – so named because their artistry was described by some as 'god-like'. Of Italian birth, Perugini worked mainly in England and specialized in portraits of elegant ladies and interiors.

A large and superb watercolour proved popular at the Farnham show. Painted by Edward Henry Corbould, 'The Butcher's Daughter' is a typically idyllic Victorian representation of a pretty country girl in picturesque costume. Much loved by the Victorians, such pictures are

△ *'Beached Boats' by S. Cursiter. 1950.* **£3,000**
◁ *Canadian landscape by Alexander Young Jackson. 1920s; 9in x 12in.* **£5,000 – £8,000**

▽ *'Miles Barton', probably by Joseph Heard. 1850s; 35in x 48in.*   **£8,000 – £12,000**

becoming fashionable again today.

Several works by the popular Victorian artist Helen Allingham turned up at the Hemel Hempstead Roadshow. Best known for her pictures of cottages and gardens, Allingham was influenced by the Pre-Raphaelite painters. Two of the watercolours brought along were, unusually, of young girls, and the third was of a scenic coastal view.

Both experts and visitors at the York Roadshow gathered to admire a portfolio containing between 60 and 70 beautiful floral illustrations painted by sisters Maud and Alice West: Alice had painted the canary in a famous 1930s bird-seed

▽ *'Gwain, Maid of Milford' by Niccolo Funni. 1870; 24in x 30in.*
£2,000 – £2,500

▽ *Two young girls in coastal scene by James Drummond. 1870; 10in x 12in.*   **£300 – £400**

△ *Watercolour portraits and scenic view by Helen Allingham*
(1848 – 1926). Portraits 10in x 12in; coastal scene 13in x 16in.
Each **£5,000 – £8,000**

advertisement while Maud had produced exquisite plant pictures for a well-known seed catalogue.

One of the most poignant and fascinating items ever to be seen at a Roadshow was undoubtedly the personalized Christmas card and envelope with decorative engraving in pen, ink and watercolour by the artist Rex Whistler. The owner had received the card in 1943 when aged just five years old. At that time his father, Sergeant Sherlock, was serving with Whistler in a tank platoon and it was in fact Sergeant Sherlock who retrieved Whistler's body after the artist was killed in battle in 1944. This moving keepsake ensured that the Yeovilton Roadshow was a memorable occasion indeed.

△ *Flower paintings*
and drawings by
Maud West (1890 –
1940). Portfolio of
60 – 70 works **£5,000**

▷ *Christmas card*
and envelope by Rex
Whistler. 1943;
6in high. **£3,000**

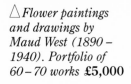

FURNITURE

BY JOHN BLY

Most furniture, particularly that which dates from the 17th and 18th centuries, reflects changes that have taken place in society. A prime example is the card table. It became popular only once gaming had been established as a fashionable pastime for the wealthy following the restoration of the monarchy in 1660.

Just as the use to which a piece of furniture was put indicates a period, so too does the shape, construction and the materials from which it is made. There can be no finer example of this than the laburnum-veneered card table seen at Cleethorpes. It displays the simple, elegant lines of a truly aristocratic piece of furniture from the 1730s. The expensive laburnum used for its veneer indicates undeniable quality, and the concertina action that provides all-round support for the top when open further emphasizes its excellence.

The York Roadshow provided a favourite from the beginning of the 17th century – a little chest in oak, the primary timber of the time. An early example of such a practical piece, it is of joined construction, with drawers suspended on side runners. Why this method was ever discontinued will remain a mystery to me, as it is certainly the most efficient means of allowing a heavy, full drawer to slide freely without unnecessary wear

and tear to the carcase. Such a simple factor also provides a clue to dating.

For me, however, the great appeal of this piece lies in the decoration. The mouldings of each drawer create the illusion of six short rather than three long drawers, and the panels are shallow-carved to represent tracing that has been pierced through and applied. Shallow carving of such 'strapwork' or 'cut-cardwork' is a technique requiring great skill and enormous patience, since the depth of the background must be maintained throughout or the illusion is spoilt.

My favourite piece from the late 18th century is the dumb waiter, partly because it is attractive, but mainly because it conjures up an image of joyous mid-Georgian mealtimes. Set on wheels or castors, the dumb waiter could be moved freely around the room to provide additional plates, cutlery, napery, dessert, cheeses or fruits. These pieces were always made in matching pairs, but most have been parted over the years, so imagine my delight at finding such a rarity – a matching pair – at the Enniskillen show.

The 19th century is dismissed by some as one of machine-production. At its best, Victorian furniture was perfect, at its worst, pretty awful. The set of four chairs from the York show fall into the

△ **FOLD-OVER CARD TABLE** *in laburnum, with concertina frame. 1730; 2ft 11in long.* **£10,000**

◁ **PAIR OF DUMB WAITERS** *in mahogany with three tiers and splay bases. 1780; 4ft 4in high.* **£15,000**

former category. Of the most glorious dark, honey-coloured rosewood, the chairs are carved in the surprisingly popular French-revival style. The backs, which are waisted and of open design, feature both 'C' and 'S' scrolls leading one over the other into deeply curved seats. Often wrongly described as Queen Anne chairs (which would date them around 1702), the design for this type of chair first appeared in the late 1820s.

My last choice, again in rosewood, is a pair of firescreens (or pole screens) from the Alexandra Palace show. In terms of style they epitomize the transition from the late Regency age through the William IV and Victorian periods. The fire screen first appeared as a popular household item in the late 17th century. Its primary function was to protect the faces of those sitting near the fire from the heat of the flames. This 'barrier' was essential, since heavy make-up containing wax and whitening ingredients was worn, and the effects of strong heat could prove catastrophic. Fire screens also had a secondary purpose; genteel young ladies passed their time stitching pretty panels of needlework to adorn the screens.

Such pieces present us with more than just a decorative item, they also present us with a tangible piece of history – a slice of life. That is why I am endlessly fascinated by furniture from different periods, and each Roadshow provides me with an unmissable opportunity to discover a truly magnificent piece.

▽ ROSEWOOD CHAIRS *1845; 2ft 9in high.* Set of 6 **£3,500**

△ FIRESCREENS, *also called pole screens. Made of solid rosewood in French rococo style. 1840.* **£1,500**

▽ OAK CHEST *The handles and feet are replacements; the carving is superb. 1603; 3ft 3in high.* **£2,000**

The desk has always played an important part in the social hierarchy – the grander the desk, the greater the importance of the owner, and vice versa.

The writing desk, or bureau, developed in France in the second half of the 17th century, and it was there that the most popular forms were first made. In English, the word 'bureau' refers specifically to a slant-fronted desk, usually above drawers, but the French *bureau* can be any one of a number of variations on the basic desk form.

The plain, flat-top version, the *bureau plat*, is the simplest form, although it is not as common as its English equivalent, the partners' desk. The *bureau à gradin*, popular in the 19th century, has a flat top surmounted by a tier of drawers or pigeon holes (most Continental desks have a top section), while the *bureau Mazarin*, named after one of Louis XIV's ministers, has a flat top and numerous drawers below but, unusually, no top section.

The *sécretaire à abattant* is an impressive piece, characterized by its large, fall-front writing surface. It first appeared in the late 17th century, but became popular only in the late 18th and early 19th centuries. It probably took so long to find favour,

▷ SECRETAIRE A ABATTANT, *probably made in Altona in Denmark (an important centre of mahogany furniture manufacture) at around the time that the town became part of Germany. This piece is very plain but features attractively figured grain patterns. Other examples have highly decorated interiors with features such as simulated brickwork or even finely painted architectural views, which can double the price. 1840; 4ft 10in high.* **£1,500 – £2,000**

△ FRENCH BUREAU A CYLINDRE
This is a scaled-down 20th century version of the 'transitional' style that was popular through the 1760s and '70s, a period covering the end of Louis XV's reign and the beginning of Louis XVI's in 1774. The marquetry and gilt metal mounts are typical of the period. 1900 – 20; 3ft 7in high. **£1,200 – £1,800**

△ DUTCH BUREAU A CYLINDRE
The diamond parquetry (geometric veneers) and crossbanding on the roll top are French-influenced neo-classical features, but the use of walnut is typically Dutch. It has original locks and fittings. 1780s; 3ft 7in high. **£2,500 – £3,500**

particularly in England, because papers had to be cleared away and placed inside before it could be closed.

The elegant *sécretaire* or *bureau à cylindre* was first used in the 1750s by Louis XV's cabinet-maker, Jean-François Oeben. The pull-down 'cylinder', made either of solid wood or of wooden slats glued on to canvas, is attractive but difficult to keep in working order. Oeben also made the *bureau à capucin*, or harlequin desk, which appears to be flat but has a spring mechanism, enabling the top section to rise up.

The *bonheur-du-jour* was popular from the 1750s onward. Pretty and compact, with a writing surface concealed in the frieze drawer, it was frequently found in a lady's boudoir.

◁ **LOUIS XV BUREAU PLAT**
The writing surface is the only straight line on this typical Rococo piece with original gilt-bronze mounts. The pattern of the South American kingwood veneer, known as 'à quatre face', was very popular in France. 1760s; 5ft high.
£5,000 – £6,000

△ **SECRETAIRE A ABATTANT** *with a 'cushion' (convex) drawer to the frieze. Each drawer has an ivory knob. 1860; 5ft high.* **£1,200 – £1,800**

VARIATIONS ON THE 18TH CENTURY CONTINENTAL DESK

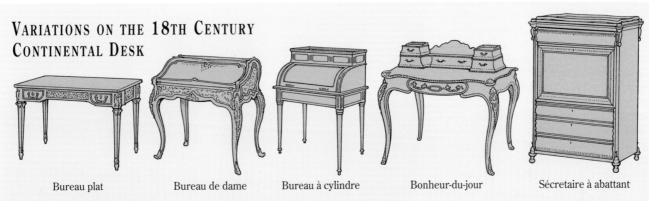

Bureau plat Bureau de dame Bureau à cylindre Bonheur-du-jour Sécretaire à abattant

A SECRETAIRE A ABATTANT

The gilt metal mounts were a later addition to this 4ft high mahogany piece made in 1820 (worth £2,000 to £3,000). Decoration in pre-Napoleonic designs was repopularized in France in the *Restauration* period (1815 – 30).

Grecian-style honeysuckle motif, one of the more restrained neo-classical motifs popular in France in the early 19th century.

Scantily dressed maiden, typical of Restauration decoration.

Elegant Neptune-like figure in a chariot drawn by dolphins (on the front of the writing flap).

COMMODES

The term 'commode' refers to two different types of furniture. In England, a commode was originally a small bedside cupboard containing (and concealing) a chamber pot. In the mid 18th century, however, a chest-type piece of furniture, also called a commode, was introduced from France. French-style commodes (which kept the same name in England, but with the stress on the first syllable) were grand pieces appropriate for a reception room, and would have been among the finest items of furniture in a household. These chests, usually with drawers and wider than they were high, became popular in England around 1740. Many English examples were beautifully designed and magnificently crafted and decorated.

English furniture maker George Hepplewhite maintained that commodes were 'never intended for use but for ornament' – in other words, decoration was all-important. Pieces were usually low to the ground, so that surface decoration could easily be seen. Drawers were frequently concealed behind a pair of doors which provided a second surface for elaborate ornamentation. Beautiful inlaid veneers were a common feature, gilt and ormolu mounts were frequently added and towards the end of the 18th century some pieces were wholly or partially painted. Most commodes were serpentine or bombé in shape, but semi-circular forms became popular in the 1770s. Plain rectangular shapes came into fashion in the Regency period.

Commodes from the 18th century are particularly rare, and the best examples command high prices.

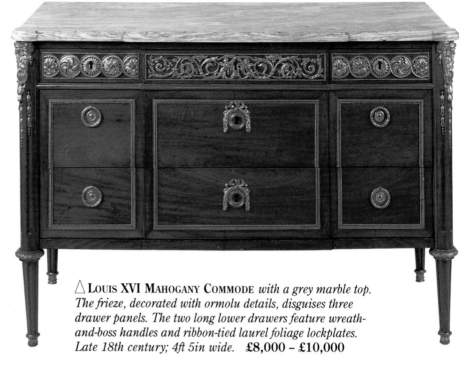

△ **LOUIS XVI MAHOGANY COMMODE** *with a grey marble top. The frieze, decorated with ormolu details, disguises three drawer panels. The two long lower drawers feature wreath-and-boss handles and ribbon-tied laurel foliage lockplates. Late 18th century; 4ft 5in wide.* **£8,000 – £10,000**

△ **CONTINENTAL THREE-DRAWER COMMODE** *This French mahogany chest of drawers is in the classically formal style characteristic of the Empire period. Among the many distinguishing features are brass mouldings which line the carcase, panels of gilt metal at the top of each corner, square gilt drop handles and a variegated grey marble top. Early 19th century; 3ft 8in wide.* **£2,500**

◁ **SERPENTINE MALTESE COMMODE** *An excellent example of Maltese craftsmanship, this four-drawer serpentine-shaped commode has panels decorated with fine marquetry (inlaid areas of veneer) and parquetry (applied veneer, using the natural veins of wood to advantage). The shaped ogee feet are inlaid, and the decoration continues up the corner stiles to the overhanging top. The multicurved apron lightens the appearance. 1775 – 1800; 5ft wide.* **£4,000 – £6,000**

COMMODE SHAPES

Variations on the basic shape range from bombé to semi-circular.

Bombé commode
1750

Rectangular commode
1750

Bow-fronted commode
1800

A CLOSER LOOK AT

A CONTINENTAL COMMODE

This late 18th century commode is finished in walnut veneer. Common woods, such as oak, were used for the carcase of such pieces, which were then finished with expensive veneers. Swedish pieces always have three drawers and frequently incorporate gilt horizontal channels and sharp-cornered veneers.

Swedish veneer, with sharp edges

Asymmetrical Rococo handles

Marquetry (Maltese commode p.20)

▽ **DUTCH MARQUETRY COMMODE** *in walnut with four drop-handled graduated drawers. The plain bow front is relieved by the shaped and moulded overhanging top. Continental domestic furniture of this period tended to be more flamboyant than its English counterpart. 1760; 2ft 9in high.* **£4,500**

◁ **SCANDINAVIAN COMMODES** *at Queensferry. Furniture expert Christopher Payne stands between the Danish commode (shown below) and the fine Swedish commode (shown above). The strong French influence is evident in the overall design and finishing details. 1775 – 1800; 2ft 8in high.* **£4,000 – £6,000**

▷ **DANISH WALNUT VENEERED COMMODE** *with a gentle serpentine front and gilt details on the feet and around the drawers. The flat sides and plain veneer indicate a German rather than French influence. The replacement top has been painted to resemble marble. Either plain wood or real marble was generally used for the tops of commodes. 1775–1800; 2ft 9in high.* **£4,000 – £5,000**

SIDE TABLES

Among the earliest forms of domestic furniture, side tables date back to before the Middle Ages. Those most commonly found today are from the period following the restoration of the monarchy in 1660 until the end of the 19th century.

The side table was an especially fashionable item of furniture during the mid 18th century, when it was used both as a writing table and a dressing table. A typical piece from this period can be distinguished by its overhanging top supported on a rectangular frame with a single drawer, and turned, tapering or cabriole legs, the latter terminating in pad feet. The finest side tables, dating from the mid 18th century are made from mahogany, but oak, ash and elm were also used for less sophisticated pieces.

As with most furniture, design was influenced by contemporary fashions and customs, and side tables with small drawers served as stylish make-up tables for fashionable men and women of the period. (When the wearing of cosmetics went out of fashion, however, so too did this item of furniture.) The three drawers were often set in an elaborately shaped frieze or apron. By the end of the 18th century, side table tops frequently had bow fronts, sometimes with two drawers to the frieze. Square tapering legs had also become popular.

Most side tables were finished and decorated on three sides only, since one side was usually pushed against a wall.

△ **OAK SIDE TABLE** in exceptionally fine condition. The joined frame and bobbin turning are of the highest quality, as is the perfect dovetail with a single nail. The rebated drawer side (grooved to fit a runner) and the cleat ends (narrow strips of wood for strengthening the top) also indicate an extremely high standard of craftsmanship. 1670s; 2ft 6in wide. **£4,500**

◁ **OAK SIDE TABLE** with its corners cut off and rounded, and a recently-made front drawer added. The drawer (shown below) is made of old and distressed timbers, but the smooth sides give it away as a recent addition. Despite the crude repairs, this table has well designed turned legs and good proportions. 1780; 2ft wide. **£550**

◁ **GEORGE II DRESSING TABLE,** *or lowboy, of unusually high quality, with cabriole legs ending in pad feet, and a deeply shaped apron. 1755; 2ft 6in wide.* **£4,500**

▷ **OAK LOWBOY** *with cabriole legs terminating in 'duck's feet'. A variation of the more traditional pad foot, the duck's foot was a popular alternative to the ball and claw foot in the early 18th century. 1745; 2ft 6in wide.* **£3,000**

THE EVOLUTION OF THE SIDE TABLE

Box-shaped tables with outside stretchers were followed by more ornate styles, before the return to classical simplicity in the late 18th century.

Oak table with bobbin-turned legs, 1690

X-stretcher table with shaped apron, 1700

Table with cabriole legs and pad feet, 1730

George III table with square legs, 1760

△ **MAHOGANY SIDE TABLE**
This type of table has been popular since its first appearance in the 1740s. This example, with a single drawer to the frieze, stands on turned and tapered legs terminating in pad feet. Less sophisticated examples were made in ash or elm, and the more elaborate tables had cabriole legs. 1750; 2ft 6in wide. **£2,500**

△ **GEORGE II SIDE TABLE**
with original 'penny ring' handles. The top of this mahogany table has re-entrant (indented) corners and the formal cabriole legs have attractive decorative carving. 1740; 3ft wide. **£3,000 – £4,000**

◁ **MAHOGANY SIDE TABLE**
The overhanging top has a caddy-moulded edge, while the junction of the frame and legs is plain. 1750; 2ft 6in wide. **£2,000**

FOLD-OVER TABLES

As with many pieces of domestic furniture, folding tables started to become popular at the end of the 17th century. By the 18th century, two main types had developed. The first was the drop leaf, in which a hinged flap at each side extended the top. In the second, used primarily for card-playing or tea, the top was hinged in the centre, and opened out to provide a larger surface, usually extending from rectangular to square, or from a half to a full circle. The open surface of a card table was lined with baize or felt; in a tea table it was polished. Most were made of, or veneered in, walnut.

There were three basic patterns of fold-over tea or card table. In the simplest design, the back right or back left leg swung out at right angles to form a support for the opened top. In slightly more expensive models, both back legs were hinged to swing out to support the top at each corner. This, obviously, gave a more sturdy surface. In a 'concertina' table, the whole frame was hinged in three

△ **EARLY VICTORIAN CARD TABLE** *The top is hinged off-centre and swivels through 90° to open. Once open, it is supported on a shaped frieze rail over a faceted baluster column, with a four-sided platform and four scroll feet. The highly figured veneers are indicative of quality. 1850; 2ft 5in high.* **£850**

places on each side to open out and form a solid friezed frame.

By the 19th century, a further mechanism had been introduced. Here, the top had an off-centre pivot and swivelled to open out and be supported by the rectangular frame. The largest number of fold-over tables found today are of this 19th century type. Generally, they comprise a shaped rectangular framework, usually with a decorative frieze rail at the front. The top sits on a central pedestal, which is supported by a platform with three or four feet. Supports varied, however: at the beginning of the century, a single central pillar was most common, but by the 1850s a wide range of pillars

and stretchers, often with carved finials in the shape of vases, orbs or spinning tops, had become popular.

The basis for all the design variations in these tables (as with most Victorian furniture) can be found in earlier periods, so rococo revival-, gothic-, classical- and Chippendale-style fold-over tables can all be found. The combination of one of these styles with the hinge and swivel mechanism, however, firmly dates a table to the 19th century.

Materials, too, can give an indication of the date of a table. Highly figured but machine-cut veneers of oak, walnut, mahogany and rosewood were combined to dramatic effect with panels of marquetry. Surfaces were also ebonized and gilded, painted or carved, and decorated with brass, tortoiseshell and other exotic veneers.

Fold-over tables started to decline in popularity at the end of the 19th century. By about 1910 they had been largely replaced by the fold-away bridge table.

◁ **MAHOGANY CARD TABLE** *The hinged top has a moulded edge, and the concave frieze is flanked by carved lotus leaves. 1830; 2ft 5in high.* **£350 – £450**

▷ **SWIVEL-TOP CARD TABLE** *The top consists of four triangles, inlaid in ivory and beech. The table itself is rosewood and has cabriole legs. 1895; 2ft 5in high.* **£500 – £700**

FOLDING MECHANISMS

The mechanism used depends on the age of the piece and on its quality: the simplest early tables had one (below) or two hinged legs; a concertina mechanism (right) was more expensive. The hinge and swivel top is a 19th century innovation.

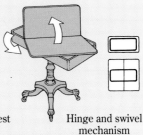

'Concertina' extending framework

Leaves open to rest on hinged leg

Hinge and swivel mechanism

△ **WALNUT CARD TABLE** *An exuberant Victorian fold-over card table decorated with highly figured walnut veneers. Although tables that rested on a central pedestal support remained the most common into the Victorian era, occasionally curvilinear supporting frameworks such as this one were made. The castors enable the table to be moved easily. 1850; 2ft 7in high.* **£2,200**

▷ **BURR WALNUT FOLD-OVER TABLE** *with a figured walnut veneer top; it is a shaped rectangle which opens out to a square. The table's elegant appearance when shut is due to the moulded edge on one flap. The pedestal is pierced into four scrolling brackets which enclose an elaborate carved finial; the cabriole legs have scrolling shellwork decoration. 1845; 2ft 4in high.* **£1,500 – £2,000**

AN 18TH CENTURY CARD TABLE

▽ *The concertina mechanism looks complicated but is a simple and logical solution to the problem of creating a solid support.*

This George II fold-over card table in laburnum has a concertina frame. This was the most expensive type of support for these tables and its presence indicates quality. Inside, the top is lined with baize and recesses provide spaces for money and candles.

Unusually in this table, the laburnum is cut and laid vertically, rather than across the grain. The edge is accentuated by lines of boxwood stringing, which were originally painted. The front legs taper and end in pad feet.

Measuring 2ft 5in high by 2ft 11in long, it was made around 1730 and is valued at £10,000.

△ *This type of hinge is standard on such tables: brass, let into each end and fastened with three screws. The hinge works on two small pins.*

▽ *The underside of a front leg shows the block-built construction and the thick, hand-cut veneers.*

18TH CENTURY CHAIRS

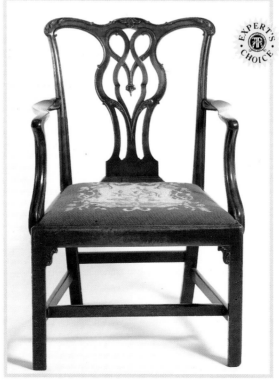

By the 18th century English seating had become less dependent on Continental influences and was starting to develop its own strong, stylistic characteristics. Chairs of the period began to evolve into different shapes for different uses: gilded and upholstered suites for drawing rooms, solid wooden seats with backs displaying a coat of arms for halls, and splat-back chairs for dining rooms.

Armchairs were no longer reserved for the most important member of the household; a suite for a salon, for example, might consist of several settees, a set of stools and another of armchairs. In all houses, however, seats were intended to stand against the wall when not in use.

The early part of the 18th century saw the introduction of the solid splat chair. Its major stylistic features were bold, curved lines; uprights shaped to the human back, and a solid vase-shaped splat running from the crest to the seat rail. (In chairs of the late 17th century there is a gap between the back and seat.)

The decorative emphasis of these early 18th century

△ EARLY 18TH CENTURY-STYLE CHAIR *made of mahogany, with late 18th century-style decoration. 1890; 2ft 6in wide.* **£2,000**

△ UPHOLSTERED WING ARMCHAIR *with scroll arms, fitted well-stuffed cushion and ball and claw feet. 1725; 2ft 10in wide.* **£14,000**

chairs was no longer on carving but on the colour and pattern of walnut, the most fashionable wood of this period. Chairs might have drop-in seats or be 'stuffed over' with fabric covering the seat rail and secured with brass nails. Arms were set back on to the sides of the seat rail to fit more comfortably with the new curved cabriole leg and to allow for wider skirts and bulky frock coats.

In the 1720s, as walnut became scarce, imports of colonial mahogany increased. This proved an excellent furniture wood, resistant to worm, strong, and with a good colour and close grain ideal for carving. Under the influence of Palladian designers, the simple lines of earlier chairs were embellished with carving of shells and acanthus on crests, splats and knees. Lion and eagle heads began to appear on arm terminals

◁ GOTHIC-STYLE MAHOGANY ARMCHAIR *with squarish back, shaped crest rail and pierced, interlaced splat. The delicate carving is typical of mid 18th century designs. 1760 – 5; 3ft high.* **£800 – £1,000**

EXPERT'S CHOICE

and cabriole legs ended in lion's paw or claw and ball feet. When carved in mahogany, these legs and feet have a character regarded in furniture terms as 'masculine'.

Designs of the mid 18th century

Thomas Chippendale's publication *The Gentleman and Cabinet-Maker's Director* of 1754 featured the most popular contemporary styles. New to these years were chairs with backs up to 3 feet high and increasingly elaborate pierced splats. The basic back was embellished in different styles: French Rococo, with curved lines and motifs drawn from nature; gothic, with pointed arches and trefoils; and chinoiserie,

▷ **TALL-BACKED BOX CHAIR** *with a frame and panel construction. A Lancashire variation, this chair has had cheek-shaped panels added to protect the sitter from draughts. The pierced and grooved frame below the wooden seat would have accommodated a rope base for a cushion. 1780 – 90; 4ft 5in high.* **£1,250**

▽ **OAK ARMCHAIR** *A provincial interpretation of the latest fashionable styles, this has an up-to-date vase-shaped splat, a crest-rail and pad feet, but the turned supports and gap between seat and back are 17th century features. 1700 – 10; 3ft 7in high.* **£350**

△ **WALNUT SETTEE** *reflecting early 18th century styles in the simple cabriole legs and pad feet, and also the influence of Palladian designers in the eagle-head arm terminals. It has been substantially restored; a perfect example would be worth three times as much. 1720; 6ft 4in long.* **£15,000 – £18,000**

▽ **LADDER-BACK CHAIR** *This country chair with simply turned uprights framing shaped horizontal rails has a rush seat and turned legs and stretchers. This traditional form was adapted and refined later in the century. 1700 – 10; 3ft 6in high.* **£300**

◁ **MAHOGANY CHAIR**
One of a set of four dining chairs of the Hepplewhite period with realistically carved drapery (detail below) forming the crest rail. Delicate interlaced arches in gothic style form a squarish back with an elegant pierced central splat. The chair also has an upholstered drop-in seat and square legs. 1775; 2ft 11in high.
The set **£5,000**

▽ **HEPPLEWHITE-STYLE CHAIRS** *with arched square backs and a dated inscription on the seat rail (right). They*

△ **MAHOGANY SIDE CHAIR** *with cabriole legs and claw and ball feet. The shaped uprights, bow-shaped crest rail and splat pierced with bold C-scrolls and lozenges are characteristic features of mid 18th century Rococo styling. 1750. 3ft 3in high.* **£2,250**

△ **SIDE CHAIR** *with plain cabriole legs and pad feet, made in mahogany. The shaped uprights and serpentine crest rail end in bold ears, above a simply pierced vase-shaped splat. The chair is one of a pair. 1745; 3ft 1in high.* The pair **£2,800**

feature square tapering legs and exhibit typical linear restraint. 1797; 2ft 11in high. Set of 8 **£4,500 – £5,000**

with blind fretwork and pagoda-like crest rails.

Leg shapes also varied. A rococo-style chair, for example, would have cabriole-shaped legs and scrolled feet, while gothic and chinoiserie designs featured straight legs and stretchers. Chippendale also featured illustrations of upholstered 'French chairs' which closely followed contemporary French designs, with padded, cartouche-shaped backs.

The move to Classicism
By the 1760s, interest aroused by the archaeological excavations at Pompeii and Herculaneum and the influence of architect-designers such as Robert Adam caused a shift in style towards Classicism. Chair backs, seats and legs became straighter and decoration was increasingly dependent on classical sources. These neo-classical chairs tended to have oval, rectangular or shield-shaped

18TH CENTURY CHAIR STYLES

In the early 18th century chairs were bold and curved, with little carving and solid splats. Carving increased in the second quarter of the century, moving from classical style to rococo, gothic and chinoiserie. By mid-century, splats were elaborately pierced, and legs were straight or cabriole shaped. By the 1760s more elegant proportions were introduced, with further classical ornamentation.

1720 – 25   1720 – 25   1735 – 40   1750 – 55

◁ **MAHOGANY CHAIR** *with pierced vase-shaped splat, and square legs. 1765 – 70; 3ft 1in high.* **£600**

▷ **1 SIDE CHAIR** *with pierced back and carved top rail. 1760; 3ft high.* **A pair £3,500**

2 LADDER-BACK CHAIR *with double-curved horizontal splats. 1770; 3ft 4in.* **A pair £4,500**

1

2

backs, and splats boldly pierced with classical forms such as lyres, urns and anthemions (honeysuckle). Rich brocade and tapestry were the most popular choices for upholstery.

In his *Cabinet-Maker and Upholsterer's Guide* published in 1788, George Hepplewhite adapted these classical forms but, by giving them slender frames and supports, made them more 'feminine' and decorative. His splats, too, were delicately carved, not only with classical motifs but also with textile-like swags, and even a stylized version of the Prince of Wales' feathers. The lightness of Hepplewhite's designs was often enhanced by the use of honey-golden satinwood which became popular toward the end of the century.

Thomas Sheraton's designs of the 1790s, although similar to those of Hepplewhite, were generally more delicate, while at the same time angular. Chairs made to Sheraton designs often appear quite fragile with their somewhat over-slender tapering supports.

The 18th century was probably the high point of English chair design, to such an extent that in the late 19th and early 20th centuries large numbers of chairs were produced in all the 18th century styles.

A CLOSER LOOK AT

A GEORGIAN SIDE CHAIR

This walnut side chair with drop-in seat has boldly scrolled uprights and a vase-shaped splat, typical of early 18th century styles. The piercing on the splat and carving on the crest rail, however, suggest a later date of 1740. This chair is 3ft 1in high and a set of four is valued at £18,000.

The seat is 22in wide: an armchair would be at least 2in wider.

Side view showing raked back and cabriole legs.

Low relief carving on the crest rail simulating drapery.

High quality carving at the knee.

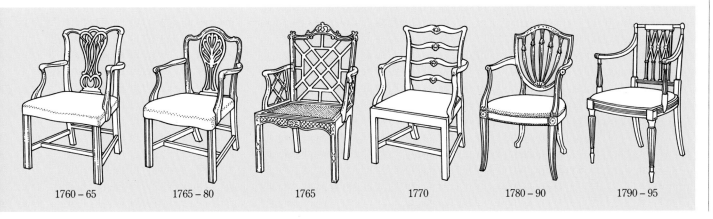

1760 – 65 1765 – 80 1765 1770 1780 – 90 1790 – 95

VICTORIAN
PARLOUR SEATING

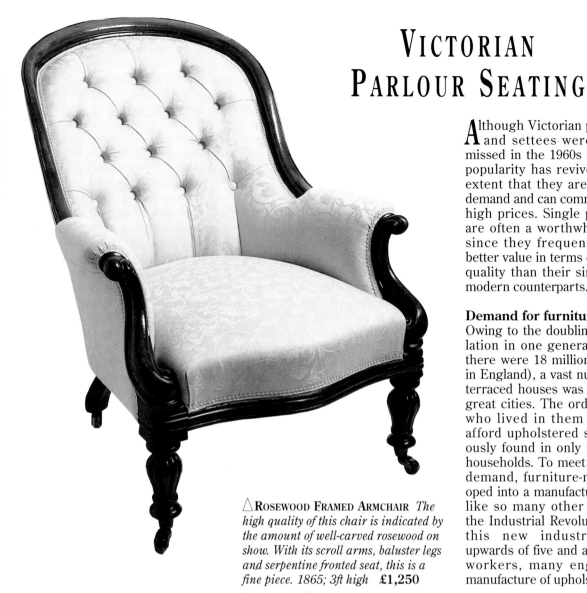

Although Victorian parlour chairs and settees were largely dismissed in the 1960s and '70s, their popularity has revived to such an extent that they are now in great demand and can command relatively high prices. Single pieces or sets are often a worthwhile purchase, since they frequently represent better value in terms of comfort and quality than their similarly priced modern counterparts.

Demand for furniture
Owing to the doubling of the population in one generation (by 1850 there were 18 million people living in England), a vast number of small terraced houses was built in all the great cities. The ordinary families who lived in them were able to afford upholstered suites – previously found in only the wealthiest households. To meet this increased demand, furniture-making developed into a manufacturing industry, like so many other crafts during the Industrial Revolution. By 1850, this new industry employed upwards of five and a half thousand workers, many engaged in the manufacture of upholstery.

△ROSEWOOD FRAMED ARMCHAIR *The high quality of this chair is indicated by the amount of well-carved rosewood on show. With its scroll arms, baluster legs and serpentine fronted seat, this is a fine piece. 1865; 3ft high* **£1,250**

▽ SIDE CHAIR *with walnut frame. The carving on the frame was achieved by shallow gouging and the top rail bears a flat-carved motif. This is a typical machine-produced Victorian chair. 1875; 3ft 3in high.* **£450**

▽ WALNUT-FRAMED SIDE CHAIR *The shaped circular seat below a balloon back and curved front legs were popular features in this period. The use of walnut indicates a mid-range piece. 1860; 3ft 3in high.* **£550**

▽ ROSEWOOD SIDE CHAIR *The date and quality of this chair can be discerned by the amount of rosewood around the frame. The deeply-waisted back, scrolling legs and serpentine front are also signs of quality. 1865; 3ft 3in high.* **£450**

PARLOUR SETS

The parlour set, generally comprising two large armchairs, four plain side chairs and a settee or chaise-longue, was fashionable throughout Europe between 1840 and 1880. There are several differences between the Continental parlour set (right) and its English equivalent (below) which help to distinguish one type from the other.

The plush settee and four chairs (right) are part of a Dutch mahogany salon suite of 1840. The settee is 4ft 6in wide, the two identical spoon-backed armchairs 3ft 6in high and the side chairs 3ft 3in high. The complete set, valued at £3,000 to £5,000, also comprises a large centre table.

English parlour sets, although often fashioned in ornate Louis XVI style like their Continental counterparts, differ in that they do not usually include a table. Furthermore, the two armchairs in the set do not match: the chair with armrests is 'his' and the other 'hers'. Unlike the pieces in French sets, which were all made to the same height, the easy chairs and settee of an English set are lower to the ground than the four balloon-backed side chairs which complete the set.

AN ENGLISH PARLOUR SET

Balloon-backed side chairs with cabriole legs

'His' armchair

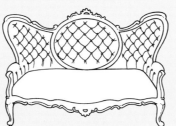
Settee with Louis XVI-style scroll carving

'Hers' easy chair

Balloon-backed side chairs with cabriole legs

Inferior materials were frequently used for the frames of mass-produced furniture, but for the new market a reasonably low price was considered more important than superior quality.

Chair styles

While grand houses boasted drawing rooms for entertaining visitors, the middle class home had a parlour furnished with upholstered easy chairs and comfortable settees.

Several styles of chair back developed during the 19th century. Until 1865, the ornate French 'Revival' style – curvilinear and decorated with foliate carving – was in fashion, but later styles were characterized

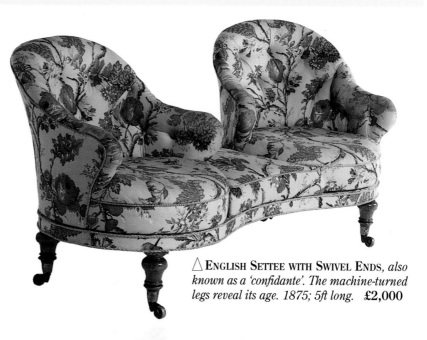
△ **ENGLISH SETTEE WITH SWIVEL ENDS**, *also known as a 'confidante'. The machine-turned legs reveal its age. 1875; 5ft long.* **£2,000**

by greater formality, demonstrated in the straighter lines and more symmetrical carved decoration.

Victorian innovations

Many Victorian easy chairs do not have arms. This was due in part to fashion: the skirts of women's dresses had become increasingly voluminous, and a lady could sit in comfort on the thickly padded upholstery of a low, armless chair, while spreading her dress around her to show it off to best advantage.

Victorians also favoured the 'conversation settee' – a sofa with intertwined, well-sprung seats designed for two or three people. Such an intimate piece of furniture provided ample opportunity to indulge in the popular pastimes of gossiping and flirting.

Other innovations which provided additional comfort were the button back chair and the coiled spring (introduced around 1820). The button back is especially comfortable because it fits the contours of the sitter's back, while the coiled spring provides effective support for the padding between the chair frame and cover. Comfortable balloon-backed chairs, with their well-filled stuffed seats, nipped-in waists and slightly sloping backs, were suitable for both the dining room and the parlour.

◁ **LOW-SEATED WALNUT SIDE CHAIR** *This type of chair is also known as a 'priedieu' because it could be used as a prayer chair – the tall back supporting the elbows of the person kneeling on the seat. The partial gilding increases the value. 1860; 4ft high.* **£1,250**

◁ **WALNUT OPEN ARM CHAIR** *in early 18th century revival style. The proportions of the chair and the construction of its frame date the chair to the mid Victorian period. 1850; 3ft 3in high.* **£2,000**

▷ **PAINTED ARMCHAIR** *in Louis XV style. It has a cartouche-shaped back, padded arms, an upholstered seat and a painted and partially gilded grooved frame. The proportions are too broad for a French piece; it may be Italian. 18th century; 3ft high.* **£600 – £800**

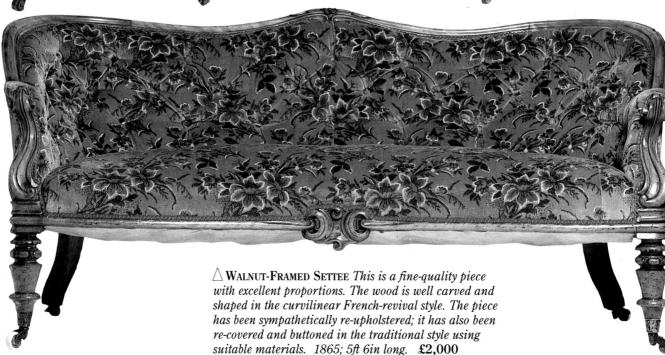

△ **WALNUT-FRAMED SETTEE** *This is a fine-quality piece with excellent proportions. The wood is well carved and shaped in the curvilinear French-revival style. The piece has been sympathetically re-upholstered; it has also been re-covered and buttoned in the traditional style using suitable materials. 1865; 5ft 6in long.* **£2,000**

Buying furniture today

Although Victorian upholstered chairs have had a reputation for shoddiness, those pieces which have survived are often very well made.

The wood used in a piece is the best guide to its overall quality. The upholstery may be in good condition, but the timber of the frame may have been worm-infested to begin with. If the chair was made of cheap wood, it may have a loose, unstable structure. The prospective buyer should check the wood that is on show, even if only the feet. If it is painted beech, the chair is likely to be poorly made, whereas if it is walnut or mahogany it should be of reasonable quality. The best upholstered chairs, however, are made of rosewood. As a rule, the more rosewood on show, the better the craftsmanship.

It is sometimes more appropriate to buy a frame in an unrestored state so that you can thoroughly inspect it yourself, and then have it upholstered as you please.

◁ **WALNUT PARLOUR CHAIR** *One of a set of four, its value is considerably enhanced by the stamp of Gillow, the makers. 1880; 3ft high.* The set **£4,000**

◁ **BALLOON BACK ROSEWOOD CHAIR** *The deeply curving back and legs of this piece are typical of the high-style French-revival Movement. 1860; 3ft high.* **£150**

▷ **ROSEWOOD CHAIRS** *from a set of six. The backs (based on the 1827 designs of George Smith) are more to the French taste than the English. 1845; 2ft 9in high.* The set **£3,500**

◁ **BALLOON BACK SIDE CHAIR,** *with the deep upper rail that became enormously popular after the 1860s. (It is one of a pair.) 1875; 3ft high.* The pair **£300**

▷ **WALNUT PARLOUR CHAIRS** *This pair (from a set of four) displays the more formal lines that characterized chairs dating from the 1870s. 1880; 3ft high* The pair **£600**

STYLES OF VICTORIAN CHAIR

Comfort was of the essence in Victorian parlour chairs. Although styles varied, chairs were invariably extremely pleasant to sit and relax in, with deeply buttoned backs gently curved to fit the sitter and plump stuffed seats with fully sprung upholstery. The coverings, too, were usually richly textured.

'Hers' easy chair
1850

Prayer chair
1860

Conversation sofa or tête-à-tête
1850

Arts & Crafts chair
1900

DRESSERS

△ **LACQUERED OAK DRESSER**
This early 18th century low dresser (above and details left), inspected by John Bly, has a shaped apron below three frieze drawers, cabriole legs at the front and plain legs at the back. It is decorated with cream lacquer in the Chinese style that was popular at the time. This was an expensive form of decoration, however, and it is unlikely that it would have been applied to such a typically domestic piece of furniture. On closer inspection, the lacquerwork can be seen to date only from the 20th century. Even taking this into account, this decorative item still has considerable value. The underside (left) shows the structure and colour of the timber. 1735 – 40; 2ft 6in high. **£2,500**

The term 'dresser' probably derives from the Norman French word *dressoire*, a side table for preparing or 'dressing' food. In this medieval practice, a light supper was prepared and left on a simple board for the knight or master of the house who might require a snack during the night. By the late 17th century, three or more drawers had been added below the board on which food was 'dressed'.

Although dressers were never considered a particularly fashionable item of furniture, they were nonetheless both popular and widespread in the late 17th century and throughout the 18th century. Essentially domestic country pieces, they were usually made by provincial craftsmen using local woods. Consequently dressers can be found in a great many different styles.

Early dressers

The tall top section common to most dressers is not present on early examples. Those from around 1630 to 1700 were essentially long side tables with a single row of drawers. Although pieces can be dated by their decoration, the most accurate guide to age is the style of the front legs. The turned baluster leg was popular from 1650 to 1700;

the flat-fronted leg in a pillar silhouette style from 1670; and the graduated spiral twist, in which the leg tapers, from 1675. A low backboard was introduced in the 1690s, together with open shelves or a row of small drawers.

A typical 18th century dresser was made up of a tall shelved top section (with or without backboards) often with a shaped cornice frieze

and a matching apron below a row of drawers. On early pieces the apron is sometimes shaped and pierced, but never carved. The front two legs are usually cabriole (a feature retained into the 19th century, long after fashion had moved on) while the back legs were almost invariably plain.

Another 18th century innovation was a backboard made up of planks

△ CLASSICAL REVIVAL CABINET *made of rosewood and decorated with marquetry panels. It has bevelled (sloping) glass around the edges of the mirrors and doors. The central section and the original superstructure have been removed and replaced. Many variations based on this form of cabinet dresser were produced. Late 19th century; 6ft 2in high.* **£650**

of uniform width – earlier dressers were fitted at the back with planks of less regular shape.

Regional variations

The best known dresser of all is the Welsh dresser, and this name is also used frequently to describe dressers in general. True Welsh dressers are usually made not of mahogany but of oak. The South Wales (or Glamorgan) dresser often incorporates a shelf at floor level called a pot board, and the West Wales (Pembrokeshire) dresser is characterized by a 'dog kennel' hole between two flanking cupboards in the lower section.

The Yorkshire dresser is the most distinctive of the regional variations. As well as a clock placed centrally in the shelf section, it has a lower section comprising as many as 12 drawers. Lancashire dressers are similar, but do not have a clock. From the mid 18th century onward, mahogany crossbanding (a contrasting decorative inlay, cut across the grain) on drawer fronts and other edges became a popular detail.

The Bridgwater dresser, made around Somerset, is unique in that each vertical side is constructed from a single piece of wood – usually the superstucture is composed of two entirely separate sections, one on top of the other. Devon dressers also boast a unique feature – panelled doors enclosing the shelves on the upper section – and Suffolk dressers

▷ ARTS AND CRAFTS-STYLE DRESSER
The solid appearance of this Indian-made piece is emphasized further by the heavy panelled doors and large metal mounts (detail above). The design is typical of the Arts and Crafts Movement, which encouraged and promoted the construction of top-quality, hand-made furniture using only the finest traditional methods. 1910 – 20; 5ft 6in high. **£2,000**

DEVELOPMENT OF THE DRESSER

The high dresser evolved from the 1680s, after which many variations on the same basic form were produced.

Low dresser with silhouette-style front legs, 1670

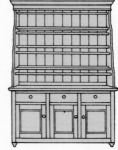

Low dresser with spiral twist front legs, 1675

Irregular backboards and turned baluster legs, 1685

Shaped frieze and apron, with cabriole legs, 1780

Welsh dresser, 1833

are known for their elaborately decorated friezes, shelves and aprons.

Popular woods

In the 19th century dressers were made mainly of pine, but in the 18th century the popular choice for top quality pieces was oak. Other plentiful local woods such as ash, elm, chestnut, and even fruitwoods like cherry or pear were also used, particularly for areas not on show such as backs and the insides of drawers. The latter types of wood are prone to deterioration, warping and woodworm infestation, so complete dressers made from them are rare.

Dressers today

In all but country areas, the dresser became less popular in the 19th century and was largely replaced by

△ COUNTRY DRESSER *in oak, with mahogany crossbanding. This piece of furniture is an example of the original low dresser form to which backboards were added later on. 1740; 2ft 10in high.* **£3,000**

△ ENGLISH OAK DRESSER *with an ogee (S-shaped) frieze below three (not six) drawers. The slats on the stretcher are unusual, because generally the area is either left open or contains a solid shelf (pot board). 1780s; 2ft 11in high.* **£2,000 – £3,000**

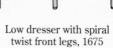

A GEORGIAN DRESSER

This 6ft high oak dresser, dating from around 1750 and valued at £4,500, has been drastically altered for the most innocent of reasons – suitability of size. The large moulded cornice rails (above) have been cut to reduce the overall height (perhaps to accommodate an immovable beam in a cottage) and replacement pieces substituted. Sometimes a whole bottom shelf would be removed for the same reason.

the more sophisticated sideboard, and later the chiffonier. Nonetheless dressers were still being made to traditional patterns well into the 1870s. The Arts and Crafts Movement helped to sustain interest, producing pieces in styles ranging from medieval to Japanese.

The most valuable dressers today date from between the 1670s and 1750s. A fine deep colour, rich patina and original feet and handles are all desirable features. Most early dressers have been repaired or altered at some time, so buyers should identify new sections.

▽ **ASSEMBLY PIECE** *from the mid Victorian period. The inlaid panels, turned and carved ball supports (right) and upright stiles carved with figures (far right) are Tudor, but the rest of the dresser is Victorian. 1860; 2ft 10in high.* **£3,500**

▷ **WELSH DRESSER,** *made of oak, from the Anglesey area. Typical features which identify a Welsh dresser are the kite-shaped ivory escutcheons (example centre bottom), plain cornice moulding and geometric inlays of coloured woods on the upper frieze. 1830; 7ft high.* **£3,500**

The patch on the inside of the drawer, above, is a tell-tale sign that the handle is a replacement. The corner bracket and cabriole leg below, however, are unmistakably original.

The fine quality tenon joints each have four pegs.

Typical Anglesey kite-shaped ivory escutcheon.

MEDIUM PINE

◁ **KITCHEN TABLE** *The clean, elegant lines of this Danish table are accentuated by the tapered square leg and the overhanging top. With its traditional dowelled joints, the only feature that distinguishes this table from one made 100 years before are the turned wooden drawer handles. 1870; 3ft wide.* **£250 – £350**

△ **LINCOLNSHIRE CHEST OF DRAWERS** *The mirror is supported by stands with turned bull's eye decoration over trinket drawers. A simple chamfer around the top, plinth and drawers relieves the flatness of this piece. The handles are not original. 1880; 2ft 11in wide.* **£350**

▽ **TYROLEAN HANGING CUPBOARD,** *with traces of its original dark green and cream painted floral decoration (many such cupboards have been stripped). 1820; 4ft 1in high.* **£800 – £1,000**

The term 'medium pine' covers items that range in size from washstands and tables to cupboards (both free-standing and hanging) and chests of drawers. Since these pieces generally fit any interior in both size and function, and are usually no more expensive than a modern equivalent, they are also often some of the first 'antiques' that people buy.

Pine furniture was common in the 19th century, and both hand-made, country pieces and machine-made examples can be found. The former are more expensive, since their traditional construction tends to give them a certain individuality. Machine-made pieces are not necessarily inferior, however. The process of mass-producing goods down to a price rather than up to a standard was gradual. In the early 19th century at least, cabinet-makers simply used machinery to help them to produce quality goods at a lower price than completely hand constructed pieces.

As the century progressed quality did in many cases decline, but signs of this are obvious even to inexperienced buyers. They include stamped plate handles, many of which have rusted; thin plywood drawer bottoms, door panels and sides and backs of chests and cupboards; and nailed joints rather than dovetails.

The quality of decoration on 18th and 19th century pine furniture was generally very good. Among the

most common decorative devices on machine-made pieces produced between 1830 and 1900 were 'split turnings' (a turned piece of wood of any length, split in half and stuck on to the front of a chest), scalloped galleries, tiled splashbacks and baluster turned legs.

Regional variations – turnings that resemble wool bobbins in areas where this was the major industry, for example – can also be found, and these can be particularly attractive. Handles were made from a variety of materials, including traditional brass, turned hardwood, black or white porcelain or, occasionally, moulded glass.

The major factor governing the price of medium pine furniture is its condition. Availability has some bearing, but there are very few items that can be called 'rare'.

◁ COUNTRY-MADE DRESSER/ CUPBOARD *constructed from broad pine boards and with a single shelf for small plates. A purely functional piece of furniture intended for a kitchen or dairy, this would originally have had a simple coat of varnish or paint. This design is generally associated with the north of England and Lowland Scotland, but in fact a cupboard of this basic construction could have been made almost anywhere in the British Isles. 1825; 3ft 10in wide.* **£275 – £300**

▽ MACHINE-MADE CHEST OF DRAWERS *(part of a 4-piece set). The shaped splashback flatters an otherwise simple piece. 1890; 3ft 7in wide.* **£275 – £350**

▽ LINCOLNSHIRE-MADE WASHSTAND *distinguished from later, inferior pieces by the dowelled joints and generous use of timber. 1860; 3ft 2in wide.* **£200**

◁ SIX-DRAWER CHEST/SECRETAIRE *The sparsely fitted desk interior (above) may originally have had drawers, and the whole piece would have been varnished or grained when it was made. It would also have been fitted with turned bun feet, to stand 4 to 6 inches higher than it does now. Secretaires are among the least common pieces of medium pine furniture, hence the value of this Scottish example. 1860; 4ft high.* **£1,000**

HOUSEKEEPERS' CUPBOARDS

The majority of large, freestanding cupboards, generally termed housekeepers' cupboards, that are brought to Roadshows date from the 19th century. Although there is plenty of well-documented evidence to show that these pieces were used before that date, the general wear and tear on such everyday furniture has meant that few early cupboards have survived in a usable state. Those pieces that have lasted in good condition tend to be made of oak – the hardiest of woods – and are generally provincial in origin.

By the 18th century, clothes were stored in wardrobes, linen presses or tallboys, while books, china and other curios were kept in bookcases or bureau-bookcases. Housekeepers' cupboards, therefore, fulfilled the two other main storage requirements: food (above all, luxury items under the direct control of the housekeeper, such as sweetmeats, sugar, preserves and pickles), and household linens (sheets, pillowcases, and so on).

The housekeepers' cupboard took many forms, but gradually evolved so that by about the 1850s it usually comprised one or two sets of

△ **HOUSEKEEPERS' CUPBOARD WITH CLOCK,** *in oak with mahogany cross-banding. 1820; 6ft 6in high.* **£3,000**

▽ **MAHOGANY GLAZED DOOR CABINET** *The design is typically early Victorian. 1845; 8ft high.* **£2,500**

△ **LARGE OAK CUPBOARD,** *with an integral clock, of the type generally used by the housekeeper of a large house for storing crockery, expensive preserves, condiments and household linens under lock and key. 1830; 7ft high.* **£5,500**

drawers, topped by a glazed, or solid (blind) door cabinet, inside which shelves, or more drawers, or a combination of the two, could be found. A clock was often included in the structure and a long sliding shelf, suitable for ironing or as an additional shelf space, was a popular feature.

Since these cupboards were generally made by craftsmen in the provinces, regional variations are common. In addition, at a time when the majority of good-quality furniture was made of mahogany, most house-keepers' cupboards were constructed of oak.

In deference to fashion, in the northern counties of Lancashire and Cheshire in particular, mahogany was often added to the edges of drawers as decoration, and door panels were veneered and cross-banded in mahogany. In Anglesey, Wales, on the other hand, kite or diamond-shaped ivory keyhole escutcheons and split turnings on each side of the drawers were the preferred forms of decoration, and it is these variations that give such pieces great charm.

◁ CABINET ON CHEST pictured (below) with owner and Deborah Lambert. The top is red walnut, while the base is mahogany, and although the inlay on both matches, the stringing was added later. The cabinet has a cushion drawer, the curved front of which forms part of the cornice, and the handles are original. Cabinet 1710, chest 1760; 6ft 10in high. £600 – £900

STYLES OF MOULDING

Mouldings can provide useful clues to dating large cupboards and cabinets. As with many other design features, regional variations are common.

1680 – 1720   1720 onward   1750 onward   1760 onward

◁ OAK CUPBOARD ON A CHEST BASE This fine-quality piece is typical of northern counties furniture. The four doors and drawers of the top prevent a 'heavy' image. The shelves in the top (see right) are for linen and/or crockery, and the baize-lined pull-out writing surface with drawer alongside for pens and pencils is for preparing household accounts. 1780; 7ft high. £4,500

EARLY ENGLISH REVIVALS & ALTERATIONS

Demand for 16th and 17th century furniture reached its peak in the mid 19th century. However, genuine period furniture did not always meet the Victorians' requirements. In London, shops were stacked with dismembered pieces of Elizabethan and Jacobean furniture, offered for sale to clients who would rebuild the various parts to create the furniture they wanted. The alternative was to buy reproduction furniture disguised to look old.

The Roadshow experts are often confronted with hall benches, court cupboards and tables which appear to date from the 16th or 17th century. Distinguishing between original pieces and Victorian rebuilds or reproductions requires a good knowledge of the periods involved, since the difference in value between the two can run into thousands of pounds. Even so, these Victorian versions are often fine antiques in their own right.

△ **RENAISSANCE-STYLE HALL BENCH**
A high-quality reproduction hall bench with lift-up seat. The finely carved late 16th century Italian motifs give it away, since they would have been unknown in England at that time. The wood is a beautiful colour. 1860; 3ft 9in wide. **£1,200**

◁ **17TH CENTURY-STYLE HALL BENCH**
A finely coloured oak bench with lift-up seat, in reproduction English 17th century style. The panelled back includes a genuine 17th century top rail (below) put together with the other, later, parts in the mid 19th century. 17th century chests were often used to form the base of such pieces. 1850; 4ft wide. **£800**

A Court Cupboard

Popular in the 16th and 17th century, the court cupboard was a piece of dining room furniture with a narrow (or court) base, usually with three tiers. This 4ft 5in high oak piece dates from the 1920s (original examples are extremely rare). The shallow colour, extraordinary amount of distressing (deliberate scratching, denting and so on) and new appearance of the interior combine to indicate its real origin. It is of good quality, however, and is worth £1,200.

Fine 17th century-style carving on the cupboard doors.

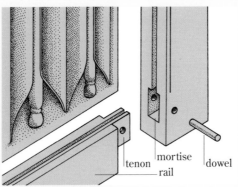

Inlay of different coloured woods in early 17th century style.

Cup-and-cover shape – a popular 16th and 17th century motif.

Crudely hand-finished panelling at the rear simulating 16th century craftsmanship.

TRADITIONAL CABINET CONSTRUCTION

To provide secure joints, rails have tenons that fit into mortises cut into vertical legs. Dowels are driven into holes drilled through both the tenons and mortises. Panels slot into grooves cut into the tops of the rails and the sides of the legs.

tenon | mortise | dowel
rail

▷ **REPRODUCTION OAK CUPBOARD,** *distressed and coloured to look like a food hutch of about 1600. 1920s; 4ft high.* **£250**

◁ **OAK FOOD HUTCH** *or larder. The basic frame dates from around 1700, but the doors were added early this century. 1915; 3ft 8in wide.* **£1,000**

EARLY OAK

Until the mid 17th century most fine-quality furniture was made of oak. Since oak is a wood that is both hard and durable, a substantial amount of this furniture has stood the test of time.

Oak was generally established as the standard timber for ecclesiastical fitments by the 9th century. This was the beginning of the great age of sacred architecture which endured until the 14th century. The sheer numbers of magnificent rood screens and other carvings that remain from this period are testimony

△ **OAK ARMCHAIR** *with tapering 'gun barrel' supports to the front. The back has been lowered and the cresting rail re-fitted with out-of-period peg tenons. 1660; 3ft 8in high.* **£1,800**

to the remarkable longevity of oak.

In the 15th and 16th centuries more easily available timbers such as elm, beech, ash, yew and fruitwoods were used for middle range furniture. Although cheaper than oak and more accessible, these woods, unlike oak, were not long-lasting and few pieces from this period have survived.

The 17th century saw a change in the pattern of family life, and it is this century that provides collectors with the greatest supply of oak furniture. The Tudor period, with its transient population, had come to an end, and as society became more settled the market for household items grew. So great was demand that in the first 30 years of the century numerous items of new furniture were developed.

By 1640 the small gate-leg table had emerged to become an integral item in the sophisticated household. Chairs with upholstered seats and

▽ **OAK DOUGH BIN** *(in which dough was left to rise). The legs are well-turned, but the bin has undergone much restoration (one of the legs has been rebuilt). 1720; 3ft 6in long.* **£450**

▽ **WELL-DECORATED DOUGH BIN** *The carved geometric pattern is combined with applied turned decoration. Each leg shows a turned baluster. 1675; 3ft 6in long.* **£600**

◁ **OAK CHEST** *with geometric carving along the bottom. It represents excellent value. 1750; 4ft long.* **£500 – £700**

▽ **OAK PANELLED-BACK CHAIR** *with an arched crest rail. The attractive bobbin-turned front stretcher contrasts with the simple turned uprights. 1680; 3ft high.* **£300 – £500**

▽ **COUNTRY CHAIR** *with solid splat back (one of a set of six). Such chairs exemplify the gentle transition from Queen Anne to Georgian style. Although simple, the overall style emulates that of a far more elaborate and high-quality piece of the same date. 1760; 3ft high. The set* **£1,500**

backs had by this time passed through the novelty stage and become more widely available. Such chairs were particularly popular because the seats and back panels could be used for displaying needlework samples stitched by the young ladies of the household.

Some early oak pieces retain traces of coloured pigment, particularly those dating from the 16th century when it was fashionable to paint furniture, beams and interior 'show-wood' in bright, primary colours. This fashion had died out by the 1640s, and thereafter decorative impact relied largely on the skills of the carver and, to a lesser extent, the inlay worker who created geometric or curvilinear patterns. Turning, too, was coming to the fore, and by the 1660s a great variety of shapes was available: bobbin, barley twist and baluster were among the most popular.

One of the most appealing qualities of oak is the extraordinary variety of depth of colour that some pieces have acquired over the years; another is the novelty and naivety evident in the design and construction of many early pieces.

The problem with much oak furniture is that it is often difficult to differentiate a genuine 17th century piece from a 19th century revival piece. In general, however, original carving should be of very good quality, well-balanced and although primitive, never crude.

▽ **BLANKET CHEST**
A good example of a panelled oak blanket chest, with original lock and hinges, fine carving and of exemplary colour. Many such chests, originally plain, were embellished with carving in the 19th century. 1640; 3ft 6in long. **£2,500**

▽ **LARGE OAK CHEST** *with early carved front panels in Gothic style (left) and a superb lock plate with decorated borders. The panels are ecclesiastical in form and date from the 15th century, but the rest of the chest was made in the 19th century. 4ft 7in long.* **£1,200**

Author, lecturer and broadcaster John Bly heads his family antiques business, established in 1891.

COLLECTOR'S · CHECKLIST

FURNITURE

To my mind, probably the most enjoyable aspect of working with or collecting antique furniture is the appreciation that every piece is an item of tangible history, and that you are handling a part of a society of an earlier period. In these pages I offer a few pointers to watch for when buying antique furniture, and give some advice on how to look after it once you have bought a piece. You should remember, however, that there is no real mystique to furniture: looking at it and understanding it is a logical process, although deeper knowledge comes with practice, experience and an understanding of manufacturing techniques.

One of the most important points about antique furniture is that you should not be afraid of it. A family dining-room table made in 1760, for example, should be used and enjoyed today. With care and normal use, it has lasted this long, and with the same treatment there is no reason why it should not continue to offer good service for another 200 years.

Just as a house needs to be lived in, so furniture needs to be used. Encourage your children to use, but not abuse, antique furniture. In this way, they will grow to enjoy our heritage.

▷ **REGENCY LYRE TABLE** *Although plain, this lyre-support occasional table is extremely fine: its rosewood veneer is of excellent colour, and the four swept legs with lion's paw feet still have their original cast brass castors. 1815; 2ft 5in high.* **£3,500**

POINTS TO WATCH FOR

1 Some chests of drawers have had as many as four sets of handles in their lifetime. Check inside the drawer fronts for extra holes, which may have been filled and disguised.

2 Some 18th century sideboards and chests have been trimmed to a narrower depth. Check that grooves for the drawer runners stop short of the backboard, and that dovetails on drawers are all of the same quality.

3 A coaster, tray or table top that has been turned will have shrunk across the grain, not along it. This is impossible to fake.

4 Woodworm is not necessarily a problem, since it can be treated. Do not automatically avoid pieces that show signs of its presence.

5 Victorian bow-fronted chests vary little from those of the 18th century in basic structure, but details such as a heavy overhanging top and bulky feet can be a guide. Check closely for disguises in both areas.

6 Marriages are common: tell-tale signs include backboards of different qualities and screw holes in the base without a corresponding hole in the top.

7 Look carefully at wood colour. On an exposed surface, it will be fresh and dry. In hidden areas, it will be darker but still dry. Where hands have held or lifted pieces, skin oils will have created a patina.

8 Authentic carving always stands proud of the outline of a piece; it is never recessed. Likewise, 18th century beading was carved from wood left on a piece of furniture for that purpose, so that the grain pattern was true; Victorian beading was carved separately and then glued in place.

◁ **WALNUT CASSONE** *or Spanish chest. Walnut was one of the most popular furniture woods in Spain until 1800. 1630; 2ft 1in high.* **£4,000**

TELL-TALE VENEERS

Veneers offer collectors some of the most important clues to the authenticity of pieces of furniture. The earliest veneers were walnut, followed in the late 18th and early 19th centuries by mahogany; walnut returned to favour in the Victorian period. Many other woods, including satinwood, rosewood and maple, have also been used at some time.

During the Queen Anne and George I periods in England, walnut veneers were usually applied to pine carcases (no-one would have used expensive oak for a piece that was to be veneered). An oak carcase and drawer front on a chest, therefore, may indicate later veneering.

In addition, after 1800 hand-cut veneers were gradually replaced by those cut by machine, which were much thinner. Hand-cut veneers are never less than ¹⁄₁₆ inch thick; a machine can produce veneers as thin as paper.

If you cannot see the edge of a veneer, look carefully at any bubbling or cracking on the surface for an indication of the veneer's thickness. If the veneer on an 18th century piece appears very thin, then either it was not applied at the time the piece was made, or the piece has been severely cleaned and the surface scraped to remove some damage.

Handles can also be a good test of the authenticity of veneers. Ensure that holes on the inside of a drawer front have corresponding holes on the outside.

PLACES OF INTEREST

Fairfax House (York Civic Trust), Castlegate, York
18th century furniture and clocks
Florence Court, Enniskillen, Co. Fermanagh, N. Ireland
Many mid 18th century pieces
Pollok House, Glasgow, Scotland
Late 18th & 19th century furniture
Victoria & Albert Museum, Cromwell Rd, London SW7
One of finest collections in country

CARE & REPAIR

1 The most important point to remember about cleaning antique furniture is that it is all too easy to remove patina and colour but impossible to replace them.

2 The safest way to clean antique furniture is to apply a little clear wax with a shoe brush, rub vigorously and then buff with a soft cloth. If any more cleaning is necessary, consult an expert.

3 Take no notice of friends' remedies, and don't use vinegar, lemon juice, olive oil, methylated spirits, or anything similar. At all costs, avoid patent cleaning mixtures. On some wax polishes, for example, the instructions for use recommend application with wire wool. *Never* do this: the combination of wax and wire wool will, in a couple of strokes, remove the patina built up over 200 years.

4 Don't expose tortoiseshell tea caddies, picture frames and other objects to direct sunlight: you will cause irreparable damage. Likewise, wooden furniture should not stand in direct sunlight.

5 Don't clean gilded handles on fine furniture. If the gilt has worn away, the handle underneath should appear bronze coloured.

▷ **OAK CRIB** *Cribs and cradles can command high prices, although rockers tend to be prone to wear. Carving is often intricate and elaborate. 1700; 3ft long.*
£1,250

'SHAKESPEARE'S TYPEWRITER'

The title is, of course, a nonsense that could not exist. The reasons why, however, can be used to determine the authenticity of much English furniture. When you look at an item, mentally check that its use, the material it is made from, its shape and its decoration were all 'invented' at the time the piece is supposed to have been made.

For example, Elizabethan satinwood teapoys never feature Roman Classical decoration. First, we did not have tea; second, satinwood was not used for furniture; and, third, cabinet-makers knew very little of Roman Classical decoration.

Styles of handles, locks, castors, screws and hinges, and the materials from which they were made, can all be dated to a greater or lesser degree, and all help to verify the authenticity of a suspect piece.

▷ **MAHOGANY-FRAMED MIRROR** *Mirror glass produced at this time is thinner than more modern glass, and has a slightly 'greyer' colour. 1815; 2ft 2in wide.* **£300**

COLLECTABLES
& TOYS

BY HILARY KAY

The 1992 *Antiques Roadshow* season took us to Orkney, our most northerly destination to date, as well as to the more familiar country towns and cities in southerly parts of the British Isles. Reviewing this year's Roadshows, I can immediately recall one particular show in Yeovilton which brought so many treasures to so many of the specialists. I was presented with a delightful toy racecourse scene, complete with grandstand, spectators, marquees, finishing post, rails and horses with riders. Although the figures were unmarked, their scale indicated that the set would almost certainly have originated in Nuremberg, where the most prolific manufacturer was the Heinrichson factory.

My toy 'bonanza' was at Bristol, where the *Antiques Roadshow* and the children's programme *Going Live!* joined forces for a special edition. Hundreds of children, most accompanied by their parents, attended this innovative event, and the majority had brought toys along. Almost without exception, these young participants were relaxed and spontaneous performers, surprisingly unintimidated by the cameras, lights

and microphones, and all bursting with questions both during and after filming.

Well-loved teddy bears jostled for attention with Sindy dolls, Pelham puppets, Hornby trains, lead soldiers and Dinky Toys. All came with a story or a tender moment. I remember a small girl who, when I asked her the name of her rather grubby and battered bear, removed her thumb from her mouth to whisper that his name was 'Wilfy'. Expressing my surprise at this unusual Christian name she went on to explain in a matter-of-fact tone ... 'we call him that because he's so *filfy!*'

Some children brought along their parents' toys, and I could see many anxious adults' glances directed towards their offspring as small, inexperienced fingers jiggled the precious playthings. One young man brought along an extraordinary trio of Dinky 'Supertoys', all identical models of a turntable fire escape vehicle (Dinky No. 956). One model was in a somewhat battered condition, having obviously been played with by both the current owner and the original owner (his father); another was in almost mint condition and contained in its original box, while

△ GERMAN WAX DOLLS
1850; 21in high.
The pair **£400 – £500**

▷ HALL 'TYPE WRITER'
1890; 15in wide.
£1,500 – £2,000

△ RACING SET, *numbering 100 pieces in total. The lead figures are two-dimensional and hand painted on both sides. Late 19th century; figures 1½ in high.* **£400 – £500**

▷ SCRIMSHAW WATCHSTAND *made of ivory and bone and mounted in a wooden frame. Hilary described it as a most remarkable piece. 1815; 2ft 5in high.* **£3,000**

the third was still in the brown paper wrapping in which the toy had originally been posted to the young man's uncle.

My position on the Miscellaneous table at the *Antiques Roadshow* recordings ensures that I see the widest possible variety of objects. Alexandra Palace brought me an unusual typewriter made by the company Hall, which had survived in remarkably good condition complete with its original mahogany case, label and instruction booklet. A gramophone by E. M. Ginn looked as if it would devour both myself and the owner as we discussed its merits on a dais, with its vast papier mâché horn towering above us, looking increasingly menacing.

It is always particularly satisfying to have an opportunity to see objects associated with the

area or town that a Roadshow team is visiting. Rochdale was one such recording, and it was made memorable by the range of devices that had been salvaged by a former employee of one of the factories from the once thriving Lancashire textiles industry. Seeing such splendid machines being scrapped all around him, he decided to save some of them to record the passing of an era. I was familiar with the machines but their owner provided me with an invaluable insight into life in the textiles industry.

I am already looking forward to the next series of the *Antiques Roadshow*. For me, part of the excitement and stimulation is not knowing what the next carrier bag at the Miscellaneous table will reveal: maybe next year I really will find my Renaissance astrolabe!

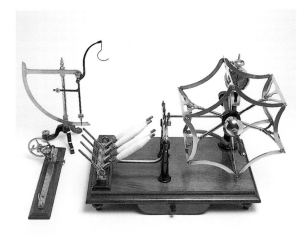

△ INDUSTRIAL MACHINERY *salvaged from the Lancashire textiles industry. 1900s.* **£1,000**

△ DINKY 'SUPERTOY' FIRE LORRIES *1960; 6in long. Mint model* **£150 – £200**; *battered model* **£3 – £4**

FANS

Ornately decorated fans, often complementing dress fashions, became popular in the 18th century. They were used by well-to-do ladies of fashion as a means of keeping cool, and also as an elegant and silent form of communication. 'The Language of Fans' was even the subject of books and articles in ladies' journals.

The sticks and guards (the outer sticks of a folding fan) were made from a variety of materials, such as sandalwood, tortoiseshell, mother-of-pearl, horn, ivory and wood, which were carved, enamelled or gilded. The paper or fabric 'leaves' were often painted with romantic scenes, heroic battles, royal portraits, songs

A fine 18th century fan might cost as much as £13,000, but a hand-painted satin or silk 19th century example can be bought for just £100. Also fairly inexpensive are Art Deco paper fans, which were given away free by certain shops in the 1920s and '30s.

△ **PRINTED AND HAND-COLOURED FAN,** *probably French. The decoration of this fine piece imitates highly ornate mid 18th century fans. The pierced and carved sticks and guards are gilded and painted with flowers and foliage. 1855; 10in high.* **£250 – £350**

▽ **IVORY BRISÉ FAN** *In a brisé fan the wide, flat sticks overlap to form the body of the fan when open. Although this one was made in China, the central illustration, in the style of Watteau, was probably painted in France. The translucent quality of the fan can be clearly seen when it is held up to the light (below left). It comes complete with its leather case, which increases the value. 1780 – 1810; 9in high.* **£1,000 – £1,500**

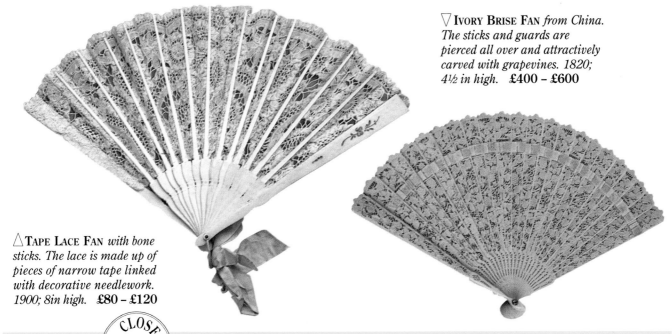

△ TAPE LACE FAN *with bone sticks. The lace is made up of pieces of narrow tape linked with decorative needlework. 1900; 8in high.* **£80 – £120**

▽ IVORY BRISE FAN *from China. The sticks and guards are pierced all over and attractively carved with grapevines. 1820; 4½ in high.* **£400 – £600**

ORIENTAL FANS

After France, China and Japan were the largest producers of carved and painted fans in the late 18th and early 19th centuries, exporting exquisitely carved ivory and sandalwood brisé examples. These included 'Fans of a Thousand Faces', such as those illustrated here, featuring distinctive tiny faces which were hand painted on pieces of ivory and then stuck to the fans. The two Japanese versions below date from about 1870. They are worth around £120 each due to their poor condition. If perfect, they could fetch £300 to £400.

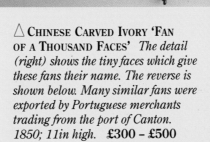

△ CHINESE CARVED IVORY 'FAN OF A THOUSAND FACES' *The detail (right) shows the tiny faces which give these fans their name. The reverse is shown below. Many similar fans were exported by Portuguese merchants trading from the port of Canton. 1850; 11in high.* **£300 – £500**

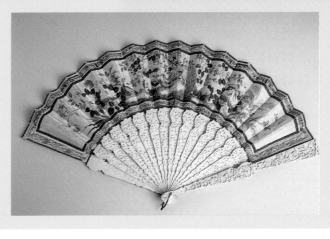

The majority of the lace brought to Roadshows is machine-made, usually from cotton. First produced in 1764, this type of lace has a regular design and a rigid background pattern, so that it is difficult to follow the direction of a single thread from one area of the design to another.

The charm of handmade laces, most of which are made from very fine linen thread, is the individual variation in their tension and construction. Over the years, three major types have been popular.

In the 16th and 17th centuries the most common types of lace were needle-point and cutwork since the geometric designs produced suited the fashions of the day. Needlepoint lace is made by building up minute layers of buttonhole stitches with a needle and thread. In whitework or cutwork lace, cut pieces of fabric are joined then decorated with embroidery.

During the 18th century, the fluid lines of patterns in bobbin lace made it more popular. The distinctive texture of bobbin lace results from the twisting and intertwining of lengths of thread which are attached to bobbins weighted with glass beads.

Although all these laces have been widely used, the emphasis since the late 18th century has been on machine-made and embroidered nets which were cheap and quick to make.

Until about 1800 most needlepoint lace was made in England and Spain.

In the 19th century production was centred in Burano in Italy, Youghal in Ireland and Point de Gaze, Belgium; today Greece and China make the majority of lace of this type. The best bobbin laces of the 18th and 19th centuries were made in Bedfordshire, Buckinghamshire, Honiton in Devon, and in Belgium; 18th century Milanese and Genoese laces are also prized.

Lace is tolerant of most conditions and rarely discolours. The best way to store fine lace is to interleave it between sheets of acid-free tissue paper. It can be also mounted on to acid-free board with cotton thread, but should never be pinned (rust marks are almost impossible to remove). Machine-made lace can be cleaned at home, but needlepoint, bobbin and cutwork lace all require specialist treatment.

◁ **IRISH CROCHET COLLAR** *This type of lace, made using a very fine steel crochet hook and fine cotton, was first produced in the 1840s. The pendant 'acorn' toggles are formed by working the crochet over wooden shapes. 1910; 13in wide.* **£30 – £50**

▽ **BRUSSELS LACE LAPPET** *This bobbin-made design is attached to the net base with small embroidered spots and needlepoint details. A lappet was worn over the head, with the panels falling down on either side of the face. 1860; 3ft 10in long.* **£30 – £50**

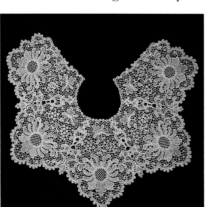

△ **CHEMICAL LACE COLLAR** *Invented in 1883, this process involved working a design by machine in cotton on a fine silk background. This was then placed in a chemical bath to dissolve the silk, leaving the design. 1900; 18in across.* **£10 – £20**

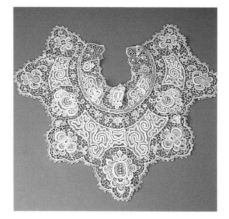

△ **MACHINE-MADE COLLAR** *This one-piece design imitates 17th century Italian needlepoint and also includes small sections of tapelace. There are bones in the neck for extra stiffening. 1905; 17in across.* **£25 – £45**

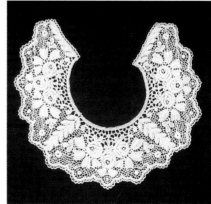

△ **LACE COLLAR,** *loosely based on Irish crochet but in fact machine-made chemical lace. The chemical process causes the cotton threads to become fluffy, which can help in identifying machine lace. 1890s; 18in across.* **£5 – £15**

△ **MALTESE HANDKERCHIEF**
*Made from cream-coloured
silk, this bobbin lace edging
has ears of wheat and Maltese
cross motifs. This traditional
design was revived in the
1830s by Lady Hamilton
Chichester to provide work
for Maltese women. 1900;
12in x 12in.* **£10 – £15**

▽ **CHEMICAL LACE** *This
clever machine-made copy
of a Brussels Point de Gaze
hand-made pattern is
worked in a soft, fluffy
cotton fibre. The design is
oversewn repeatedly on a
special machine to give it
its raised texture. 1910;
2ft 9in long.* **£20 – £30**

△ **MACHINE-EMBROIDERED
DRESS FLOUNCE** *This
detailed whitework design
was worked on to a fine silk
gauze ground. The lace
was probably intended to be
part of a wedding dress, but
was never used. 1910 – 14;
3ft 4in x 12ft.* **£50 – £100**

▽ **HANDKERCHIEF OF MIXED
LACE** *The central piece is
fine lawn with a whitework-
embroidered monogram and
flowers, surrounded by a net
border of Brussels bobbin lace
swags, ribbons and an outer
border of flowerheads. 1860;
16in x 16in.* **£25 – £50**

▷ **HONITON LACE
COLLAR** *Honiton
lace of the mid 19th
century was very
high quality, but
this crude later
example is known
as 'slugs and snails'
because of the poorly
formed shapes.
The diamond and
plaited centres of
the flowerheads are
traditional. 1900;
20in.* **£20 – £40**

SEWING BOXES

In the 19th century, every well-educated lady was expected to be a competent needlewoman. There were seamstresses to do the more mundane tasks while the lady of leisure, often in company with her friends, could occupy herself with more decorative work.

All the necessary equipment for needlework was stored in a portable sewing box. Although usually made from rosewood, walnut or mahogany (often inlaid with mother-of-pearl, marquetry or parquetry), leather, cloth and boullework sewing boxes can all be found. Inside was a lift-out tray fitted with compartments designed to hold thread spools, tape measure, thimbles and pincushions, and depressions, pockets or loops to prevent scissors, needlecases and other items from rattling around when the box was moved from room to room.

The materials from which the fittings were made varied. In the days before disposable cottonreels, skeins of wool, silk and cotton were wound by hand on to thread spools made from wood, ivory or mother-of-pearl, and sometimes elaborately decorated. Sewing boxes contained at least one pair of scissors, but usually more, with steel blades and silver or gilt handles which were often decorated or inlaid with gem-stones. Similarly, thimbles might be made from silver, gilt or porcelain and could be engraved with their owner's name or initials.

Needlecases were usually ivory, although decorated silver examples, sometimes inset with precious stones, also exist. A sewing box contained several of these cases, each holding the needles appropriate to a different kind of work: embroidery, beadwork, lacework and so on. A cloth tape measure, which wound into a carved ivory or wooden case, was also an indispensable element of the sewing box.

The invention of the sewing machine in the mid 19th century led to the gradual decline of the well-fitted sewing box, so that by the 1920s many contained little more than an unadorned steel pair of scissors, a thimble and packets, rather than cases, of needles.

▽ **FRENCH RED TORTOISESHELL BOX** *with boullework decoration. The most ornate needlework tools tended to come from France, where flat sewing cases were more usual than true 'boxes'. The red velvet-lined interior is fitted with mother-of-pearl thread spools and needlecases, silver thimbles and scissors. The tray can be lifted out and there is further storage space beneath. 1820 – 30; 9in wide.* **£500 – £700**

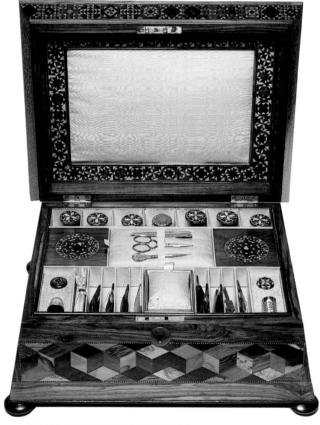

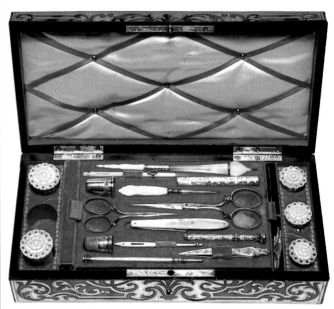

▷ **FINE-QUALITY ENGLISH ROSEWOOD BOX** *The exterior parquetry is continued in the interior of the box on the inside of the lid, on the individual compartment lids and on the thread spools. 1830; 14½ in wide.* **£400 – £700**

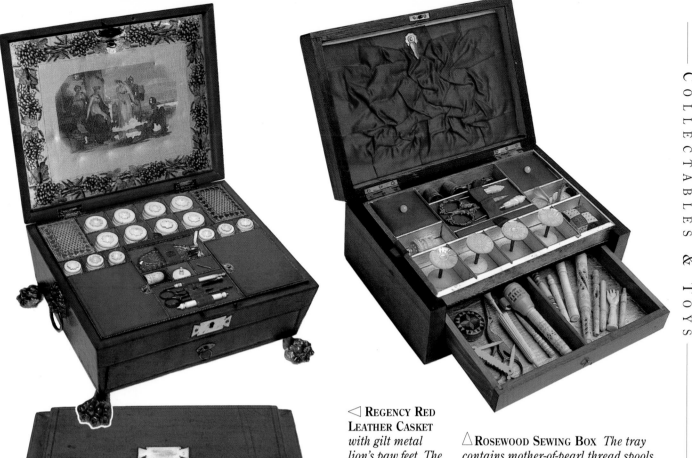

◁ **REGENCY RED LEATHER CASKET** *with gilt metal lion's paw feet. The metal plaque on the lid is engraved with the owner's name. In addition to the usual thread spools, pincushions, thimble, scissors, and needlecases, this box also has a fitted scent bottle, often found in early sewing boxes. 1810; 12in wide.* **£300 – £500**

△ **ROSEWOOD SEWING BOX** *The tray contains mother-of-pearl thread spools, an ivory-cased tape measure, scissors and thimbles. The ivory needlecases, including umbrella- and hand-shaped novelties, are stored in the drawer. 1860 – 80; 12in long.* **£120 – £180**

▽ **UTILITARIAN VELVET CASE** *with crimped lining and the minimum of articles fitted. The popularity of the sewing machine, mass-produced needles, and pre-wound disposable thread spools spelled the end of the fully equipped sewing box in the early years of this century. 1930; 6in long.* **£15 – £25**

THE CHATELAINE

Originally intended for the housekeeper to hold keys and other items for use in an emergency, chatelaines were also produced as ornaments for ladies. This one in silver contains thimble, scissors, button hook, pen and notebook, and tape measure, and is worth £300.

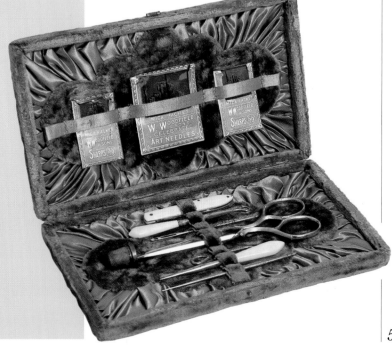

SCALES

There is an almost infinite variety of sizes and styles of weighing scale, but all are operated by one of two basic mechanisms: the balance beam or the spring balance. With a balance beam scale, weights on one side of a beam counterbalance the object to be weighed on the other. With a spring balance, the weight moves a spring which is linked to a calibrated dial.

The smallest scales were usually made from brass and used for weighing spices, precious metals, jewels and chemicals (these are generally referred to as analytical scales). Those that date from the 17th century are as precise as contemporary scientific or navigational instruments and are popular with collectors. Also desirable are sovereign scales, used for checking the weight of coins.

Most of today's collectable scales were mass produced in the 19th century for use in shops, railway and post offices, and in the home. Many of these machines are finely detailed and engineered, usually in brass, cast iron or a combination of the two. Condition is all-important, and any decoration – such as piercing, engraving, or enamelling on the base, tray, balance arms or support – adds to the value of a scale, which should be complete with its original weights.

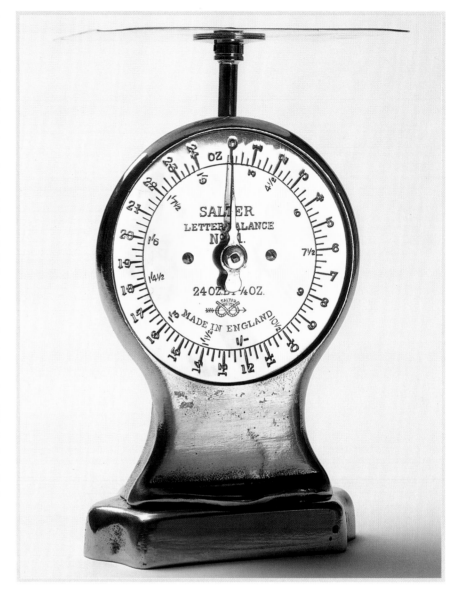

▷ **POST OFFICE SCALES** *have been made in many styles and sizes. This is a standard Salter (one of the biggest English scale manufacturers) 24oz letter balance in brass and steel. 1930; 7in high.* **£30 – £50**

◁ **GRAIN SCALES** *were used throughout the 19th century in local corn exchanges to check by weight the quality of grain on offer. This elegant instrument in cast iron and brass, made in London, is a fine example. 1820; 17in high.* **£300 – £400**

▽ **PORTABLE GRAIN SCALE** *with a sliding weight on a fixed beam: the further out this sits, the greater the weight to be counterbalanced. Complete with its box and a board for levelling the grain, it is a finely engineered piece in brass. 1840; 5in high.* **£200 – £250**

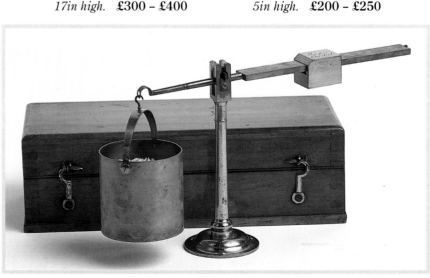

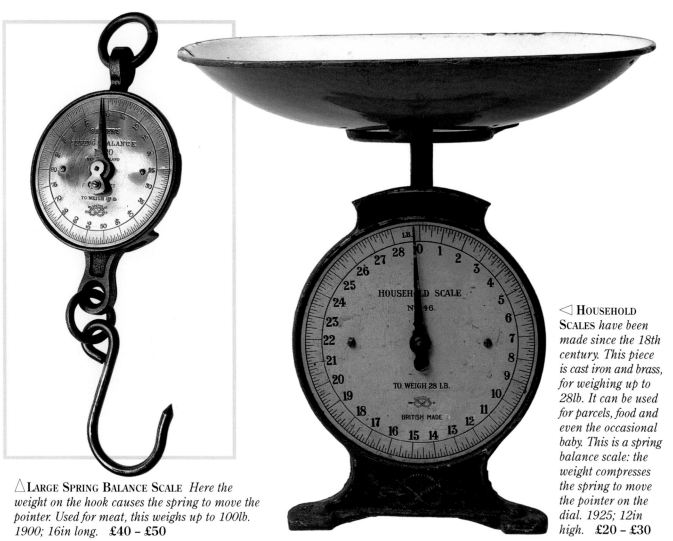

△ **LARGE SPRING BALANCE SCALE** *Here the weight on the hook causes the spring to move the pointer. Used for meat, this weighs up to 100lb. 1900; 16in long.* **£40 – £50**

◁ **HOUSEHOLD SCALES** *have been made since the 18th century. This piece is cast iron and brass, for weighing up to 28lb. It can be used for parcels, food and even the occasional baby. This is a spring balance scale: the weight compresses the spring to move the pointer on the dial. 1925; 12in high.* **£20 – £30**

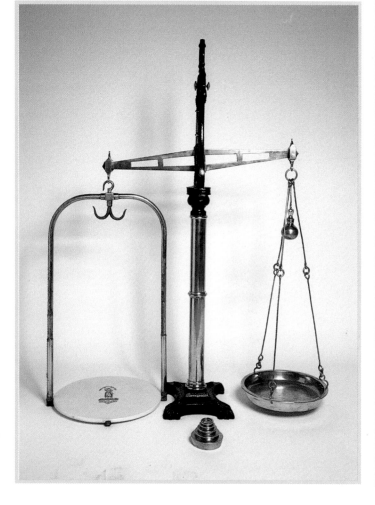

△ **BRASS BALANCE BEAM SCALE** *Weights are placed in the left-hand, circular tray to balance the dry goods in the removable scoop. These are fine scales, but the weights are missing. 1870; 20in high.* **£150 – £200**

▷ **SET OF SHOP BALANCE SCALES** *complete with porcelain slab and brass weights. Meat and other goods could be hung from the hook. Such high-quality scales are very desirable today. 1860; 2ft 6in high.* **£400 – £500**

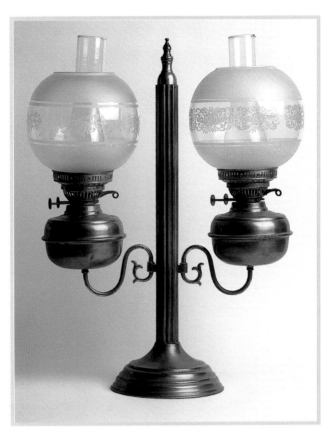

◁ **ADJUSTABLE DOUBLE LAMP** *in brass with glass shades and funnels. The stepped base is weighted with an iron core for stability. The scroll arms of the reservoirs add a touch of elegance. 1880 – 1900; 2ft high.* **£280**

▷ **VICTORIAN BRASS OIL LAMP** *with twin-stripe vaseline glass shade and glass reservoir. This may have been made at the glassworks of James Powell at Whitefriars in London. 1890; 2ft high.* **£200**

OIL LAMPS

Since they are so easily adapted for electricity without any loss of value, and since their price compares well with modern pieces, oil lamps today are very collectable. Their heyday was from about 1860 – when the discovery of vast reserves of oil enabled the production of cheap paraffin – until the turn of the century, when first gas, then electricity, became more widely available.

London had gas lighting by 1816, and other large towns and cities gradually followed the capital's lead. In workplaces and homes which could not be connected to gas, however, the paraffin lamp provided more powerful illumination, diffused over much greater distances, than the candles and wick-burning lamps which had been used for centuries.

Most paraffin lamps consist of a brass column supporting an oil reservoir, chimney and globe (or shade) made from glass. The more expensive the model, the more elaborate the column, and the better the quality of the reservoir and decoration of the globe. Acid-etched or coloured globes, as well as coloured glass reservoirs, were common in lamps intended for the drawing room, while a plain glass chimney, with no globe was more usual for a kitchen lamp.

The brilliance of the flame could be adjusted by turning a small knob above the oil reservoir (the wick winder), which raised the position of the wick. Extinguisher plates that snapped over the burning wick to put out the flame were often fitted on more elaborate models.

Little is known about the makers of oil lamps, although it is sometimes possible to attribute the glass globe to a particular manufacturer. Similarly, the wick mechanism occasionally bears a maker's name.

◁ **RAILWAY LAMP** *Made for Rhodesian Railways by Sherwoods of Birmingham, this has a heavy base to prevent it toppling with the movement of the train. 1910; 22in high.* **£60 – £80**

▷ **GLOBE-SHADED LAMP** *Most lamps intended for the grander rooms had a globe over the chimney to diffuse the light. Here, the red-lobed rim casts a pink glow. 1900; 23in high.* **£150**

◁ **COLUMN LAMPS** *The ruby glass reservoirs in these lamps enable the remaining level of oil to be easily determined. The solid brass column (left) is a typical late 18th century candlestick shape; the round column is made from turned, striated marble on a brass stand. The knobs for adjusting and trimming the wicks are clearly visible. 1880 – 90; 2ft 4in high (left), 2ft high (right). The pair* **£625**

▷ **BRASS LAMP** *The manufacturer of this fine late Victorian oil lamp avoided the more common column support. The reservoir is decorated with a mask motif and it stands on three exuberant winged cabriole legs with lion's paw feet, reminiscent of the neo-classical style of the early 19th century. The triangular base is made from pale marble. 1890; 19in high.* **£400**

AN OIL LAMP

A typical, good quality table lamp, this has a fluted brass column supporting a ruby glass reservoir. Although the chimney is made from plain glass, the globe is decorated. Valued at £200, it dates from the 1890s and is 28in high.

◁ *The globular shade has a matt surface to diffuse the light, giving it a softer glow. The decoration is acid-etched so that it looks like true engraving, but the lines are shallower.*

◁ *The fluted and twisted column and domed foot add a touch of elegance to this everyday article. The ceramic base provides the stability needed in a tall lamp.*

TYPES OF LAMP

Variations on the basic principle of an oil lamp – a reservoir of fuel feeding one or two lights – produced many different designs.

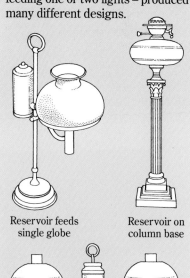

Reservoir feeds single globe

Reservoir on column base

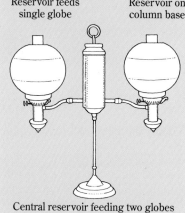

Central reservoir feeding two globes

Victorian innovation and enterprise were responsible for the development of two of the most common novelties brought to Roadshows: the magic lantern, and the zoetrope. Both were concerned with moving images as a means of amusement, and the magic lantern was the forerunner of the cine projector, the most popular mass entertainment of this century.

The zoetrope (from the Greek *zoe* meaning life and *tropos*, turn) creates an almost perfect illusion of movement using the scientific principle of 'persistence of vision'. A simply constructed toy, it consists of a tin cylinder (similar to a cake tin), open

△ **THE GREAT ZOETROPE,** *also known as a 'Wheel of Life'. Lids are often missing or broken, making this complete example rare. 1875; 16in high.* **£500 – £700**

at the top, and with vertical slots around it. This spins on a centrally mounted pin, supported on a wooden base. Strips of drawings consisting of up to ten consecutive images are placed inside the tin, and the whole is spun. As the viewer looks through the slots, the pictures appear to make one moving image.

Zoetropes were rather limited in appeal, and fell from favour early this century. They are therefore

△ **GERMAN ZOETROPE,** *made from tin plate. The coloured picture strips here depict a horse rider, tumbling acrobats and a tightrope walker. 1870; 17in high.* **£300 – £400**

fairly rare and even basic tin plate models can command several hundred pounds at auction.

Athanasius Kircher, a German, is credited with having conceived the 'modern' magic lantern around 1645. This more sophisticated device is based on the *camera obscura*, or pinhole camera, in which a bright image is projected through a hole in the dark box on to the wall of a darkened room. Instead of bright sunlight, Kircher used a candle, the light from which was concentrated by a concave mirror, and in place of the small hole he used glass lenses to focus the image on a white wall. As with

▷ **MAGIC LANTERN WITH CHROMATROPE** *In addition to square glass slides, this lantern can be used with chromatropes. When the chromatrope is inserted into the lantern and the handle turned, a moving kaleidoscopic image is produced on the screen.* **Lantern 1890; 18in long.** **£60 – £80**
Chromatrope 1870; 7in long. **£100 – £150**

◁ **CHILDREN'S MAGIC LANTERN** *This is a basic instrument, made for use in the nursery. It is complete with four boxes of amusing coloured glass slide strips which include views of New York and Washington, in addition to children playing in the snow and having fun. Slides for family viewing were often of a more educational nature. This also has its original box, which is reflected in the value. As is clear from the graphics on the box's label, this instrument was produced for an international market. 1910; 10in long.* **£80 – £120**

▽ **GERMAN MAGIC LANTERN** *by Ernst Plank. Complete with its original box, this was made for children to play with in the nursery. In most magic lanterns, petroleum oil or incandescent lime was used as the source of light, although some were later converted for use with electricity. This lantern still has its original set of slide strip stories. 1910; 10in long.* **£80 – £120**

the *camera obscura*, the room had to be darkened so that the viewer could see the often faint image. In the 19th century, with the addition of more intense light sources, better quality lenses and many of the technological advances which led to the development of photography, the magic lantern became a popular way to entertain the family.

Beautiful instruments were made by the Victorians, with brass and mahogany the most popular materials used in their construction. Many fine-quality magic lanterns with informative and educational slides were produced for family entertainment in the drawing room. In addition, however, more basic models, complete with brightly coloured slide strip stories, were made for children.

▽ **BINGOSCOPE SAFETY CINEMA** *This children's cine film projector is complete with films and fake leather trunk. 1928; trunk 14in long.* **£40 – £60**

▽ **SHUTTER AND LENS** *from an early cine projector. The sprocket and 'Maltese cross' control the shutter and movement of the film so that a continuous moving image is produced. 1900; 12in long.* **£125**

SNUFF BOXES

▷ **RAM'S HORN SNUFF 'MULL',** *decorated with quartz cairngorms – the traditional stone for mulls of this type. (The instruments for blending the snuff are attached.) 1865; 14in long.* **£650**

△ **PAPIER MACHE BOX** *decorated with a Napoleonic battle scene. This box is priced so highly because it was given to the owner's father by a member of the aristocracy. 1830; 3in wide.* **£1,200**

▷ **TWO SNUFF BOXES** *The shoe is carved from wood, the other is papier mâché inlaid with mother-of-pearl. 1860; 3in long.* Each **£25 – £40**

▷ **COMMEMORATIVE SNUFF BOXES** *in papier mâché, one showing William IV, the other Caroline, wife of George IV. Top 1820, bottom 1830; 3in wide.* Each **£400 – £500**

By the beginning of Louis XIV's reign in 1643 snuff-taking was all the rage throughout French society. The practice was introduced to England in 1660 by Charles II, who had been greatly influenced by the European courts, and its popularity quickly spread. Once snuff-taking had become firmly established in high society, the snuff box evolved from a simple, practical container into an important status symbol, reaching a peak of development in the 18th century.

Snuff containers were made in a variety of materials; the finest were of gold inset with enamel plaques, or of finely painted Continental porcelain, but many far less grand examples were also produced in cheaper materials ranging from silver, pewter, brass and horn, to tortoiseshell, papier mâché and wood. Curiously shaped 'novelty' snuff boxes were particularly popular, such as those in the form of a shoe. Collectors today would have difficulty rivalling Frederick the Great, however, who owned 1,500 boxes, or Madame de Pompadour who owned a different snuff box for every day of the year.

ENAMEL BOXES

The small enamel box, an essential fashion accessory for stylish ladies and gentlemen in the mid to late 18th century, contained a wide variety of social necessities, among them toothpicks, beauty patches and pills. Boxes were made from sheet-copper coated with a layer of opaque white enamel on which a design was painted or transfer-printed. The finest examples also had gilded mounts to protect the edges. Boxes came in a variety of shapes and sizes, some with mirrors in the lids, and decoration ranged from portraits and landscapes to mottoes and intricate designs.

The centre of the enamel trade at this time was the Black Country, in particular Bilston which produced a variety of decorative enamel items collectively known as 'toys'. Battersea, too, made enamel boxes in all sizes and patterns, and the transfer-printing technique used both there and at Bilston was subsequently adapted for use by major ceramics manufacturers, notably Worcester.

△ **ENAMEL BOX WITH MOTTO**
A great many boxes are decorated with hand-painted or printed mottoes, reflecting how frequently such thoughtful gifts were exchanged between friends and lovers. 1780; 2½in wide.
£100 – £150

▷ **HUNTING SCENE ENAMEL BOX** *The enduring popularity of decorated enamel items was largely due to the combination of bright colours used and delicate brushwork. This is a fine example and typical of its date. 1780; 1½in wide.* **£200 – £300**

▽ **STAFFORDSHIRE ENAMEL BOX** *charmingly decorated with a curled, sleeping dog. 1790; 1in wide.* **£300**

▽ **THE TONTINE INN** *at Sheffield. Boxes decorated with buildings or scenes were bought or given as commemorative gifts and souvenirs. 1810; 1½in wide.* **£200**

▽ **PILL OR PATCH BOX**, *the motto of which suggests it would have been given to a close friend who had moved away. 1800; 1in wide.* **£80 – £100**

▽ **ENAMEL BOX** *with a loving motto. Although attractive, this box is chipped and its 'collectability' thereby reduced. 1800; 1in wide.* **£50**

ORIENTAL CARVINGS

Chinese ivory carvings tend to be unadventurous in general. The majority are of religious figures such as minor Buddhist deities ('immortals') or Buddha himself. As with religious images the world over, the unchanging nature of the worshipped figure was emphasized, hence a carving of an immortal made in the Ming dynasty looks much like one made 400 years later. This has resulted, predictably, in a great many forgeries. A considerable number of supposedly early-looking carvings have been produced this century for export and the tourist trade.

As well as bearing spurious reign marks, usually from the Ming or Qing dynasties, many ivory figures have been 'aged' by smoking. Figures are left in a smoking chimney, resulting in cracking and staining which give pieces an authentically 'antique' appearance. In fact ivory does not darken significantly over the years and Chinese ivory figures with reign marks or brown staining should be viewed with great caution.

Few Chinese carvings were exported until the end of the 18th century when work baskets, boxes, fans, card cases and letter racks began to be made for the Western market, their quality ranging from fair to good. The decoration of exports

◁ CHINESE FISHERMAN IMMORTAL *in ivory, with details filled in black. Figures of this type can be difficult to date, and such pieces are best avoided (see box below right). 19in tall.* **£300 – £400**

▽ JAPANESE IVORY KINGFISHERS, *with finely detailed engraving and inlaid eyes, on a lotus pod made of stag antler. A quite superb piece, it is signed 'Kofu'. 1900; 11in long.* **£4,000 – £6,000**

△ JAPANESE WALRUS IVORY FISHERMAN *with Raiden, the Taoist god of thunder, in clouds above the head. The name 'Tamayuki', which is engraved on a red lacquer plaque on the base, denotes a studio rather than a single maker. 1900; 12in tall.* **£300 – £400**

IVORY AT THE ROADSHOW

Antique ivory is regularly brought along to Roadshows and some pieces are fine works of art. The ivory for the majority of these pieces was obtained long ago, before the world began to condemn the slaughter of elephants which supports the ivory trade. The same is not true of ivory obtained over the last 50 years, which should *never* be purchased. New ivory is notoriously difficult to date and collectors should not buy *any* ivory unless they are quite certain of its age.

was quickly standardized, with small figures and minutely detailed landscapes among the most common.

Around this time the Chinese began making modest quantities of soapstone carvings for export, and by the 19th and 20th centuries the early trickle had become a flood. Some of the first pieces are superbly carved, but later examples are poor.

If Chinese carvings lack inspiration, the reverse is true of Japanese pieces. Highly individual, they are full of verve, action and humour. Few early carvings have survived, with the exception of large wooden sculptures of temple guardians and Buddhas, and *netsuke* (toggles) carved in a variety of materials.

The carving industry underwent profound changes when Japan opened up to the West in the mid 19th century. The kimono was replaced by Western-style clothing in the 1860s, and with the introduction of pockets, pouches and *inro* (small, multi-layered boxes worn on the belt) became unnecessary, so making *netsuke* redundant. Some carvers continued to make *netsuke*, adapting them to Western tastes, while others turned to making larger figures and groups, known as *okimono*, from elephant or walrus ivory.

Today there is a strong market for the finest Japanese carvings, particularly in America and France, and interest is also increasing steadily in Japan itself.

JAPANESE MINIATURE IVORY CABINET

Only seven inches high and made in about 1880, this cabinet would have been produced specifically for export. Such pieces are fairly rare: they are made from 'sheets' of ivory, for which very large and expensive elephant tusks were required. This example is well lacquered in tones of gold and black (in places the lacquer has been built up to give a low relief), and the interior is decorated with motifs of birds and flowers. Expert David Battie (pictured here with the owner) valued the cabinet at between £2,000 and £3,000.

△ **JAPANESE IVORY FIGURE** *of a poultry farmer possibly testing an egg for freshness by scrutinizing the air sac. An exceptionally well carved, amusing piece. 1900; 10in tall.* **£2,000 – £3,000**

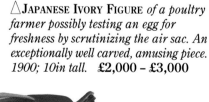

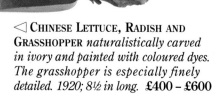

◁ **CHINESE LETTUCE, RADISH AND GRASSHOPPER** *naturalistically carved in ivory and painted with coloured dyes. The grasshopper is especially finely detailed. 1920; 8½ in long.* **£400 – £600**

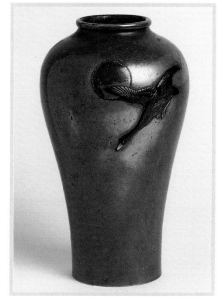

◁ **JAPANESE BRONZE PHEASANT,** *well cast with a dark patination relieved by details picked out in copper and gold. Birds, particularly game birds, are less common than other animal subjects and much sought after. Originally one of a pair which would have been worth £4,000 to £6,000, this single example is nevertheless very saleable. 1890; 12in long.* **£1,500 – £2,000**

The Bronze Age in China began around 1500BC and it was shortly after this date, in the Shang dynasty, that superbly crafted bronze food and wine vessels for ritual use first appeared. Such early pieces are exceptionally rare today and can command prices of up to as much as half a million pounds.

In Japan there was no comparable bronze age. Here, iron was the most prized metal and it was used primarily for making ceremonial teapots and kettles. But bronze was not entirely neglected: it was the preferred metal for replicas of Buddha. In fact Japan holds the record for the largest bronze figure in the world.

Made over 1,000 years ago, it stands 53 feet high and can be seen today at the temple of Nara in central Japan.

According to expert David Battie there is little more to be said about Chinese bronzes until the 19th century. During both the Ming and Qing dynasties (1368 – 1912) domestic items continued to be made, but these were mostly incense burners in the form of animals, human figures, or Buddhas which tended to be somewhat unimaginative and repetitive in design.

Bronze-making began to flourish once more in China in the 19th century, when a substantial number of pieces were made for export to

△ **JAPANESE BRONZE VASE** *with a goose flying by the moon, inlaid in a gold and silver alloy called 'shibuichi'. The plumage is particularly well engraved. The natural patination has suffered due to polishing, thereby halving the value of the piece, and repatination is costly. 1900; 9in high.* **£150 – £200**

◁ **BRONZE INCENSE BURNER AND VASE** *The vase (near left) is one of a pair worth around £200. Once bronze has been polished, as here, it is difficult to distinguish it from brass. These pieces are typical of the millions exported from China at the turn of the century. 1920; Incense burner 11in high.* **£150 – £200** *Vase 10in high.* **£50 – £60**

JAPANESE INFLUENCE

This fine Japanese-style teaset was in fact made by the American company Gorham & Tiffany in 1883. Made of iron and decorated with flowers and sea creatures in alloys of gold and silver, the set is worth around £1,500. Japan was reopened to trade in the 1850s and the enormous number of goods exported to Western markets profoundly influenced a wide range of artists and craftsmen.

Europe. These can be identified by their often crudely chased decoration of inlaid metal dragons flying in clouds. Those marked simply 'China' date from about 1891 to 1902, while those with a 'Made in China' mark date from after 1902.

The end of the 19th and the beginning of the 20th centuries saw the greatest period of Japanese bronze work. To meet the increasing demand in the West for fine-quality Oriental objects, Japanese metalworkers made bowls, tea wares, figures, vases and a variety of other pieces that rival any by their more famous Russian contemporary, Fabergé.

Trained in the tradition of samurai sword-making, Japanese metalworkers were skilled in employing a wide range of decorative techniques, such as the application of alloys. Different coloured alloys, created by treating a metal (frequently gold or silver) with acid, were applied to the surface of otherwise plain pieces. Tones of red, black and grey were particularly popular.

▷ **JAPANESE BRONZE DISH** *signed on the back by Inue, one of the better makers. It is inlaid in gold, copper and alloys with a naturalistic floral design typical of export wares. 1900; 15in wide.*
£600 – £900

▷ **JAPANESE SPILL (TAPER) VASES** *in bronze, decorated with mandarin ducks, symbols of marital fidelity. The decorator has made clever use of silver in the prunus blossom and stream. 1900; 4½ in high.*
£500 – £800

TINY JAPANESE 'KODANSU' *or decorative boxes of drawers. They were both made by Komai, a leading metalworker who specialized in inlaying gold into iron. Many of these intricately crafted boxes have been badly affected by rust – these are in fine condition. 1900; 3in high. Each*
£2,000 – £3,000

BRONZE FIGURES

▷ **MAN AGAINST NATURE**
*This fine-quality statue of
a man wrestling a lioness
is typical of the 19th
century approach to
classicism. Made in
France, it has an
excellent patina and
its original marble
base. 1880; 2ft high.*
£1,800 – £2,250

▽ **CLASSICAL-STYLE BRONZE** *after a
marble original of Belvedere Antinous.
It is either Florentine or French, and is
paired with a Medici Venus (the pair is
worth £15,000 – £25,000). Late 17th
century; 20in high.* **£5,000 – £7,000**

△ **SEATED LADY** *Many 19th century
French bronze figures could be attached
to furniture or used as supports for
clocks. This statue was originally part
of a clock, but could also stand on its
own. 1860; 11in high.* **£300**

▽ **VENUS,** *Roman goddess of love, was a
popular 19th century subject and statues
of her exist in parian porcelain and
marble, as well as bronze. This is similar
in style to works by the French sculptor
Pradier. 1890; 12in high.* **£600 – £800**

During the 16th and 17th centuries
craftsmen in Continental Europe
produced small, high-quality statues,
cast mainly in bronze, that were
inspired by pieces from Greek and
Roman antiquity. Generally made
only in small quantities, these figures
were popular into the 18th century.

At the height of the Rococo period
bronze was used only for furniture
decoration, but the classical revival
of the late 18th century and the
growing number of travellers in
Europe keen to bring home statue
replicas provided a new stimulus for
bronze-making. Most of the figures
that survive today are 19th century
pieces, made in France or Italy.

The growing market for sculpture
in the late 19th century triggered
experiments to develop a cheaper
metal than bronze. The result was
spelter, a low grade zinc alloy which
could be coloured and finished to look
like bronze. Many classical figures of

the late 19th and early 20th centuries are actually made from spelter. Lighter and softer than bronze and more easily damaged, it is also often poorly cast and finished.

The introduction of new modelling materials, including spelter, together with improvements in metal casting techniques, generated an enthusiasm for decorative sculpture. Classical figures and historical subjects proved popular, and the fascination for naturalism during the 19th century stimulated a fashion for sculptures of the female figure which became increasingly dominant at the end of the century. Initially, however, animal sculpture was more successful. French artists dominated the 'animalier' school from the 1830s; among the most famous were Antoine-Louis Barye (1795 – 1875) and Pierre-Jules Mène (1810 – 70), who modelled both domestic and wild animals as well as hunting and racing scenes, and artist Paul-Joseph Gayrard (1807 – 55), noted for his particularly fine humorous bronzes.

Prices for classical bronzes are affected by the quality of casting – which can vary considerably – the rarity of the model and subject matter, and the patination (the colour of the bronze that develops over the years). The sculptor is also significant: a model bearing the signature of an identifiable artist and the founder's mark is always desirable.

▽ '**MONKEY STEEPLECHASE**' *by Gayrard. Although a good cast, this piece has been polished and repaired, which reduces its value. 1850; 10in wide.*
£1,000 – £1,500

▽ **CIGAR LIGHTER** *and cheroot holder, with a gas feed line for permanent desktop mounting. This humorous-style bronze was produced by Fay et Cie in Paris. 1890; 10in wide.* **£700 – £800**

▷ **CECIL BROWN BRONZE** *This is a replica of the Imperial Camel Corps memorial in London's Embankment Gardens. A connection with T. E. Lawrence would enhance the value. 1920; 17in high.*
£1,000 – £1,500

◁ '**SWEETHEART'S FAREWELL**' *Russian bronzes are rare but this example by Gratchev is finely detailed and of good quality. 1900; 10in high.*
£2,500 – £3,000

ORIENTAL CLOISONNE

The technique known as cloisonné is a complex one which was practised first by Chinese and then by Japanese craftsmen, although, surprisingly perhaps, it was introduced to the East from the West (enamelling on metal was a speciality of the Limoges region of France in the Middle Ages).

The cloisonné method involves fixing a pattern of wires on to a metal body (usually brass or copper, but occasionally precious metals were used) according to a drawn design. The small cells formed by the wires, called *cloisons*, are filled with enamel made from a paste of coloured ground glass, and the piece is fired. When drawn from the kiln it is a runny mess, but polishing transforms it into an exquisite creation, somewhat similar in appearance to stained glass. Indeed, Japanese craftsmen are known to have spent periods of up to a year on the polishing stage in order to produce the finest pieces.

Cloisonné is a variation of the champlevé technique (champlevé preceded the development of cloisonné in Europe) in which cells are simply gouged out of a cast bronze base, rather than formed by wires, and then filled with enamel. In later forms the 'barriers' are incorporated into the original mould.

The Chinese began making cloisonné in the 14th century. Their repertoire of designs and colours was fairly limited, however: most designs were of fruit, mythical beasts or scrolling foliage with flowers and

△ JAPANESE CHAMPLEVE FIGURES *of three Chinese deities. The dark patination of the features is original and should never be polished. 1880s; 6–10in high.* Each **£600 – £900**

CLOISONNE MOTIFS

The most common motifs are dragons, the lotus and the eight precious objects of Taoism. Each motif has a special meaning.

Dragon with flaming pearl (regeneration)

Lotus blossom (purity, truth, creative power)

Paired fish (fertility, conjugal happiness)

Endless knot (longevity, giving and receiving)

Wand or sceptre (wish-granting)

Fan (official's insignia, attribute of deities)

◁ JAPANESE MOONFLASK, *so-called because of its shape. This is an early Japanese example of cloisonné, though the style is reminiscent of Chinese pieces. The roundels on the front and back (inset) show a carp turning into a dragon as it leaps a waterfall (symbolic of a student passing his exams). 1860s; 13in high.* **£700 – £1,000**

◁ CHINESE INCENSE BURNER *decorated with encircled 'shou' characters, which symbolize long life, and lotus blossoms. A fine piece, it is heavy and the bronze has been gilded on its exposed surfaces. It bears the reign mark of the Emperor Kienlong (1736 – 95). 5½ in high.* **£2,000 – £3,000**

△ **PAIR OF CHINESE COVERED CUPS** *decorated with flying dragons on a black background (a popular design). The turquoise enamel and gilt edges are typical features. 1920s; 7in high.* **£300 – £400**

figures, and the predominant colour was generally blue. Although few in number, the designs were applied to a vast range of forms, including vases, bowls, dishes, boxes and animals.

Cloisonné marks are rare and should be discounted as an accurate means of dating. Particularly unreliable are those marks which read '*ta Ming nien chi*', which translates as 'Made in the Period of the Ming

Dynasty'. Marks such as this indicate that the piece was made in Japan in the 19th century. Chinese pieces from the 19th and 20th centuries are often marked '*ta Ming*'. A black background generally indicates a piece from the 1920s or '30s, while earlier examples have a rough, distinctly pin-holed quality.

Chinese cloisonné greatly influenced both European and Japanese

▽ **CHINESE CLOISONNE VASES** *These are unusual in that they are marked on the base. The casting is heavy and the decoration is superb. Mid 18th century; 6in high.* Each **£1,500**

△**CHINESE CLOISONNE** *Both the bowl and the vase bear a false Ming mark. Early pieces were never enamelled in green. 1930s. Bowl 11in wide.* **£150** *Vase 13in high.* **£30 – £40**

craftsmen: Japanese figures (of which very few were made) are always Chinese in style and they are based on the eight Taoist 'immortals' or deities. In general, Japanese cloisonné is more desirable than the Chinese variety, being notably lighter and finer.

Original dark patination is frequently apparent in both cloisonné and champlevé pieces: neither type should ever be polished.

△ **CLOISONNE CENSER AND COVER,** *very attractively decorated with exotic birds. It has a copper body, which means it could be easily damaged, but this example is in perfect condition. 1890; 6in high.* **£250 – £350**

A CLOSER LOOK AT

A FRENCH JARDINIERE

At first glance this magnificent 5ft 3in high jardinière, or flower stand, looks Oriental, but closer inspection reveals a mark which identifies it as having been made in 1874 by the celebrated French company of metalworkers, Christofle of Paris. The actual jardinière is Japanese in style, with crane handles, gilt bronze celestial clouds and a distinctive design of waves and cranes, while the simulated bamboo pedestal is more Chinese in character. It is worth £8,000 to £12,000 (the maker's mark adds about £1,000 to the price).

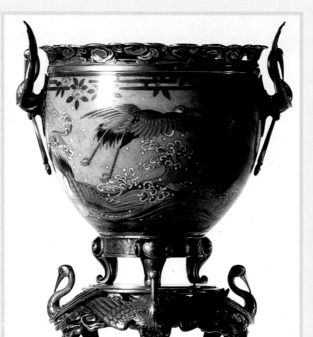

▽ *Expert Eric Knowles maintains that this jardinière from the Cleethorpes Roadshow is the finest such piece that he has ever seen.*

Waves and a flying crane superbly executed in cloisonné.

Gilt bronze crane handle with pendant loop.

Gilt metal mount in the form of a crane on the bronze stand.

Manchurian crane motif, modified by French craftsmen.

TIN BOXES

Printed tins first started to appear in any quantity in the 1870s, after the development of the lithographic printing process. From this time on, manufacturers of biscuits in particular (Huntley and Palmer were the first company to take advantage of the new process), chocolates and confectionery, tea and coffee, tobacco and medicinal products, vied with one another to design and produce decorative promotional tins.

'Juvenile' tins, made as stocking fillers for children in such shapes as castles and drums and often intended for later use as money boxes, were produced from the 1890s. The most inventive period, however, was just before and after World War I, due to a combination of advances in both food production methods and box manufacturing techniques.

Tins with royal connections are always popular. Some of these were made to commemorate jubilees or coronations, but during the Boer War and World War I, members of the royal family endorsed tins containing chocolates, cigarettes and other goods to be sent to soldiers. Since they were made in large quantities, these are not particularly valuable.

Prices for tins vary enormously, depending on shape, design and designer, rarity and condition. Age is no guarantee of value: a 1920s plain tin is worth a few pounds; a rare 1950s design considerably more.

▷ FAIRY TREE MONEY BOX *Tins in unusual shapes or by well-known artists are of special interest to collectors. This money box, made for Crawford's biscuits, features a design by Mabel Lucie Attwell, the children's book illustrator. 1925; 14in high.* **£200**

▽ COMMEMORATIVE WARES *Special packaging to celebrate royal occasions has been popular since Queen Victoria's Jubilee in 1887. This tin for Rowntree's chocolates was produced for the Coronation of Edward VII. 1902; 6in long.* **£10 – £15**

▽ TOFFEE TIN *Exotic shapes have most appeal. Here the tin underlines the trade name of Mackintosh's Beehive toffee. 1930; 7in wide.* **£40 – £80**

▷ BISCUIT TIN *The base of this lavishly decorated tin (below right) bears Huntley & Palmers' award for excellence from the Paris Exhibition of 1878. 1898; 9in long.* **£50 – £100**

ADVERTISING MATERIAL

PEARS' SOAP *One of the great names of late Victorian advertising was Pears, best known for its sentimental images (below). The figure (left), modelled by Italian sculptor Giovanni Focardi, was made by Watcombe Terracotta, Devon. It was later widely copied in plaster and other materials (right).* Printed advertisement *1910; 6in high.* **£5**
Figure left *1880; 25in high.* **£1,000**
Figure right *1900; 16in high.* **£200**

YOU DIRTY BOY!

From the original Pears Soap sculpture.
"YOU DIRTY BOY" (after G Focardi)

"This is the way we wash our hands,"
"Wash our hands,"
"Wash our hands,"
"This is the way we wash our hands,"
"With PEARS' SOAP in the morning."

▽ **YORKSHIRE RELISH DISH**, *an adaptation of the Willow pattern, and probably made in Staffordshire. This is typical of many domestic wares made for advertising purposes by the late Victorians. 1880; 4in across.* **£30**

The appeal of advertising material lies in its variety, its essentially decorative quality and its relative cheapness and accessibility. It is also hard to ignore the fact that advertising is by its very nature ephemeral, so that practically every poster or figurine, dish or bottle, tin or packet that survives has done so by chance.

Advertising as we understand the term is largely a Victorian innovation, a natural by-product of that intensely commercial and inventive period. Almost unknown at the beginning of Victoria's reign (when food manufacturers, for example, supplied goods to retailers in large quantities for the retailer to package for his individual customers), by the end of her reign, it had become a major and potent social force.

There are many reasons for its swift development. Mass production techniques enabled food manufacturers to package goods individually, thereby shifting the responsibility of publicity from retailer to manufacturer. The Trade Marks Act of 1875 gave rise to and then protected the brand name. The spread of the railways provided manufacturers with a truly national market place for the first time, and the growth of the Empire meant new, seemingly limitless, markets to be tapped.

Newspapers had carried advertisements of sorts since the 17th century, but in Victorian England the railway station, with its transient but captive audience, became the most natural setting for product advertising. Old photographs show stations and hoardings covered in slogans, posters and placards, making all manner of exaggerated claims. Nor was the Royal Family exempt from exploitation. Manufacturers claimed, without any foundation, the royal seal of approval for their goods.

The Victorian era is perhaps best characterized as the 'adolescence' of advertising, and represents all that is brazen, exuberant and highly competitive in the medium. Although a more orderly approach became common later, advertising material was probably never as decorative or such fun as in these early years.

The first advertisements relied essentially on typography to convey their message. Notable examples include theatre and circus playbills, with their adventurous selection of wood-cut typefaces, boldly printed in black and red. Developments in colour printing techniques from the 1860s onward, however, brought the colourful picture poster into existence. By the end of the century, posters and leaflets, bottles and packaging, enamel

DRINKS AND DRINKING

▽ **FAMOUS NAMES** *Ashtrays, trays, jugs and other items used to promote brands of drinks, while of recent origin, are desirable. 1930 – 60; Each £15 – £50*

▷ **CERAMIC TOUCANS** *Many models of the Guinness toucan were made by Carlton Ware, but the set of wall plaques is the most collectable. 1960; 5 – 10in long. The set £300*

Items connected with drinking have always been popular collectables, partly because of the extraordinary diversity of available material. For 100 years, brewers and drinks manufacturers have been making great efforts to promote their products, turning pubs and bars into richly decorated and colourful places in the process. The range available includes glasses, bottles, jugs, ashtrays, signs and placards, calendars, figurines, bottle openers and corkscrews, trays and even small pieces of furniture. Some familiar brand names such as Guinness have a particular appeal, but many lesser known and more modern wares are also of interest, and beer mats should not be overlooked.

signs, vehicles, stationery, tableware and a host of related domestic products were being used to communicate the manufacturer's claims.

For many collectors the Victorian and Edwardian eras represent the golden age of advertising, but every period has its own distinctive style and appeal. The jazz-influenced 1920s and Art Deco modernism of the 1930s are popular periods in which to specialize. Today material from the 1950s and '60s, decades that are well documented by design and social historians, is fast becoming highly collectable.

Other collectors choose to specialize by subject, with smoking and drinking, costume, food and domestic products, and travel and transport among the most popular areas. It is also possible to base a collection on materials such as pottery, glass, wood, tin or Bakelite; or to focus on objects, with ashtrays, matchboxes, figurines and bottle openers all common themes.

Enamel wares are always popular, and some of the best known advertising signs for brands of cigarettes, petrol, tea, chocolate, soap and drinks have been reproduced, a reflection of the current enthusiasm for nostalgia. Modern copies, which lack the quality and richness of the originals, reveal the decorative appeal of old styles.

◁ **ENDURING STYLES** *Labels are always interesting, as few survive in good condition. 1930; 2 – 5in. Each 50p – £5*

▽ **ROBERTSON'S GOLLIES** *The golly has been Robertson's trademark since 1928. These plaster bandsmen are typical of collectable golly wares. 1960; 3in high. The set £40 – £60*

CHILDREN'S BOOKS

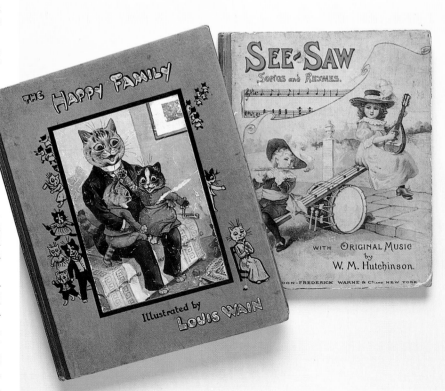

The first children's books, horn books, were not books at all but sheets of vellum or paper mounted on wood, ivory or bone and inscribed with a cross, the letters of the alphabet, the vowels, a prayer and Roman numerals. A sheet of transparent horn protected the paper, and a hole in the handle meant that the 'book' could be tied to the child's belt. Genuine early horn books are very rare. The more common late 18th and early 19th century examples are curios: by this time children were learning to read by other methods.

The earliest known book published exclusively for children is Kunst und Lehrbüchlein (1580). It is also the first printed book to show a child holding a horn book and the first to show a child holding a doll.

British printers soon followed the Continental lead, producing 'chap' books – one sheet folded to make 8, 12 or 16 pages – to be sold at fairs and markets by pedlars or 'chaps'. Subjects ranged from popular legends such as Jack the Giant Killer, Tom Thumb and Reynard the Fox, to religious tracts, simplified travelogues and biographies. Recreational publishing for children became a recognized market only in the mid 18th century, and not until the 19th century were children's books widespread.

The first publisher to promote children's literature that was amusing and instructive, rather than morally uplifting, was John Newbery (1713 – 67). Among his publications were *Pretty Little Pocket Books*, priced at 6d (2½p); in addition many well-known titles, some of which were later reworked,

◁ **RAPHAEL TUCK** *were pioneers in the children's book world of the late 19th century, with high-quality illustrations and immaculate chromolithography. 'In Dolly Land' is typical of their work, printed on linen for durability and with bold, bright illustrations. 1890; 6in.* **£20**

▽ **POPULAR CATS** *Louis Wain's cat illustrations were popular from the 1890s until World War I, and all his works are now sought after. 'See Saw' was produced by Frederick Warne, best known for their editions of Beatrix Potter. Cats 1914; 7in.* **£250** *See Saw 1880; 6in high.* **£30**

were first published by his company. Among the authors who worked extensively for Newbery was Oliver Goldsmith (1730 – 74) whose *Goody Two Shoes, Giles Ginger-bread, Roman History* and *History of the Earth and Animated Nature* he published.

By the end of the 18th century there were six other publishers specializing in juvenile literature. The Industrial Revolution and the rise of a moneyed middle class gave publishers, authors and artists a ready market. Some of the most prolific authors were women of the leisured classes, including Maria Edgworth, Lady Eleanor Fenn and Mrs Barbauld.

By the mid 19th century, another change was apparent: model children gradually gave way to more realistic characters. The

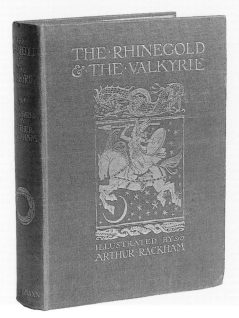

△ **BEANO ANNUALS** *Although the first Beano annual was produced for Christmas 1939, early editions are difficult to find since publishers D.C. Thomson recommended their readers to sell copies for salvage during World War II. From 1943 to 1953 the annual was entitled the 'Magic Beano Book'; its most famous character, Dennis the Menace, appeared in 1951. 1951 – 90; 11in high.* Each **£20 – £50**

◁ **DICK BARTON SPECIAL AGENT** *was first broadcast in 1946 and proved such a success that the BBC decided to issue the first six scripts, with a minimum of artwork added, in annual form. This formula was repeated each year the series ran, until 1951. An edition of this first annual, in very good condition, would be worth £50. 1946; 10in high.* **£25**

ARTHUR RACKHAM

Rackham (1867 – 1939) is one of the most highly acclaimed children's illustrators. Although he found fame in 1900 with an edition of *Grimm's Fairy Tales*, his artistic style and publishing practice were not truly defined until 1905, when he produced a beautiful, signed, limited edition of *Rip Van Winkle*. From then on, he produced about a book a year with magnificent colour plates mounted on to the page. Alongside an ordinary edition, he also issued a signed, limited edition in a special parchment, vellum or white buckram binding. This 1910 ordinary first edition, with buckram binding and 34 watercolour plates, is worth £150.

titles that best chart this progress are Lewis Carroll's *Alice in Wonderland* (1865) with its appealing but slightly bad-tempered heroine, and Robert Louis Stevenson's *Treasure Island* (1883). The cruelty of Thomas Hughes' *Tom Brown's School Days* (1857) and miseries of Eric in *Eric, or Little by Little* (1858) by F. W. Farrer underline this move towards realism, or at least towards realistic feelings.

At the same time, bindings were being remodelled. Paper and leather or vellum gave way first to bold machine-blocked cloth with blind or gilt stamping (which leave an impressed title and/or image), then to colour. By the 1880s in Germany Lothar Meggendorfer was producing moving picture books, which were widely imitated by other publishers. The second half of the 19th century also saw the introduction and proliferation of children's magazines, forerunners of the modern comic.

The 20th century

The meteoric rise in popularity of the comic and comic book has led to a wealth of books and, particularly,

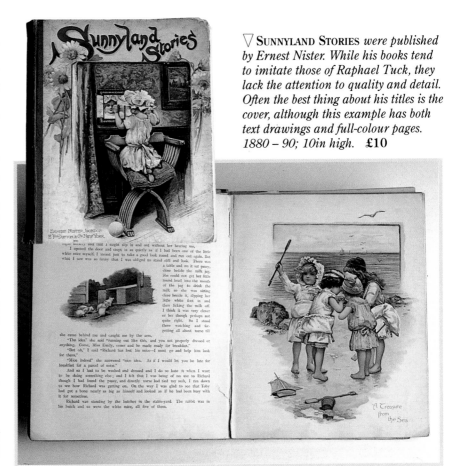

▽ SUNNYLAND STORIES *were published by Ernest Nister. While his books tend to imitate those of Raphael Tuck, they lack the attention to quality and detail. Often the best thing about his titles is the cover, although this example has both text drawings and full-colour pages.* 1880 – 90; 10in high. **£10**

ANNUALS

The first annuals were simply collections of the year's weekly or monthly magazines, bound together with a title page and perhaps a frontispiece illustration. Charles Dickens' *Christmas Books* and Kate Greenaway's *Almanacs* were new works designed for Christmas, but the annual as we know it, using the ingredients of the weekly or monthly magazine with additional layouts and illustrations, is a 20th century innovation. Interest in annuals has increased lately, and prices are unstable.

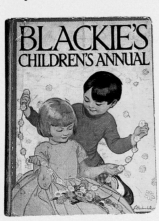

◁ BLACKIE'S CHILDREN'S ANNUAL, *introduced in the early 1920s, lacked distinction. Although it had bright covers, the insides were printed on thick, coarse paper with only the occasional colour plate.* 1923; 11in high. **£5**

△ CARTOONS AND COMIC STRIPS *Mickey Mouse, introduced on film in 1928, was the first Disney creation to have an annual; he was followed by Donald Duck in 1936, Snow White in 1937, and Pinocchio in 1939. Rupert first appeared in 'The Daily Express' in 1920 and has remained popular, with an annual every year since the 1930s. Bobby Bear and the Lion started life in comics: The 'Lion Annual' is based on 1950s science fiction.* Mickey 1940s; 9in. **£8** Lion 1958; 9½in. **£5**

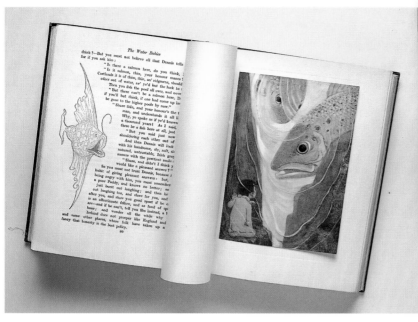

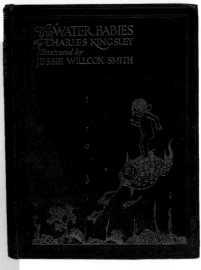

▷ **THE WATER BABIES** *by Charles Kingsley was first published as text only in 1863. Its characters and magical settings, however, lent themselves to illustration. This edition was illustrated in bold realistic style by American Jessie Wilcox Smith. 1920; 9in high.* **£45**

annuals derived from their central characters. The adventures of Dan Dare, Rupert, Batman and Superman, and copies of the *Beano* are now being traded among collectors at many times their original cover prices.

High-quality children's books of the 20th century include Beatrix Potter's (1866 – 1943) deceptively simple illustrations and writing; the stories of A. A. Milne (1882 – 1956) and Kenneth Grahame (1859 – 1932); the fabulous world of Arthur Rackham; and the rich, rebellious works of Roald Dahl (1915 – 90).

The major consideration when collecting children's books is their condition. Almost by definition, they are not well kept. The most highly prized examples therefore are those in near perfect state.

▷ **STYLES AND QUALITY** *The simple, inexpensive (it is printed on pulp and uses only red and black) layout of the Mickey annual is nonetheless very effective. Rupert, on the other hand, is printed in colour throughout on good quality paper, and offers something for children with varying levels of reading skill. The Rupert-inspired Bobby Bear does not have the same educational value. Rupert 1970s; 9½ in.* **£5** *Bobby Bear 1940s; 9½ in.* **£8**

EARLY TIN PLATE VEHICLES

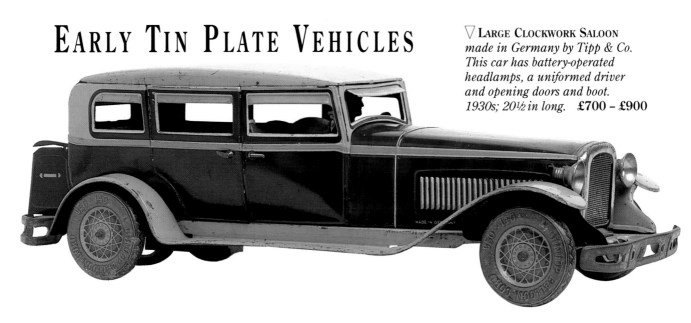

▽ LARGE CLOCKWORK SALOON
*made in Germany by Tipp & Co.
This car has battery-operated
headlamps, a uniformed driver
and opening doors and boot.
1930s; 20½ in long.*   **£700 – £900**

The first tin plate vehicles were made in Germany in the early 19th century. Carriages were the main modes of transport at that time, and they were accurately represented in the dainty toy carriages that were made for children. This mirroring of contemporary society – which continued over the decades – is one of the principal reasons why the collecting of tin plate vehicles is so popular today.

As the various methods of transport changed, so the toy vehicles were adapted to encourage children to update their old models with the latest designs. Before 1908, most toys were cut from tin-plated steel sheets and shaped, soldered and painted by hand. After this date, however, they began to be manufactured by the offset lithographic process, which quickly became more widespread and increasingly important. In this process designs and decoration were printed on to flat metal sheets, which were then cut and shaped by machine, and held in position by metal tabs. This more mechanized process meant that tin plate toys could be produced more cheaply and in greater quantities, so tin plate vehicles, which had once been expensive luxuries that only the rich could afford, became available to the general public at more reasonable prices. (As well as vehicles, tin plate has also been used for making character toys, animal figures, robots and novelty toys.)

In the 19th century, Germany was the largest manufacturer and exporter of tin plate toys, subtly adapting the colours or lettering on their vehicles to appeal to specific countries. American toy production began in the mid 19th century, but as few toys were exported to Europe,

△ TIN PLATE LIMOUSINE *made
by the German manufacturer
Gebrüder Bing. Running on
spoked wheels, this clockwork car
has a driver, opening rear doors
and a handbrake. 1920s;
10½ in long.*   **£500 – £700**

▷ RARE FOUR-SEATER TONNEAU
*made in Germany by Gunthermann.
This lithographed clockwork vehicle
contains four hand-painted military
figures and runs on spoked wheels
with real rubber tyres. 1908;
7¾ in long.*   **£800 – £1,200**

France and England became Germany's main competitors.

The appeal of tin plate vehicles began to to wane from about 1934 onward as die-cast toys (which were cheaper to make) started to become more popular. The last tin plates were the magnificent Cadillacs, Chryslers, Buicks and Fords produced in Japan in the 1950s and '60s. The rarest of these can fetch several thousand pounds.

◁ **OPEN LORRY** *made in Germany by J. L. Hess. It is powered by a flywheel mechanism primed by winding the starting handle. 1920; 10in long.* **£600 – £900**

A CLOSER · LOOK AT ·

A TIN PLATE MOTORBUS

This 8-inch-long open-topped motorbus, valued at £1,200 to £1,500, was first patented by Ernst Lehmann in 1907. It is an accurate copy of the full-size vehicles which would have been familiar to children at this time. Decorated by the lithographic process, the bus is finely detailed, with a uniformed driver behind the steering wheel and a staircase to the top deck. It runs on spoked wheels powered by a ratchet and spring mechanism. The various components of the bus are joined together by small tabs that are slotted into openings and then folded over securely.

The clockwork mechanism of the bus (above) is driven by a simple key-wound ratchet and spring system (below).

▽ *The underside of the front of the bus reveals the front axle, which is controlled by the steering wheel.*

◁ *The Lehmann dumb-bell trademark is displayed on the front of the bus. A folded-over metal tab can be seen below each headlamp.*

WAX DOLLS

Of all the materials that have been used over the years for making dolls, wax gives the most natural-looking and human-like features. However, it is also difficult to work with and expensive, and so its use was confined to nativity figures for a long time before it was considered suitable for mere 'playthings'.

The wax used was beeswax: it was bleached and coloured, and strengthened with special additives. Exact recipes varied, with individual families of makers guarding their formulas and passing them on from one generation to the next.

One of the earliest wax dolls dates from 1758. By an unknown maker, she has clothes by one of the Powell family, whose members dressed dolls from the 1740s until 1911. Wax dolls are still made, but their high cost puts them firmly in the collectors' market. The real heyday of wax doll-making was from the 1800s until the 1930s.

Types of wax doll

Dolls fall into one of three categories: solid wax, poured wax, and wax over composition or papier mâché. Solid wax dolls tend to be older, less common and smaller than poured wax or wax over composition varieties. Also, they tend to have fairly simple expressions and lack many of the refinements of later poured wax dolls.

The main drawback with wax over composition heads is that the thin

◁ **POURED WAX DOLL** *with wax lower arms and legs, and a cloth body. Her blonde hair is inserted into the scalp in clumps, then cut into a fringe at the front. The brown staining on her face is a result of ageing. Made in England, she still has her original clothes and bonnet. 1880; 16in tall.*
£400 – £600

USEFUL TERMS

POURED WAX A hollow head created from several thin layers or one thick layer of wax, depending on the maker. Molten wax was used to coat the inside of a mould, and the excess drained off; this could be done more than once with different coloured waxes to build up a realistic-looking 'skin'.
SOLID WAX The least common type of wax doll, with a head made entirely of wax, either carved from a block or cast in a mould.
WAX OVER COMPOSITION A head made from papier mâché or wood pulp dipped into or brushed with molten wax. If the base had painted features, white wax was used; alternatively, the wax itself was coloured.

▷ **ENGLISH POURED WAX DOLL** *with blue glass eyes and blonde human hair. She has her original blue satin dress, trimmed with net and pink and white fabric flowers, cotton underclothes and pink kid slippers. The wax of her head and lower arms has faded slightly. 1880; 14½ in tall.* **£500 – £800**

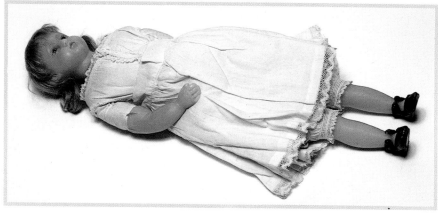

layer of wax expands and contracts at a different rate from the composition head and so is prone to cracking. Although this can detract from a doll's aesthetic appeal, it does not significantly affect value.

Types of eyes

Eyes and hair varied according to the type of doll. A solid wax doll had her eyes painted on or beads attached to the face with a drop of molten wax. Most poured wax dolls, by contrast, had proper eye sockets. After the mould was removed, holes were cut into the wax and glass eyes fixed to the inside of the head. The heads of poured wax and wax over composition dolls were fairly strong, and able to take the extra weight of eyes that opened and closed. These so-called 'sleeping eyes' were also attached to the inside of the head, but with plaster, rather than molten wax.

Types of hair

The simplest way to give a doll hair was to carve or mould it as part of the head, then paint it (this method was often used for solid wax dolls). An alternative was to make a wig, by attaching human hair

△ **ENGLISH DOLL** *with poured wax head and lower limbs and a cloth body. Her glass eyes are attached inside the head and the cotton clothes are original. 1880 – 1910; 16in tall.* **£400 – £600**

▷ **MOTSCHMANN-TYPE DOLL** *named after the well-known German maker Charles Motschmann, who in fact only patented the type which originated in Japan. These dolls usually have wax over composition heads, solid shoulders, hips, lower arms and legs, unstuffed cloth limbs and a squeaker in the chest. Her christening robe is original. 1860 – 1900; 12in tall.* **£200 – £300**

▽ **PAIR OF WAX OVER COMPOSITION GERMAN DOLLS** *with cloth bodies, upper arms and legs, and lower arms made of kid. Both are slit-head dolls; their brown mohair ringlets are sealed with wax into slits in their heads. Pairs of such dolls, with complementary (as here) or matching clothing and accessories, are not uncommon. The wax is slightly cracked, but this has not affected their value. 1840; 21in tall.* The pair **£500 – £700**

EXPERT'S CHOICE

or mohair to a cotton or linen base.

The most satisfactory way of producing a convincing head of hair, however, and the most common in wax dolls, was to make a series of very small slits all over the wax head, insert a few hairs (again, mohair or human hair) into each, then heat-seal the slits again. This method had two distinct advantages: it made the hair appear to be growing from the top of the head, and it meant that the hair could be styled. Hair colour and texture also varied; a baby doll might be given fine blonde hair, an older child or adult thicker, darker locks. A simpler method, found in cheaper wax over composition dolls, used a single slit at the top of the head into which a clump of hair was inserted. Such dolls are often referred to as 'slit-heads'.

Body shapes

Wax dolls varied in body shape too. During the 19th century, the first 'baby' dolls were made with chubby

▷ **GERMAN WAX OVER COMPOSITION DOLLS** *with wax arms and legs and cloth-stuffed bodies. Their eyes are glass fixed into the head, and their hair is inserted into the wax. Everything about them – clothes, underclothes, bonnets – is original, hence their value. 1870 – 80; 20in and 24in tall.* The pair **£600**

CLOTH AND KID BODIES

Wax heads were generally placed on cloth or kid bodies. Using kid had several advantages, including that it was easier to shape and to 'gusset' so that the doll could adopt more realistic poses. It was, however, expensive. The majority of wax dolls therefore have cloth bodies, usually white calico stuffed with either cow hair or (for cheapness) sawdust. The body itself was made in separate sections – torso,

upper arms, upper legs – and stitched together. The head and shoulders were almost always made as one piece, with holes at the back and front (often reinforced with metal eyelets) so that they could be stitched to the torso.

In the 1850s, German maker Charles Motschmann patented 'floating' limbs, in which the upper arms, upper legs and midriff were made from unstuffed tubes of cloth.

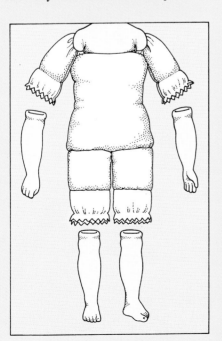

Most wax dolls had the head and shoulders, lower legs and lower arms made of wax, and a body of stuffed cloth sections stitched together. The wax parts were moulded or carved with holes at the back and front so that they could be stitched to the cloth. These bodies usually had little shape and were used for baby dolls.

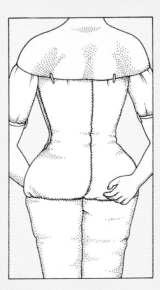

Kid was easier to shape than cloth and an adult waist could be modelled.

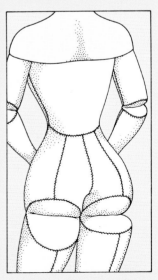

Gussets were introduced on kid bodies at elbows, thighs and knees for added realism.

bodies and no waist. A child's body was more elongated, but again had little real shape. An adult female doll, on the other hand, had a narrow waist, and broader chest and hips.

The nature of wax means that it is very susceptible to changes in temperature and to light, fading readily. It also breaks, stains or becomes rubbed easily, with protruding parts such as noses being particularly vulnerable.

▽ **GERMAN DOLL** *Although this wax over composition doll has replacement lower arms and a new human hair wig, her dress and underclothes are late 19th century originals. 1890; 13½ in tall.* **£100 – £150**

▷ **BROWN-EYED DOLL** *made in Germany. She has a wax over composition head and shoulders and lower limbs, eyes fixed inside her head and a brown mohair wig. Her cotton clothes and brown leather shoes are of the period. The wax on her face is somewhat worn. 1900 – 10; 21½ in tall.* **£150 – £200**

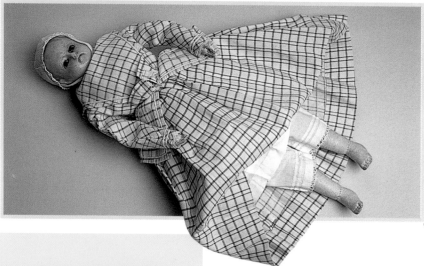

DOLL MAKERS

The best known London makers of poured wax dolls were the Montanaris (mother and son), working between 1849 and '84, and the Pierotti family who began working in the 1840s and whose last member retired in 1935. Both families referred to themselves as 'wax modellers' rather than 'doll makers', and in fact the Montanaris' fame rests on their family of dolls representing Queen Victoria and her children, shown at the Great Exhibition of 1851.

The Montanari family signed some of their dolls' bodies. The Pierottis did not, although since their dolls were retailed by Hamleys, many dolls bearing the Hamleys stamp are in fact by the Pierottis. Names scratched into the wax are an unreliable method of attribution, since this can be done at any time.

Other 19th century makers include Lucy Peck, Thomas Peacock and Charles Edwards, who also made wax over composition dolls. The majority of these dolls, however, were made in Germany, and tend to be anonymous.

△ **BABY DOLL** *This doll's original body has been replaced by one made from kid. There are many reasons why this might have happened: the seams of the cloth body may have burst, allowing the sawdust stuffing to escape; the sawdust might have been subject to an attack of woodworm; or the owner may have preferred the extra realism that a kid body could give. Her wax over composition head, cotton dress and undergarments are all original. 1860 – 70; 16½ in tall.* **£100 – £150**

AUTOMATA & CLOCKWORK TOYS

Automata are mechanical amusements which, when wound up, imitate the movement of a person or animal. These toys were intended essentially for adults, although naturally they had great appeal for children, too.

What are generally recognized as true automata were not invented until the 18th century, when diminutive human figures with stilted movements began to be produced. These were first seen at public shows in Paris, but by the 1760s they were also being made in London by John Merlin, a clockmaker, who produced a variety of automata for public entertainment.

Early mechanical figures were very large and complicated to make, as well as being expensive to buy. In response to a growing demand from ordinary people for cheaper figures, many small factories and workshops were established in Paris, and by the first half of the 19th century they were producing a considerable number of well made but affordable automata. Most of these were clockwork-powered, but later figures were powered by electricity.

Roullet & Decamps were one of the most prolific makers of the late 19th and early 20th centuries, and other Parisian firms, such as Bontems and G. Vichy, ensured that France remained at the forefront of automata production. Many of the

△ **FIDDLING MONKEY AND 'SAILOR'S FAREWELL'**, *both probably made by the French firm, Phalibois. The monkey fiddles, and the small doll waves while the sailing ship is buffeted by waves.*
Monkey *1875; 16in.* **£800 – £1,200**
Doll *1890; 16in.* **£400 – £600**

▽ **LETTUCE-NIBBLING RABBIT** *The clockwork movement causes the creature to rise and prick up his ears. Rabbit automata were very popular at the turn of the century. This French model is similar to one made by Roullet & Decamps. 1905; 6in high.* **£400 – £600**

larger manufacturers of conventional dolls, such as Jumeau and Simon & Halbig, supplied parts for automata dolls. Good examples of their early swimming automaton, marked on the head with the letters 'S+H', can fetch up to £800 today.

Fake automata, which have recently appeared on the market, can be identified by the unrealistic amount of dust and surface grime present, giving the impression that the toy has just been discovered in an attic. All too often, however, brand new material and construction are revealed if the doll's clothes are peeled back. Fakes are difficult to spot, so inexperienced collectors should be wary of tempting offers that seem too good to be true.

▽ **'THE MARRIAGE PROPOSAL'** *This type of French picture automaton was very popular at the turn of the century. Once in motion, it produces many surprises – figures pop up and eyes and limbs move. 1900; 11in high.* **£400 – £600**

△ **DOLL AUTOMATON** *of the more traditional box type. When set in motion, the musical movement in the base plays and the doll raises her glasses to her eyes. Like many conventional dolls, she has a bisque head. 1885; 15in high.* **£500 – £800**

▽ **WALKING AND GRUNTING PIG** *Probably made by Decamps, this pig is covered with kid skin. Other popular animal automata included monkeys, rabbits, bears, cats, dogs and birds in cages. 1900; 10in long.* **£1,000 – £1,500**

△ **DANCING PUNCHINELLO** *The doll moves when the handle is turned and music plays from an internal movement. French-made, hand-wound toys such as this were cheaper than clockwork versions. 1885; 11in high.* **£600 – £900**

▽ **MUSICIAN PIGS WITH GIRL CONDUCTOR** *by Schuco. These highly collectable toys were marketed as Walt Disney's Three Little Pigs. When wound, the girl conducts and the pigs play their instruments vigorously. 1935; 5in high.* **£500 – £700**

TOY SOLDIERS

Model soldiers have been made for thousands of years. In ancient Egypt they were used to represent armies in the Pharaohs' tombs, and Roman children are known to have played with lead figures of soldiers.

Solid and flat-cast lead soldiers have been popular for a few hundred years, but lead alloy figures have only been mass produced since 1893, when William Britain perfected the hollow-cast method. Although manufacturers such as Johillco and Reka Ltd copied their methods, Britains were responsible for more than half the lead soldiers produced until the mid 1960s, when cheaper plastic figures were introduced.

The earliest Britains figures, most of which have oval bases, are unmarked, but they can usually be identified by the high quality of their casting and painting. To protect copyright, paper labels were stuck to the bases of figures after 1900 (from about 1905 cast lettering was used) and after 1907 bases were square, not oval. The Britains range was extensive, including railwaymen and zoo animals, as well as soldiers.

The condition of toy soldiers is all-important for valuation, and an original box can as much as double the price of a set. Beware of overpriced figures – a fine set of 1st Life Guards from the 1920s, for example, can cost as little as £70 to £90.

▽ **BRITAINS MOUNTAIN ARTILLERY,** *set no. 28, first issued in 1895. This is the first version of the set – the figures still have oval bases and the forelegs of the mules are raised. This set is unboxed. 1900; 3–4in high.* **£100 – £150**

△ **BANDSMEN FIGURES** *The drummer is from a nine-piece Britains set of 'Bands of the Line', while the earlier bugler in khaki dress was made by Johillco (John Hill & Co.). 1914 – 20; 2in high.* **Each £10 – £15**

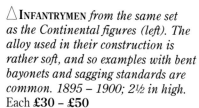

△ CONTINENTAL FIGURES, *probably made by the Heyde factory in Germany. Solid-cast, they depict a standard-bearer, a fusilier and a mounted officer of the Napoleonic era. 1895 – 1900; 2½ in high.* Each **£30 – £50**

△ INFANTRYMEN *from the same set as the Continental figures (left). The alloy used in their construction is rather soft, and so examples with bent bayonets and sagging standards are common. 1895 – 1900; 2½ in high.* Each **£30 – £50**

△ BRITAINS AMBULANCE WAGON *of the Royal Army Medical Corps, set no. 145. There is an earlier and more valuable version of this set, distinguished by a grey wagon and heavier collar harness, and flatter horses' ears. 1924; 3½ in high.* **£150 – £200**

▷ BRITAINS MOUNTED BAND OF THE 1ST LIFE GUARDS, *set no. 101, one of Britains' most popular sets, with arms that slot into place. The uniforms of the soldiers were based on the Household Cavalry of 1898. This playworn set is unboxed. 1900; 3in high.* **£400 – £600**

SPACE TOYS

The beginning of the Space Age in the 1950s (the first Sputnik satellite was launched in 1957) greatly influenced the design and styling of cars, fabrics, furniture and electrical appliances. Science fiction, space adventure stories and comic strips, featuring space heroes such as Buck Rogers and Dan Dare, became popular. The movie industry responded by producing more and more films about space and many early space toys were 'spin-offs' from these films. With the advent of television, toys inspired by popular programmes such as *Thunderbirds*, *Fireball XL5* and *Space 1999* also became available.

The great majority of space toys were produced in Japan during the 1960s. Most were made of lithographed tin plate, with perspex or plastic detailing. Because they were manufactured relatively recently – from the 1950s through to the present day – and were generally made in large numbers, condition is of paramount importance. Collectors are only willing to pay high prices for toys in mint condition and in their original boxes. If a toy is battery operated, the batteries should always be removed after use since any leakage of battery fluid will cause corrosion, seriously affecting the toy's value.

△ **SPACECRAFT AND SPACEWALKER** *by the Masudaya company. These brightly lithographed spacecraft are made of tin and have plastic detailing. The tin circling spacewalker is rare: such figures tend to become detached, then lost, over the years. 1960s; 8½ in long (left).* The pair **£200 – £300**

▽ **REMOTE-CONTROL MOON EXPLORER VEHICLE** *by Yonezawa. Complete with lights, motor sound, moving antenna, and its original box, it is in excellent condition. An interesting design feature is the rocket-shaped remote control, which houses the batteries. 1960s; 8½ in long.* **£120 – £200**

△ **MASUDAYA 'MARS' AND YOSHIA 'SPACE ROCKET'** *Battery powered, both have survived in excellent condition. 1960s; 'Mars' 14½ in long, 'Space Rocket' 13½ in long.* The pair **£350 – £450**

▽ **'MOON EXPRESS'** *by the Japanese company, Alps. It glows in different colours and emits a realistic motor noise. In excellent condition, it still has its original box. 1960s; 14in.* **£120 – £200**

△ **TWO 'SATELLITE' SPACECRAFT** *by Masudaya. When the battery-powered mechanism is started, the astronauts float above the craft on a jet of air. 1960s; 8in diameter.* The pair **£200 – £300**

△ **TWO 'SONICON ROCKET' VEHICLES** *by Masudaya. Powered by remote control batteries, they are in good condition, with only minor scratches. 1960s; 13in long.* The pair **£300 – £400**

▷ **'MOON PATROL VEHICLE'** *by Yonezawa, with flashing lights and moving radar. This toy has survived in near mint condition, and comes in its original box. 1960s; 13in long.* **£500 – £600**

Hilary Kay is a director of Sotheby's and an expert on collectables, toys and games.

COLLECTABLES & TOYS

Collectors are drawn to toys and games for many different reasons; to form a collection, to own a great rarity, or finally to acquire a certain toy they have coveted since childhood. Dolls are much sought after, and in collecting terms the most desirable early dolls are the wooden variety dating from the 17th century. The best of these, which must be in good, original condition, can fetch as much as £30,000. At the other end of the scale are fabric and soft dolls from the late 19th century, and some good examples can make over £1,000. Teddies and other soft toys are also highly collectable, in particular well known cartoon characters.

The 'Golden Age' of tin plate, from 1900 to 1914, produced trains, boats and vehicles, the best produced by German makers, which are much sought after today. There is considerable demand too for modern toys such as battery-operated novelty figures, robots and space toys, and these can be found more and more frequently today at specialist auctions and toy fairs. Good condition is always of paramount importance, whether a toy or a game and, if possible, games should come with their original box.

One of the great advantages of collectables over other categories of antique is that there are almost endless subjects in which to specialize: scientific instruments; cameras; domestic appliances; textiles and items related to all forms of travel. I find the decorative influences linking a utility object to the era in which it was made particularly fascinating, such as the high Victorian rococo scrolling motifs on the cases of musical boxes. One of the most interesting aspects of the collectables field is that it is constantly evolving, so keep all your old records and mementos, they might one day become highly collectable.

◁ **A MERRYTHOUGHT FOX** *named Anthony. Elephants and rabbits were more popular; a fox is quite rare. 1930s; 13in high.* **£200**

POINTS TO WATCH FOR

1 Check the back of bisque dolls' heads for manufacturer's marks and the mould number. These enable the doll to be identified and valued.

2 When buying antique costumes, check seams and lining for alterations (many 18th century robes were adapted for use as fancy dress costumes a century later).

3 Look in the left ear of a soft doll or animal: if a small embossed metal rivet pierces the ear it is likely to be a highly collectable product of the German manufacturer Steiff.

4 Biscuit tins and other packaging must be in near mint condition to have much financial value.

5 To be of any interest to collectors board games must be complete with their original playing pieces, dice and instructions.

6 The backs of cigarette cards are just as important as the fronts, so take great care when removing cards that have been stuck down.

7 Recently made dolls' prams have been imported into Europe in vast numbers from the Far East; once 'aged' they are difficult to tell at a glance from Victorian originals.

8 Check whether teddy bears or soft toys have been patched, darned or re-sewn – such repairs will badly affect the toy's value.

9 Many cast-iron mechanical money banks were copied and reproduced in Taiwan in the 1970s: these are worthless to collectors.

10 Don't buy tin plate toys that are rusty – if badly affected, the decoration (and toy) are likely to be unrestorable.

▽ **HORNBY DUBLO 3-RAIL ELECTRIC TANK GOODS TRAIN** *produced by Meccano. 1950; engine 6in long.* **£150 – £200**

Media Toys

A relatively recent category of collectable, 'media toys' are becoming increasingly popular. Based on television series, films or comic book characters, the toys appeal mainly to a younger generation of collectors who grew up with the programmes. Films such as *Dick Tracy, Star Wars, Who Framed Roger Rabbit?, Indiana Jones, Robocop* and *Batman,* have spawned their share of toys. Toy shops in the 1960s, '70s and '80s tempted children to part with their pocket money in exchange for the movable figures, die-cast space vehicles and speaking dolls based on favourite film characters. In the same way, television programmes such as *The Monkees, Thunderbirds* and *The Avengers* inspired a range of related items. Media toys are not difficult to find, but condition is very important, with collectors insisting on the toys being in their original boxes and packing before purchasing them.

Care & Repair

1 Never leave a cylinder musical box playing if there is a possibility of the power running out half way through a tune; this puts undue pressure on both the cylinder pins and the comb teeth.

2 Don't use abrasive cleaners or abrasive materials on metal collectables; the value of a scientific instrument, for example, can be seriously affected if the original lacquer has been removed through vigorous cleaning.

3 Framed textiles, such as samplers, fade with age. To help delay the fading process, hang them on walls that do not receive direct light: dark passages and hallways, for example, are ideal.

4 Keep collectables with moving parts in as dust-free an environment as possible, and remember to lubricate the moving parts occasionally with one or two drops of light sewing machine oil.

5 To clean tin plate, lead, cast-iron and die-cast toys, use a silicone spray polish and a soft cloth. Never use abrasive cleaners or polishes.

6 Check wooden toys for wood-worm occasionally. From time to time place teddies and soft toys in a plastic bag with insectide pellets to prevent infestation. But do not use this method if children will be playing with the toys.

7 Never polish bronze; polishing removes the attractive patina that this metal develops as it ages.

◁ **Edison Gem Phonograph** *which plays two- and four-minute cylindrical records. 1880s; horn 21in long.* **£350**

'Kitchenalia'

Stimulated, perhaps, by excellent historical television series such as *Upstairs Downstairs* in the 1970s and, more recently, *The Victorian Kitchen*, a great deal of interest has developed in collecting bygone kitchen equipment, mechanical gadgets and other appliances for use in the home.

Labour-saving devices became increasingly necessary from the latter part of the 19th century when labour that had been destined traditionally for domestic service was lured into the burgeoning manufacturing industries and, later, into the armed forces and munitions factories during World War I. Upper and middle class families who had previously relied on a steady supply of servants to enable their homes to function efficiently were desperate to find alternative methods by which the chores of household management could be eased.

A wide variety of labour-saving devices was invented and produced to help in the preparation of food, including choppers, peelers, mixers, beaters, mincers, and marmalade and ice cream makers. Elsewhere, domestic servants were aided by mechanical sweepers, vacuum cleaners, and sewing and knitting machines.

Collectors of kitchenalia should look for mechanical devices in good original condition, preferably complete with their protective cover or case, and best of all with the operating instructions.

▷ **Edwardian Paraffin Iron** *on an Art Nouveau stand. The paraffin in the reservoir at the back was fed through a tube to burners in the base. 1905; 8in long.* **£30 – £40**

Places of Interest

Bethnal Green Museum of Childhood, London E2
Outstanding toys and games
Museum of Childhood, Edinburgh
The noisiest museum in the world
Museum of London, London EC2
19th & 20th century ephemera

POTTERY, PORCELAIN & GLASS

BY DAVID BATTIE

After attending over 100 Roadshows and handling around 30,000 pieces of pottery, porcelain or glass, surely I should be heartily fed up with the whole business? But the fact is, I am not. I am hooked on works of art, and not just my own subjects but everyone else's as well.

No two Roadshows are the same, and over the years my interests have changed. Some time ago I remember pondering on why one of our directors collected only *blanc de Chine* porcelain. After all, why collect something white when you can have coloured? I now realize that there is no such colour as white; there are probably over a hundred different shades of white, each one specific to a factory, country or period in history. Throw or cast a pot, glaze and fire it, and you have pure form, unobscured by colour or pattern. Each of the 30,000 pieces that I have handled over the last 14 years of the Roadshow has added a little – and in some cases a lot – to my knowledge.

Sometimes, the moments of discovery missed by the camera are those I remember best. On one occasion I unwrapped an excellent piece of English porcelain dated around 1820; it was an unusually shaped, superbly painted flower vase with beaded borders. Who had made it? I struggled for five minutes throwing out suggestions – Spode? Various Worcesters? Rockingham? Mason's? Swallowing my pride, I showed the vase to Terence Lockett and Henry Sandon. No luck there either: I had to admit defeat. Then, as I turned the piece over in my hands for the last time, I spotted a small insect on one side. It rang a bell. Where had I seen that insect before? Bingo! The answer was at home, on a plate from Charles Bourne of Fenton (1817 – 30). For me, making that small attribution was more satisfying than winning the football pools.

The '92 series kicked off to a great start. An extraordinary collection of Japanese and Chinese porcelain and works of art at Alexandra Palace included a Chinese blue and white pen tray with the reign mark of the Emperor Wanli (1573 – 1619)

△ **COALPORT VASE** *A 'jewelled', pierced vase, in superb condition. 1895; 10in high.* **£2,500 – £3,500**

◁ **MANDARIN PALETTE VASES** *in elongated form. (One vase is damaged.) 1770; 22in.* Pair **£4,000 – £6,000**

△ RARE CHINESE PEN TRAY, *well painted and in good condition. 1573 – 1619.* **£12,000 – £15,000**

▽ MOONFLASK *Early Japanese cloisonné in distinctly Chinese style. 1860s; 13in high.* **£700 – £1,000**

on the base. The Chinese tradition of writing any old mark on the bases of their pots has led to considerable confusion, but this piece was 'mark and period' and, at £12,000 to £15,000, the best piece of Chinese ware I have handled on the Roadshow so far. The owner's father had in fact taken the piece to Sotheby's in the 1940s where it had been valued at £46. How times have changed!

A pair of vases with covers painted in the bright 'Mandarin' palette was also an unusual find. Unlike the pen tray, these had been made for export to the West, as was the work table from the Queensferry Roadshow. I am particularly fond of ivory and it is always shown to best advantage combined with black, as with the lacquer example here. Most such work tables are damaged due to wear and tear, but this one was in superb condition.

We see numerous Chinese cloisonné pieces at Roadshows, mostly dating from 1900 to 1930, which are rarely worth more than tens of pounds. Very occasionally a fine, early Chinese example comes in which is worth £1,000 or so, or a superb piece of Japanese of similar value. Also quite rare are mid 19th century Japanese pieces. One such example was the moonflask from 'Ally Pally', which curiously, considering its rarity and historical importance, was worth only £700 to £1,000.

A great admirer of teapots, I recently discovered that I own over 20. One that I would dearly love to possess was brought to the Stratford-upon-Avon show. Entitled 'Sally Sikes', it was a Staffordshire creamware pot dated 1781 and painted in underglaze blue, with a prim miss seated at tea in a garden. It is these unexpected finds that we all hope for as the next eager visitor arrives at the porcelain desk. Roll on the next series!

▽ UNDERGLAZE BLUE TEAPOT, *neo-classical in design; chipped, but desirable. 1781; 5½ in high.* **£600 – £900**

▽ LACQUERED WORK TABLE, *made in China for export to Europe. 1830 – 50; 2ft 5in wide.* **£2,500**

UNDERSTANDING CHINESE CERAMICS

POTTERY, PORCELAIN & GLASS

Ceramics, the earliest entirely man-made objects, have been found in even the most primitive societies, and in China they have been produced for some 10,000 years. Many of the examples shown here are prohibitively expensive for the collector, but imperfect pieces dating from as early as the 10th century can sometimes be had for as little as £200.

Early ceramics

Chinese Neolithic pieces differ little from the first ceramics used by other early peoples, and were mainly cooking and storage utensils. Made from coils of clay, they were fired without a glaze in a brushwood fire. Glazing was introduced in about 1500BC, and by the beginning of the Han dynasty (206BC) high-fired pottery, heated to 1200°C, had been developed.

Apart from domestic wares, most of which have perished, large numbers of ceramic pieces were made for burial with the dead, and it is these that are of greatest interest to collectors. During the Tang dynasty, superb *sancai* (three-colour) glazed camel, horse and warrior figures were interred with their owners. The earliest pieces to resemble true, hard-paste porcelain were also made at the beginning of the Tang dynasty, some 1,000 years before Europeans discovered the formula.

Porcelain contains the vital ingredient, kaolin (china clay), which is mixed with ground *petuntse* (china rock). Its distinguishing features are translucency, toughness and a musical note if it is struck. Common types of early Chinese porcelain include *dingyao* and y*ingqing* (also known as *qingbai*), made from the 10th to the 14th century. The former has a creamy tint, and the latter is bluish. Both were engraved or moulded with patterns under the glaze. Prices for such pieces range from £100 to £10,000.

Yuan dynasty (1260–1368)

One of the most important developments in porcelain took place in the early 14th century during the Yuan dynasty. It was found that cobalt, painted under the glaze on an unfired object, would survive the high firing temperature and turn blue. Subsequently Jingdezhen (pronounced 'Ching-tê-chen'), the centre of porcelain manufacture in China, produced a great many large pieces in underglaze blue for export to the Middle East.

▽ CELADON DISH *impressed from a mould. This has a floral design and an unusual notched rim. Poor examples can cost around £200. 10th–11th century; 7¼ in high.* **£20,000 – £25,000**

◁ EARTHENWARE JAR *from the early Tang dynasty. It is unusual both for its form (masks and rings at the shoulders, and dragon handles) and for the touches of black. 7th century; 14½ in high.* **£10,000 – £20,000**

▽ YINGQING DISH *with a carved lotus under a pale green glaze. The rim is unglazed because such pieces were fired upside-down. Quite good examples can cost £300 – £400. 13th–14th century; 5½ in across.* **£3,000 – £5,000**

CHINESE DYNASTIES

TANG	618 – 906
FIVE DYNASTIES	907 – 960
LIAO	907 – 1125
SONG	960 – 1279
Northern Song	960 – 1127
Southern Song	1128 – 1279
JIN	1115 – 1234
YUAN (MONGOLS)	1260 – 1368
MING	1368 – 1644
Hongwu	1368 – 1398
Jianwen	1399 – 1402
Yongle	1403 – 1424
Xuande	1426 – 1435
Zhengtong	1436 – 1449
Jingtai	1450 – 1457
Tianshun	1457 – 1464
Chenghua	1465 – 1487
Hongzhi	1488 – 1505
Zhengde	1506 – 1521
Jiajing	1522 – 1566
Longqing	1567 – 1572
Wanli	1573 – 1619
Taichang	1620
Tianqi	1621 – 1627
Chongzhen	1628 – 1643
QING	1644 – 1912
Shunzhi	1644 – 1661
Kangxi	1662 – 1722
Yongzheng	1723 – 1735
Qianlong	1736 – 1795
Jiaqing	1796 – 1820
Daoguang	1821 – 1850
Xianfeng	1851 – 1861
Tongzhi	1862 – 1874
Guangxu	1875 – 1908
Xuantong	1909 – 1912
REPUBLIC OF CHINA	1912 – 1949

◁ COPPER-RED VASE *with scrolling foliage. Copper-red is difficult to fire because the colour tends to turn silver or grey. This example was sold for a record price in Hong Kong in 1988. 14th century; 12½ in high.* **£1,200,000**

Ming dynasty (1368–1644)

At first the new underglaze blue porcelain proved unpopular in China, but by the reign of the Emperor Yongle (1403 – 24) pieces were being made for use at court. In the middle of the 17th century, thousands of pieces were exported every year. A particularly popular style was called *kraak*, named after the 'carrack' – the type of Portuguese ship in which porcelain was transported to Europe. Bowls and dishes in this style range in price from £300 to £3,000.

Before the mid 17th century the small amount of porcelain which was enamelled over the glaze was reserved almost exclusively for the domestic market, and rarely exported. Wares made for court use are marked with the Emperor's name on the base. The Chinese custom of copying earlier pieces, including the reign mark, often with great accuracy, was intended as a gesture of respect, not to deceive.

Transitional period (1620–1644)

The Ming dynasty started to disintegrate after the death of Emperor Wanli in 1619, and finally collapsed in 1644. During the unrest the Imperial kilns at Jingdezhen were destroyed and far less porcelain was produced. Despite this, provincial potters developed new shapes and designs, in a style that became known as 'Transitional'. Prices for these pieces start at about £100.

Qing dynasty (1644–1912)

The accession of Emperor Kangxi in 1662 stabilized the Qing (pronounced 'ching' or 'king') dynasty, and porcelain production increased once more. Innovations included *famille-verte* decoration, with its distinctive green enamel and, at the end of Kangxi's reign, a pink enamel known as *famille-rose*.

During the 18th century the export of Chinese porcelain became a massive industry. At its height, more than three million pieces reached Europe each year. Most were tea and dinner wares in underglaze blue or *famille-rose,* but a few special sets decorated with the coats-of-arms of titled families were also ordered. Trade waned after the 1770s as European porcelain factories began to flourish, particularly in England. However, exports again increased in the second half of the 19th century, to satisfy the mania for all things Oriental that was gripping the West. Most successful at this time were brightly coloured Canton-style pieces and reproductions of Kangxi blue and white ware.

△ **BLUE AND WHITE JAR** *This rare design features a dragon on one side and a phoenix and clouds on the other. The vigorous painting and vivid blue are unusual, so, despite a small crack and chips, it is valuable. A poor piece could cost just £100. 1425 – 50; 5in high.* **£15,000 – £18,000**

▽ **TRANSITIONAL BEAKER VASE** *The tall form is typical of the period, as are the figures (one with a banner), the V-shaped leaves and the purplish tone of the blue. 1620 – 44; 16½ in high.* **£4,000 – £6,000**

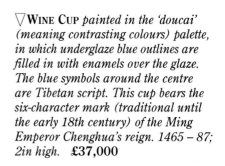

▽ **WINE CUP** *painted in the 'doucai' (meaning contrasting colours) palette, in which underglaze blue outlines are filled in with enamels over the glaze. The blue symbols around the centre are Tibetan script. This cup bears the six-character mark (traditional until the early 18th century) of the Ming Emperor Chenghua's reign. 1465 – 87; 2in high.* **£37,000**

▽ **FAMILLE-VERTE COMPAGNIE DES INDES JUG** *with painted flowers and scroll handles in lizard form. One of a pair, this would have had a matching basin. A perfect 'famille-verte' wine cup could cost as little as £80. Late 16th century; 11in high.* **The pair £10,000 – £15,000**

USEFUL TERMS

CANTON Undecorated white porcelain made at Jingdezhen and coloured, enamelled and gilded at Canton.
CELADON Stoneware with a distinctive glaze, which ranges from grey-green to olive-green.
COMPAGNIE DES INDES Chinese porcelain shipped to Europe by the French East India Company.
COPPER-RED Porcelain underglazed with copper oxide to produce red.

FAMILLE-ROSE, FAMILLE-VERTE Porcelain with enamelled colour in which pink, or green, predominates. *Famille-jaune* (yellow) and *noir* (black) pieces were also produced.
KRAAK Late Ming blue and white porcelain, exported to Europe.
STONEWARE Earthenware fired to porcelain temperatures (1250°C), so that it is impervious to liquids without the need for glazing.

POTTERY, PORCELAIN & GLASS

97

CHINESE BLUE & WHITE PORCELAIN

Although the Chinese discovered porcelain in the 7th century, decoration was limited until the 14th century, when the next great breakthrough took place. It was found that cobalt oxide under the glaze turned blue when fired; this was the beginning of Chinese blue and white, a style that has been popular ever since.

Competent pieces were achieved very quickly (the earliest dated blue and white objects, from 1351, are now in the Percival David Collection in London). Curiously, the colour scheme was unpopular at the Chinese court and most was made solely for export to the Middle East, particularly Persia. The majority of these pieces were large dishes, suited to the Middle Eastern custom of eating

△ **RARE PEN TRAY** *with the reign mark of Wanli, 'ta Ming Wanli nian zhi' – 'made in the reign of the Great Ming Emperor Wanli', on the reverse (left) in a single line rather than the usual two rows of three marks. In good condition, it was valued for probate by Sotheby's in the 1940s at £48, which shows how dramatically prices have risen. 1573 – 1619; 7½ in long.* **£12,000 – £15,000**

▷ **EXPORT VASES**
Two vases from a garniture of five: there would also have been two trumpet-shaped vases and one similar to the left-hand example. Both are chipped; a perfect piece is worth £250. 1780; 12in high.
Each **£100**

△ **GLOBULAR JAR** *made during the Transitional period. The painting is slightly less well handled than usual, but the subject – figures and a man on horseback – is very attractive. 1660; 13in high.* **£1,500 – £1,800**

A GARNITURE

Garnitures were sets of three, five or seven jars and vases made to decorate a mantelpiece.

from communal dishes (a contrast to the Chinese tradition of eating from small individual bowls).

One of the characteristics of these early pieces is a defect known as 'heaping and piling'. Unable to control the amount of cobalt flowing from his brush on to the dish, the painter left thick patches, which appeared as dark spots on the glaze when the piece was fired. Today, far from viewing it as a flaw, collectors positively prize this effect: in fact it was copied in the 18th century when the Emperor Yongzheng began to appreciate early examples.

Blue and white pieces from the 14th and 15th centuries can now be extremely expensive, but prices vary widely. Once blue and white was accepted by the Chinese court at the beginning of the 15th century, pieces bearing the Emperor's *nien hao*, or reign mark, started to be made. This mark usually consists of six (although sometimes only four) characters and it can cause huge variations in price between otherwise identical objects. A poor quality 10-inch-high Ming vase without a mark can be bought for a few hundred pounds, while good marked pieces have realized almost £1 million at auction.

In the mid 16th century, a style of decoration known as *kraak* became popular in Europe on imported Chinese porcelain. Large dishes and bowls are most common, but all pieces have the same recognizable characteristics. They are thinly, and often rather crudely potted, and usually have kiln

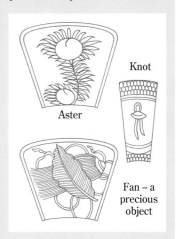

△ **TWO LARGE MEAT DISHES** *from a dinner service. These have survived in large numbers and are bought by interior decorators rather than collectors today. If perfect they would be worth £300 – £450, but these are damaged. 1760 – 80; 14in and 13in wide.* Each **£80 – £120**

◁ **EXPORT DINNER PLATES** *of the type sent to Europe in vast quantities. In one year alone over 3 million pieces were imported into Britain: what is surprising is not how much has survived but how little. Soup plates fetch less than dinner plates – they don't hang flat against a wall. 1750 – 75; 7 – 9in wide.* Each **£60 – £90**

KRAAK

Kraak is a corruption of 'carrack', the vessel that brought Chinese export porcelain to Europe. It was widely copied in Holland and England, as well as Japan and Persia.

▷ **TYPICAL DISH** *with a hairline crack, but of fair quality. 1600; 19in wide.* **£2,000 – £3,000**

◁ **UNUSUAL KRAAK BOWL** *in that it is considerably shallower than most examples. 1640; 11in wide.* **£800 – £1,200**

TYPICAL SYMBOLS
Kraak pieces were painted to a formula: the central pictorial element was surrounded by panels of flowers, knots and precious objects on the rim.

Aster

Knot

Fan – a precious object

△ **SOUP TUREEN** *It is popularly believed that these tureens are based on European silver designs, but this would not appear to be the case here. Quite how they evolved is something* of a mystery, but pieces of this shape were standard during the 18th century. Sauce tureens were the same shape, but smaller. 1750; stand 16in wide. Tureen and stand **£1,000 – £1,500**

△ **SHIELD-SHAPED FLASK** *This rare Transitional flask is painted blue with warrior decoration. It would have started life with a cylindrical cover. 1650; 7in high.* **£300 – £500**

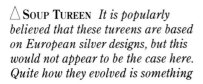

◁ **EXPORT SALT** *Salts are rarely found today. Some have three or four feet, but this is the most common form. 1770; 3in wide.* **£60 – £80**

▷ **SHELL-SHAPED BUTTER DISH** *One of a pair, the shape is based on silver designs. 1750; 5in wide.* The pair **£600 – £800**

DYNASTY MARKS

In many reigns, there were two ways of writing the marks: one in regular script (the examples on the left) and one based on archaic seal characters (those on the right). The marks illustrated below are some of those most commonly seen.

MING

大
明
宣
德
年
製

南圖內
鸞圖內
鷤蕊矑

Xuande (1426 – 35)

大
明
成
化
年
製

宬
宬
宬

Chenghua (1465 – 87)

QING

大
清
康
熙
年
製

南嚻川
纝霤川
纝繎精

Kangxi (1662 – 1722)

大
清
乾
隆
年
製

凮靐川
纝纝川
纝纝精

Qianlong (1735 – 95)

大
清
雍
正
年
製

南孂川
纝丠正
纝繎精

Yongzheng (1723 – 35)

大
清
光
緒
年
製

南嚺川
纝纝川
纝繎精

Guangxu (1875 – 1908)

grit adhering to the rim of the foot. Quality steadily deteriorated over the 100 years that *kraak* was made, and the blue varies from a deep, warm purplish tone early on to a silvery grey later. Today, most pieces have hair cracks, but for sheer decorative value *kraak* is hard to beat.

Between the 1620s (when the Ming dynasty started to collapse) and the 1640s (when the Manchu Qings established control) a style arose that became known as the 'Transitional'. Shapes changed and figures, often taken from popular novels, began to dominate decoration. Most Transitional pieces are surprisingly heavily potted, but all are well painted. This style has just begun to be appreciated and prices are consequently rising, but good pieces can be found for a few hundred pounds.

The first Qing emperor, Kangxi, a porcelain connoisseur, re-established the Imperial kilns at Jingdezhen, which had been sacked during the unrest. In his reign, blue and white, much of it based on the shapes and styles of European silver design, flooded the market. The range available today is wide, but tea wares are the most common.

Porcelain was made for use at court throughout the 18th century and pieces bearing reign and date marks from this period have risen sharply in price over the last few years. Collectors should always view reign marks with suspicion, however. Not only did the Chinese 'dedicate' pieces to earlier emperors, but modern pieces, produced in South Korea and Taiwan, are now flooding into this country, with marks that are accurate enough to fool the unwary.

In the late 19th century 'china-mania' swept England, and stores such as Liberty & Co. imported blue and white by the shipload. Especially popular at this time were pairs of vases, most decorated with prunus blossom on a 'cracked ice' background. A 10-inch pair is worth £200 to £500, a 15-inch pair up to £1,000. Pairs are worth three times more than singles. Again, damaged pieces exist and these are excellent candidates for conversion into lamp bases.

CLOBBERING

This Chinese blue and white plate has been 'enriched' in Europe with coloured enamels. This technique, known as 'clobbering', is frowned upon by collectors, largely because in many cases it was so badly done (the best comes from Holland). This 9-inch-wide plate dates from 1760 and is valued at £40 to £60.

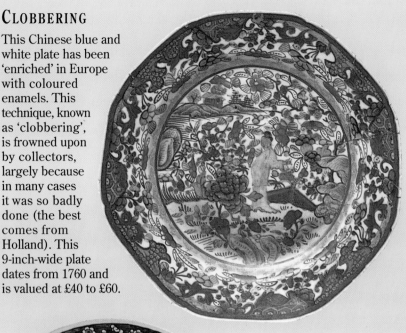

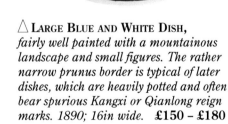

▽ **SPILL VASE OR BRUSH POT,** *imported from China around 1971. At this date the vase would not yet have been 100 years old (that is, a 'genuine' antique) and therefore could be legally exported. Such pieces can be recognized by the red sealing wax on the base. Modern transfer-printed copies are also being made for export. 1880; 11in high.* **£120 – £150**

△ **LARGE BLUE AND WHITE DISH,** *fairly well painted with a mountainous landscape and small figures. The rather narrow prunus border is typical of later dishes, which are heavily potted and often bear spurious Kangxi or Qianlong reign marks. 1890; 16in wide.* **£150 – £180**

◁ **QUINTAL VASE** *The name derives from the series of five holes. This is a 19th century reproduction of a popular 17th century design, made to take tulip or hyacinth bulbs. Most are painted, as here, with dragons and peonies or other flowers. This one is cracked; a perfect example would be worth £300 to £500. 1870; 9in high.* **£70 – £100**

◁ **FAMILLE-VERTE DISH** *painted with lotus flowers and scrolls. The underside bears a mark (inset) showing a leaf enclosed by two concentric rings. The tiny chips on the rim are to be expected on a piece of this age, and they barely affect its value. 1700; 15in wide.* **£2,000 – £3,000**

▽ **FAMILLE-ROSE TUREEN AND STAND** *This popular form was also frequently decorated in underglaze blue. 1765; 11in high.* **£2,500 – £3,000**

CHINESE EXPORT PORCELAIN

The first known contact between Continental Europe and China was during the 13th century. In 1271 the Italian adventurer Marco Polo visited the Mongol emperor Kublai Khan, returning to his homeland with, reputedly, a selection of delicate Chinese *yingqing* wares.

Small quantities of Chinese porcelain continued to make their way overland to Europe through the middle ages and up to the 16th century. These pieces, fit for princes and kings and treated as objects of wonder, were mounted in gold and silver and set with jewels, and given as diplomatic gifts.

Early exports

Trade in ceramics between China and the West developed significantly in the early 17th century along the sea-trading routes of the Portuguese, Dutch and British East India Companies. Underglaze blue ware, known as *kraak porselein,* was the chief export in this period, and it was usually decorated with images

▷ **MANDARIN PALETTE VASES** *in the elongated form so popular in the late 18th century. They were probably part of a set of five which would have included another similar vase and two more of 'trumpet' (wide-rimmed) form. One of this pair has been damaged. 1770; 22in high.* The pair **£4,000 – £6,000**

△ **FAMILLE-VERTE WINE POT** *which would have been used as a teapot in Europe. The handle (usually damaged) is intact, but the end of the spout and the knop have been replaced in silver. 1680; 6½ in wide.* **£2,000 – £3,000**

of precious objects and flowers around a central tableau of deer, birds or flowers. Large *kraak* dishes measuring more than 18 inches across can fetch between £1,500 and £3,000 today, while a piece with a hairline crack can cost as little as £300 – a modest sum for genuine Ming porcelain.

Coloured export porcelain

After the Qing dynasty succeeded the Ming dynasty in 1644, a new, more colourful style of porcelain decorated with overglaze enamels was developed specifically for the European market. The *famille-verte* palette with its bright leaf-green hue predominated, and variations such as *famille-jaune* (yellow) and *famille-noire* (black) followed.

In the 19th century it was fashionable to strip and redecorate earlier pots in famille-noire colours. Such pieces are much sought after by interior decorators today, particularly in France. Many biscuit porcelain figures were also decorated at a later date. Most popular of these are the pairs of Buddhist lions, or 'Dogs of Fo', which sell today for up to £1,000.

The next important development was *famille-rose*. Although the most famous palette, it was not in fact of Chinese origin. This pink enamel derived from gold was brought to China by missionaries in the early 18th century: it found immediate favour and was used extensively on both domestic and export wares.

While the East India Company continued to increase its trade in blue and white ware during the 18th century, the representative, or 'supercargo', on board ship dealt privately in the more profitable

△ **FAMILLE-VERTE DISH** *The style of decoration is more to Chinese taste than is usual in export ware. 1700; 13in wide.* **£1,000 – £1,500**

◁ **RARE COSMETICS BOX AND COVER** *with famille-verte decoration. Few such boxes were made, and most have been broken. Larger versions were made for Chinese domestic use. 1700; 3½ in wide.* **£400 – £600**

▽ **FAMILLE-VERTE TUREEN** *The shape is similar to that of European silver porringers, from which it may have been copied. A pair is worth four times as much as a single example. 1700; 13in wide.* **£3,000 – £5,000**

△ **FAMILLE-ROSE PLATE** *The brownish-red dressing around the rim was intended to limit the chipping caused by firing, which worsened through use of the plate. The technique was only partially successful. 1760; 9in wide.*
£150 – £200

▷ **SMALL BRONZED VASE** *with a poorly painted design of warriors on horseback, on a ground deliberately crackled to simulate age. The enamels are a combination of the famille-verte and famille-rose palettes, framed by bronzed bands. The handles, also bronzed, represent the 'Dogs of Fo'. The appearance is a little too 'dirty' for today's tastes, and the price is accordingly low. 1870; 12in high.*   **£20 – £30**

▽ **EXPORT SALT,** *the design of which is more usually seen in silverware. The centre is finely painted with a bouquet of flowers in the famille-rose palette. Two to four dinner guests would share one salt, helping themselves to this condiment using the points of their knives. 1750; 3in wide.* **£100 – £120**

coloured ware, on his own behalf or on behalf of china dealers in London. This ware was usually decorated in Canton with flowers, figures, fish and animals, both real and mythical. Rarer subjects included bagpiping Scotsmen, English mansions, political satires, ships (often named and dated) and views of the port of Canton. Such pieces are much sought after today, with prices ranging from £3,000 to £20,000. Less expensive are Chinese armorial items bearing the coats-of-arms of British families: prices for these start at around £300 per plate.

The Mandarin palette

Styles in coloured export ware changed little until the 1770s, when the purplish pink Mandarin palette began to dominate. Figures on a terrace were a popular decoration, with panels framed in underglaze blue and much of the ground covered in 'diaper' decoration. Mandarin bowls and vases were often richly gilded, but today that gilding has mostly worn off. So popular was the palette that it was copied by many factories, including Worcester in England.

▷ **FAMILLE-ROSE JUG** *Attractive utilitarian wares such as this fine jug, with its intertwined handles and delicate pattern, were extremely popular. 1785; 8in high.* **£500**

◁ **FAMILLE-ROSE TEA CANNISTER,** painted in the Mandarin palette (the pink can be clearly seen on the clothes and in the background). The base was modelled separately before being attached. 1780; 9in high. **£120 – £150**

△ **MANDARIN PALETTE TEAPOT** decorated with a scene of figures on a terrace. It has a famille-rose lid from a different piece of a similar date. Lids rarely fit well, however, even on matching teapots. 1770; 5½ in high. **£30 – £40**

▽ **FAMILLE-ROSE PUNCH BOWL** which also features the Mandarin pink. Pieces decorated with European subjects, such as this hunting scene, are more expensive than those with Chinese designs. 1760; 11in wide. **£1,800 – £2,000**

19th century export porcelain

Large quantities of *famille-verte* and *famille-rose* dishes and vases were imported from China in the 1880s and '90s, most decorated with panels of figures and many bearing the incised reign mark of Emperor Chenghua (1465 – 87). This custom of using old marks on new pieces in honour of ancestors can cause confusion. Well painted examples from the late 19th century are very rare, but since pieces are both decorative and saleable they are in demand, with prices ranging from around £100 to £2,000.

USEFUL TERMS

IDENTIFYING RESTORED CHINA

This 12-inch-wide bowl (pictured with expert David Battie) dates from about 1770 and is decorated with typical *famille-rose* panels of flowers and pink diaper borders. When struck, it rings out clearly, apparently indicating that it is uncracked. It is in fact damaged but has been restored (detected by sliding a sharp knife over the enamel until it catches on a restored, unglazed area). This reduces its value from £1,000 to £150 to £200.

BRONZING Iron oxide used to simulate bronze, popular from 1870 – 90.
DIAPER Repeated geometric pattern of small squares or diamonds.
'DOG OF FO' Mythical guardian spirit in the shape of a lion-pekingese.
GROUND Background colour, usually monochrome.
MANDARIN PALETTE Ornate, late 18th and early 19th century enamel decoration, dominated by reds, purples and gold.
YINGQING Chinese porcelain made from around 960 to 1350, with carved or moulded floral designs and a distinctive blue-green glaze.

MEISSEN

Early Meissen porcelain (from 1713) was creamy in colour and bore no maker's mark. Many designs were derived from Chinese *blanc de chine* wares and decorated with moulded cherry blossom sprays. Figures from this period were also based on Chinese designs.

By the mid 1720s enamel painting was well-established at Meissen. The Oriental influence was still very strong and is evident in the superb chinoiserie fantasies painted by J. G. Herold, who had joined the factory in 1720, and the many designs derived from Kakiemon ware.

Meissen porcelain had become far whiter by 1725 and the famous underglaze blue crossed swords symbol was introduced. Previously, pieces had been left unmarked or given one of a number of symbols.

By 1740 Oriental designs had been superseded by harbour and battle scenes which gave way to flower and bird subjects based on prints in scientific textbooks. From the 1750s Meissen enamel painters also produced romantic figure scenes inspired by the work of Boucher.

Highly collectable today, Meissen figures were the mainstay of the factory's production until the 19th century. Popular subjects included shepherdesses, monkeys, artisans and street traders. The finest figures, however, were pantomime characters sculpted in the late 1730s and early '40s by J. J. Kändler.

▽ **SUCRIER (SUGAR BOWL) AND COVER**
Ozier (basket weave) borders of this type were a popular form of decoration. 1750s; 4in high. **£600 – £800**

◁ **CHOCOLATE POT AND COVER** *painted in enamels and gilded, in the style of a Japanese original made at Arita. The ear-shaped handle is typical of the period. Covered jugs were made in considerable numbers, but the hole in the lid (into which a stick for stirring the drinking chocolate was inserted) of this piece is a rare feature. Sometimes the hole is found in the centre of the knop. The base of this unusual piece shows the Meissen crossed swords mark (above). 1740s; 8in high.* **£1,500 – £2,000**

▽ **ENAMELLED SNUFF BOX,** *closed (left) and open (below). The exterior is well painted in enamels and has a moulded border. The interior, painted using a stipple technique, reveals a scene of cupids playing. The gilding on the silver mount has worn off and the box is cracked. In perfect condition, it would be worth £5,000 – £6,000. Late 1740s; 3in wide.* **£1,000 – £2,000**

TYPES OF GILDING

Gold was applied to Meissen porcelain in several ways. The technique used for early white Meissen ware involved sticking gold leaf to the body with glue. This method did not produce a durable finish, however, and more permanent results were achieved by applying gold leaf to the body and firing it at a low temperature.

During the late 1820s Meissen developed gloss-gilding, a process which enabled liquid gold to be painted in intricate patterns, as on the two plates (right). This gold layer was not particularly hard-wearing, however, and on many pieces whole sections of decoration have worn off.

△ GLOSS-GILDED PLATES *This type of gilding is rarely seen in such good condition. Both of these fine examples are marked with the Meissen crossed swords (above). 1840s; 11in wide.*   Each £140 – £160

THE MEISSEN INFLUENCE

Augustus the Strong tried and failed to keep the formula of hard paste porcelain a secret. In the 18th century Meissen workers ran away to other factories in Vienna, Italy and Germany, taking with them the secret formula. As well as using the formula, rival factories also imitated Meissen's designs. Sèvres was instructed by Louis XV to make porcelain in the manner of Meissen, and English factories, usually slow to adapt to new ideas, were influenced by Meissen, particularly in their figures.

▽ DUTCH VASES *made by the Dutch Oude Loosdrecht factory, in a style popularized by Meissen. The market for Dutch porcelain is limited. 1770s; 7in high.*   The pair £1,000 – £1,500

◁ LUDWIGSBURG COFFEE POT *closely modelled on a Meissen original. The Ludwigsburg factory was established in 1737, but only began producing fine porcelain after 1759, when an itinerant craftsman, J. J. Ringler, sold them the formula for hard paste porcelain. 1760s; 9in high.*   £1,000 – £1,500

▽ MEISSEN-STYLE TEA CANNISTERS *The example on the left was made at the Höchst factory, where Ringler worked from 1750 – 2. It bears a faint spoked wheel mark on the base (below). The other piece was made at the Berlin factory and is marked with an underglaze blue sceptre. If the lids had survived, the price of each piece would be doubled. 1770s; 3½ in high.*   Each £1,000

SEVRES PORCELAIN

◁ **RARE WHITE VASE** *with Art Nouveau style decoration in enamels and gilding, and a gilded bronze stand. Sèvres pieces from the 19th century are almost as rare as those from the 18th. The factory's management changed frequently in the second half of the 19th century, although some excellent artists were in charge of decoration. Sèvres pieces are usually marked (below); the marks on this piece indicate the potting year 1880 (top) and a decorating year of 1881. 1881; 5¼ in high.* **£300 – £500**

Although soft-paste porcelain had been made in France since the late 17th century, Louis XV, like other 18th century monarchs and princes, wanted his own hard-paste porcelain factory. In 1745, he granted Charles Adam and Eloy Brichard the rights to make porcelain in the manner of Meissen. They founded a factory at the disused royal palace of Vincennes, but moved to a purpose-built site at Sèvres, between Paris and Versailles, in 1756. Three years later, the factory came under direct royal control, with Madame de Pompadour, Louis' mistress, as one of its patrons.

As an operation dedicated solely to the glory of the French king, rather than a money-making enterprise, Sèvres could impose far higher quality controls than most factories. To begin with, Sèvres produced soft-paste porcelain, which was always more difficult to control in the kiln than hard paste, and made to an exacting and complex formula. The results, however, were unsurpassed: a pure white body with a soft glaze into which the brilliant enamels sank, producing a delicacy unequalled elsewhere. In addition, Sèvres took as source material prints by such well-known artists of the French Rococo as Fragonard and Boucher; superb painters were employed to execute the work and, at a time when porcelain styles were based on wares in gold and silver, leading goldsmiths were chosen to design the shapes.

Sèvres made few figures, but was responsible for discovering biscuit-ware – unglazed porcelain figures resembling marble. The factory produced a range of biscuit figures which were more sought after and expensive in the 19th century than they are today. Biscuit figures were more expensive than coloured since even the slightest flaw was apparent.

Sèvres finally succeeded in making hard-paste porcelain in 1769, and made hard and soft wares in tandem

△ **VINCENNES TUREEN, COVER AND STAND,** *painted by Charles-Nicholas Dodin on a 'bleu lapis' (deep blue) ground. This piece has been traced in the factory records, where it is listed as 'mediocre', probably due to the slight bubbling in the glaze. 1754; 9½ in wide.* **£3,000 – £5,000**

▷ **ROSE POMPADOUR FLOWER BOWL,** *superbly painted with flowers in a gilt-edged panel. The pink colour, Mme de Pompadour's favourite, was not used after her death in 1764. 1759; 6¾ in wide.* **£7,000 – £10,000**

until the early 19th century when soft paste was dropped. Unfortunately, with no aristocracy to support the factory in the decade after the Revolution, quality declined and some poor pieces were produced.

In addition to the interlaced Ls (for Louis), Sèvres pieces also have a painter's mark and a date letter. Inevitably, all these marks have been copied.

SEVRES MARKS

Interlaced Ls with date letter
A – Z 1753 – 77; AA – PP 1778 – 93

| Year mark 1845 – 48 | Decorating year 1855 – 70 | Potting year 1852 – 70 |

| Château designation | Le Guay (painter) 1778 –1840 | Dodin (painter) 1754 – 1802 |

△ **SAUCER AND MUSTARD POT,** *lacking its cover, combined in the late 19th century to be used as a cup and saucer. The overall quality is good and the decoration is typically Victorian. 1890; saucer 4in diameter.* **£100 – £150**

▷ **BISCUIT PORCELAIN GROUP** *from a design by sculptor E. M. Falconet and entitled 'L'Education de l'amour'; the figures represent Smell, Sight, Reading and Painting. Biscuit groups from the 18th century are never marked. 1763; 12½ in high.* **£3,000 – £4,000**

IN THE STYLE OF SEVRES

Sèvres' standards and the difficulty of working with soft paste resulted in high wastage in the first, white, firing. Any piece (with the exception of the most complex) was rejected if it was flawed. Unlike most factories, however, which destroyed rejects or sold them for decoration elsewhere, Sèvres stored theirs. When the factory was in financial difficulty in the early 19th century, these pieces were sold. Many were bought by Staffordshire decorators and painted there in Sèvres style.

Identifying such pieces is not easy. The matter is made worse by the many copies made in the 19th century, when 18th century works of art of all sorts were being collected. Most of these were highly elaborate, with popular ground colours such as the factory's famous *bleu celeste* and *rose Pompadour*, and with applied ormolu mounts. Perhaps only 5% of all Sèvres-style pieces were actually made by the factory at the date they claim. They are, nevertheless, very saleable.

△ **SAMSON HARD-PASTE CUP AND SAUCER,** *in the style of Sèvres. Edmé Samson founded his Paris works in 1845, producing copies of many other factories' output. These pieces are now highly collectable. 1860; 3in high.* **£120 – £180**

◁ **NAPOLEON-STYLE CUP** *based on a Sèvres original, but of poorer quality. The mark is painted. 1900; 3½ in high.* **£150 – £200**

△ **MINIATURE SEALS** *from the Chelsea and Girl-in-a-Swing factories, inscribed in French with messages of dedication and love. One has a gilt metal mount to hold the agate seal in place. Although such seals were particularly expensive from the 1920s to the '50s, they are less so in real terms today. 1749 – 54; 1 – 1½ in high.* **Each £600 – £800**

▽ **DIANA THE HUNTRESS** *A Chelsea/ Derby figure of the goddess Diana. The well-painted spotted greyhound at her feet makes this group, which would originally have almost certainly been one of a pair, particularly attractive. 1780; 11in high.* **£700 – £900**

CHELSEA & DERBY FIGURES

The Chelsea factory, founded in 1744, was the English equivalent of Meissen, making expensive figures and other ornamental wares in the contemporary Rococo style. Although the soft paste used was difficult to handle, standards of modelling, painting and gilding were extremely high.

All early Chelsea figures are rare. These include the all-white pieces of the 'Triangle' period (1745 – 50), and the raised-anchor, improved-paste wares produced after 1750. At this time, a supposed offshoot of the Chelsea factory, known as 'Girl-in-a-Swing' from the first identified piece, was also making figures and other wares; these too are rare and expensive. Most figures of this period were based on Meissen or French faïence originals, but the factory's models of birds were taken from British ornithological books.

Pieces produced during the 'Red Anchor' period display all that is best about 18th century English porcelain. The figures are superbly modelled and painted in a clear white paste which shows off the enamels and gilding to best effect. Meissen was still influential, but many Red Anchor

▽ *A typical red anchor mark, 1752 – 56.*

designs were original. During the 'Gold Anchor' period (1756 – 69), however, quality declined and the pieces started to lose their charm.

In addition to full-size figures, both the Chelsea and Girl-in-a-Swing factories produced miniatures. Most of these so-called 'toys' were in the form of scent bottles or seals.

The Derby factory started production around 1750, and initially made only ornamental wares, including figures. The animals of Andrew Planché, in particular, most of which

CHELSEA AND DERBY MAKERS' MARKS

Chelsea and Derby were both popular factories in the 19th century, and numerous copies made in France, Germany and elsewhere exist. Most have some sort of mark, often wrong for the apparent period. All marks should be treated with the utmost caution, particularly the gold anchor which is still in use on figures today.

Chelsea 1752 – 56 in red, 1756 – 69 in gold. Gold also used for Derby decorated at Chelsea 1769 – 75 | Chelsea/Derby 1769 – 84 gold or colour

Derby 1769 – 75 usually gold | Derby 1782 – 1825 various colours | Derby 1785 – 1825 blue, copy of Meissen mark

◁ **CHILD MUSICIANS** *made at the Chelsea/Derby factory. In common with many such figures, the inspiration here is from a contemporary Meissen group. 1780; 10in high.* **£600 – £800**

▽ **PAIR OF SWEETMEAT FIGURES** *These Chelsea Rococo figures are based on Meissen originals. Some slight damage has reduced the value by around £1,000. 1760; 7½ in high.* **£2,500 – £3,000**

are white and have a 'dry edge' at the base where the glaze stops short, are vigorously modelled.

Following the employment of William Duesbury in 1756, Derby started to produce more domestic wares, at the same time continuing to make figures that were still largely based on Meissen originals. Slip-cast and lightweight, by the 1760s these were being fired on blobs of clay in the kiln, which left (usually three) instantly recognizable 'patches' on the base.

In 1770 Duesbury bought the Chelsea factory and, increasingly influenced by Sèvres, started to manufacture biscuit figures. Quality, however, declined during this Chelsea/Derby period. In 1784 the Chelsea factory was closed, and all production transferred to Derby.

△ **MONKEY MUSICIANS** *This rare group, compiled from two sets, was possibly modelled by Samuel Keyes. It was inspired by the Meissen monkey band of the mid 18th century. 1835; 3 – 4in high.* Each **£600 – £800**

◁ ▷ **CHELSEA/DERBY SHEEP GROUPS** *The figures in these attractively modelled and well-coloured pieces are set against flowers and foliage that are in unusually good condition. 1780 – 90; 6in high.* The pair **£1,300**

ROYAL WORCESTER

Only one English porcelain factory founded in the 18th century has survived into the 20th: Worcester. Although it was set up in 1751 on the banks of the River Severn by Dr John Wall and William Davis, Worcester's origins date back to a factory established in Bristol around 1750 by Benjamin Lund, who was granted a licence to mine Cornish soaprock as an ingredient for his porcelain. These early products are very rare and include a famous underglaze blue-decorated moulded sauceboat marked on the underside 'Bristoll' (sic).

The secrets of Bristol porcelain-making were bought by the Worcester proprietors in 1752, along with rights to the soaprock. As a result, it is difficult to differentiate early Worcester products from those made in Bristol. Since Worcester had the experience gained in Bristol to build on, its experimental period was short, lasting from 1751 until 1754. From then until the early 1770s was the high point of 18th century production. After that, the excitement of the early painting was replaced by a dull competence.

Worcester's success was due to the soaprock formula: its tea wares, unlike those of Bow

▷ **UNUSUAL MUG** *painted with a rare pattern of a Chinaman, with a vase of flowers on a table and a kneeling boy to one side. The blue patterns used by the factory have now been named: this one, in two shades of cobalt blue, is called 'The Gardener'. 1765 – 70; 5½ in high.* **£700 – £1,200**

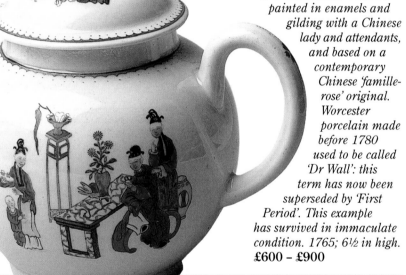

▽ **SAUCE TUREEN, COVER AND LADLE,** *painted and gilded with the 'Lord Henry Thynne' pattern, named for the eldest son of the Marquis of Bath (crescent mark inset). 1775; ladle 7in long.* **£2,500**

◁ **'FIRST PERIOD' TEAPOT** *painted in enamels and gilding with a Chinese lady and attendants, and based on a contemporary Chinese 'famille-rose' original. Worcester porcelain made before 1780 used to be called 'Dr Wall': this term has now been superseded by 'First Period'. This example has survived in immaculate condition. 1765; 6½ in high.* **£600 – £900**

△ CUP, TEA BOWL AND
SAUCER *(a 'trio') decorated
with a black overglaze transfer
scene known as 'l'Amour' and
engraved by Robert Hancock
who developed the technique
at Worcester. Overglaze is
very prone to wear: price
depends on condition. 1775;
saucer 5in.* **£250 – £350**

◁ BARR, FLIGHT & BARR
*cup and saucer bat printed
(a variation of transfer
printing, which gives the
finest of all reproduction) in
black with classical subjects
on a simulated gold marble
ground. The impressed mark
(inset) is often accompanied
by written marks on larger
pieces. 1804 – 13; cup
2½ in high.* **£250 – £350**

and Chelsea, could withstand boiling
water without cracking. Early pieces
were decorated in underglaze blue,
with designs based on popular
Chinese imports. Oriental figures and
landscapes were common, though not
slavishly copied from the Chinese,
but given an amusing chinoiserie
twist. Many of these pieces have a
blue-painted crescent mark and,
often, a painter's mark near the rim.

Identifying early English porcelain
is not easy and there is still much
research to be done. Early Worcester,
if held to the light, usually shows a
greenish tinge to the paste, and
there is often a line of glaze missing
next to the foot rim on the underside.

Printing was used both under and
over the glaze, the former in blue,
the latter mainly in black, but also in

▷ SWEETMEAT FIGURES *designed by
James Hadley, whose moulded
signature appears on the rear. Both
have printed marks, including the last
two figures of the year. 1865; 8in high.*
£600 – £900

▽ **GRAINGER'S GLAZED PARIAN VASE** *pierced by Alfred Barry. Barry's work is not as fine as that of George Owen, but all Grainger's work has risen in price in the last few years. This example is damaged: a perfect piece would be worth double. 1880; 5in.* **£150 – £200**

▽ **MEDIEVAL CRAFTSMAN,** *one of a series by James Hadley. Hadley modelled numerous matching sets and this is not among the most common. The bronzing makes this a little gloomy, although there is a printed mark. 1878; 4in high.* **£200 – £300**

MAKERS' MARKS

Many marks on Worcester pieces, and those produced by factories assimilated into Worcester, can help in dating output precisely. In the third quarter of the 19th century a date code system, which gives the year of production, was introduced.

 'open' crescent on painted wares 1755 – 83

 cross-hatched crescent on printed wares

fretted square, on heavily decorated wares 1755 – 75

Barr Flight & Barr, impressed 1807 – 13

Barr Flight & Barr, Worcester
Flight & Barr, Coventry St, London Manufacturers to their Majesties and Royal Family

Flight, Barr & Barr 1813 – 40

Kerr & Binns figure indicates year 61 = 1861

standard mark 1862 – present here 1866

DATE MARKS

A 1867	P 1879	From 1891 'Royal Worcester, England' was written out and other marks added to indicate year.	1918 one dot either side of star	
B 1868	R 1880		1927 six dots to left, five to right	
C 1869	S 1881			
D 1870	T 1882		1928 rectangle	
E 1871	U 1883	1892 – 1915: A dot system was added to the mark.	1929 diamond	
G 1872	V 1884		1930 division sign	
H 1873	W 1885	1892 one dot to left of crown	1931 two interlaced circles	
I 1874	X 1886	1893 one dot either side of crown		
K 1875	Y 1887	1915 12 dots either side of crown	1932 – 1941: Three interlaced circles. Dots were added in the same manner as the earlier periods	
L 1876	Z 1888			
M 1877	O 1889	1916 – 27: A star added under the mark and the dot system repeated.		
N 1878	a 1890	1917 one dot to left of star	1941 – 8: No change to date mark	

ROYAL CHINA WORKS
G&Cº ESTABLISHED 1801
WORCESTER
1889 – 1902

George Grainger & Co. was taken over in 1889 and closed in 1902. Letters under the mark indicate year of manufacture.

A 1891	E 1895	I 1899
B 1892	F 1896	J 1900
C 1893	G 1897	K 1901
D 1894	H 1898	H 1902

Models by James Hadley
Hadleys WORCESTER England
printed mark 1902 – 5

LOCKE & CO. WORCESTER

on porcelain 1895 – 1904

tones of red and brown. Worcester overglaze prints, a peculiarly English development, have not been bettered. Some pieces were also decorated in coloured enamels, using the print as a guide.

Colour painting and grounds

In addition to blue printing, coloured painting developed rapidly, initially of chinoiserie, and then of European landscapes, birds and flowers within a finely painted gold border. Under the influence of Sèvres, the factory introduced coloured grounds, the most common of which was royal blue, but turquoise, yellow and a watery green can also be found. Some porcelain was sent to London for decoration at the studios of James Giles. Many of these pieces bear a reproduction of the Meissen crossed swords mark; the Sèvres interlaced Ls were also fabricated.

In the last quarter of the 18th century, Rococo gave way to neo-classical designs, and silver shapes were copied for tea wares. Decoration

was often simple, limited to borders in underglaze blue and gilding. Quality fell, however, and, plagued by financial difficulties, Worcester was bought by Thomas Flight in 1783.

The 19th century

Under Flight's management and that of several of his successors (with variations of the names Flight and Barr), the factory rose to heights unsurpassed by any other of the early 19th century.

This golden age of superb potting and painting, in which the proprietors proudly proclaimed their ownership with a lengthy series of painted marks, came to an end with an in-glorious amalgamation with the Chamberlain factory in 1840. There was a period of fairly limited, but good-quality work during the following decade under Kerr and Binns, but the next major revival in Worcester's output came in the 1880s.

Highlights of the late 19th century include fine-quality figures and painted services and vases, as well

△ PAIR OF HOODED WARBLERS *perched on Cherokee roses, modelled by Dorothy Doughty, whose sister Freda produced studies of children for the factory. Dorothy's bird models were introduced in 1935. 1961; 12in, 10in.* Pair **£1,500 – £2,000**

△ BARR, FLIGHT & BARR PLATE *This very rare plate is part of the Stowe service produced by the company for the 2nd Marquis of Buckingham in 1813, and bearing his coat of arms. 1813; 9¼ in diameter.* **£1,200 – £1,800**

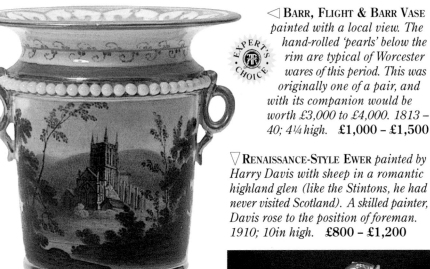

as the extraordinary pierced wares produced by George Owen. Noteworthy painters of this period include Charles Baldwyn, who specialized in birds and whose works now command more than £1,000 each; the Stinton family, whose members covered their vases with heather and highland cattle, although none had ever crossed the border; and Harry Davis, who specialized in sheep.

There were other factories making porcelain in Worcester (the Royal prefix was added in 1851) besides that founded by Dr Wall. Chamberlain's was initially established as a decorating shop, before absorbing the main factory. Others included Grainger's, Locke's and Hadley's, all of which were eventually taken over by Royal Worcester.

The factory used numerous marks during its lifetime, many of which can be mistaken for others, although several can help in dating pieces fairly precisely.

◁ BARR, FLIGHT & BARR VASE *painted with a local view. The hand-rolled 'pearls' below the rim are typical of Worcester wares of this period. This was originally one of a pair, and with its companion would be worth £3,000 to £4,000. 1813 – 40; 4¼ high.* **£1,000 – £1,500**

▽ RENAISSANCE-STYLE EWER *painted by Harry Davis with sheep in a romantic highland glen (like the Stintons, he had never visited Scotland). A skilled painter, Davis rose to the position of foreman. 1910; 10in high.* **£800 – £1,200**

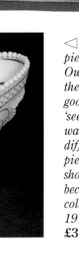

◁ COURT SHOE *pierced by George Owen, signed on the base, and with good-quality gilt 'seeding'. Owen was master of the difficult craft of piercing. These shoes are rare and becoming highly collectable. 1919; 7¾ in long.* **£3,000 – £5,000**

MASON'S IRONSTONE

Englishman Miles Mason was a London-based dealer in Chinese and other ceramics, and a man of some importance in the 1790s, until the Napoleonic Wars in Europe and unrest in China disrupted his trade. Mason's immediate recourse was to begin manufacturing porcelain in Liverpool (little is known of this venture) and earthenware in Staffordshire. The Liverpool undertaking was closed in 1800 and a factory set up at Lane Delph near Newcastle-under-Lyme. Like many of the county's other manufacturers at this time, Mason's firm produced decorative wares as well as ranges of useful items such as teasets, dessert wares, dinner services, in the new hybrid hard-paste bodies.

The Ironstone body for which Mason is famed was a tough, heavy earthenware which could be decorated to imitate the porcelains of the day, and had a similar 'ring' when struck, but was cheaper to produce. Mason's son took out the patent on their body in 1813, using the word 'Ironstone' for the first time. This early Ironstone, a hard-looking, dense grey-white material usually without crazing, was immediately successful, particularly in America where it is still widely collected.

Mason's Ironstone ranged from utilitarian blue and white dinner services, through brightly enamelled dessert services comprising 30 or more pieces, to elaborate vases and covers, some four feet high. Apart from the body itself, there is one characteristic common to all Mason's work, and that is his ponderous eccentricity. Give Mason a rococo scroll and it will out-rococo any other; likewise, his Japanese-style flowers are golder, redder and more boldly Imari than those of any other manufacturer. Mason's work is stamped with a confidence that his was the original, the strongest, and the best Ironstone body.

Mason's Ironstone continues to be made today: modern pieces can be distinguished by their cream colour and thick, clear, crazed glaze.

MASON'S IRONSTONE MARKS

Mason's pieces usually bear the Royal Arms and a banner. Other marks have been used, but all modern pieces are marked 'Made in England'.

Rare mark used only on some china pieces

1891 – 1902 date mark

△ VASE AND COVER *decorated with bold Imari-style flowers and gilding. It has been heavily restored: in good condition it would be worth £2,000, and a pair might realize £5,000 to £10,000. 1830s; 2ft 4in high.* **£600 – £800**

◁ POT POURRI VASE, *one of a pair with pierced covers, based on Chinese originals. The design was printed in black, then coloured by hand. 1830; 16in high.* The pair **£1,000 – £1,500**

▷ VEGETABLE TUREEN WITH COVER *transfer-printed with Imari-style flowers, then hand coloured. This is cracked; if perfect it would be worth up to £500, while a soup tureen would be worth up to £1,200. 1820; 7in high.* **£120 – £150**

A CLOSER · LOOK AT ·

AN IRONSTONE DESSERT SERVICE

Dating from the early years of Ironstone production, around 1820, this service displays all that is best from the factory. The forms, which derive from contemporary silver design, have been taken to extremes in characteristic Mason style. The wave to the rim of the stand and the scallops on the shaped rectangular dish are much bolder than any other manufacturer dared to produce; this is part of the appeal of Mason's work. The Japanese-style floral decoration is colourful and flamboyant and the whole difficult to improve upon.

Sadly, today most services are being broken up, with single pieces commanding high prices.

▷ *A fruit stand or comport, worth £400 – £600. The hole through the stem is very unusual, but the 'wave' to the rim is typical.*

▽ *An original dessert service usually comprised more than 30 pieces, with its exact composition determined by the individual purchaser.*

◁ *The original Mason's mark, which is still in use today on mass-produced earthenwares.*

▷ *Detail from the shell-shaped dish. This would have been one of a pair and is worth £250 – £300 alone.*

THE OCTAGONAL JUG

The eight-sided jug was Mason's most popular design, and usually included a green enamelled 'dragon' (as here) or snake handle. Such jugs are still in production today, and modern examples can be recognized both by their pink maker's mark and by the appearance of the body, which is cream rather than grey-white in colour and has crazing. Although various designs were originally produced to adorn octagonal jugs, the Imari-style flowers used here proved the most popular. These jugs were available in six different sizes and were widely copied by other manufacturers. Dating from around 1840, the jugs here measure 10 inches and 8 inches high and are worth £100 and £80 respectively.

TOBY JUGS

The origins of the Toby jug go back a long way. Novelty jugs and drinking vessels in the form of bears were made in Germany during the 16th century, and owl jugs were produced in Staffordshire potteries in the late 17th century. It was not until the mid 18th century, however, that the instantly recognizable English Toby jug began to be produced, although similar pieces had been made earlier in the 18th century from Dutch Delft (tin-glazed earthenware).

The name 'Toby jug' probably derives from the nickname – 'Toby Philpot' (or 'Fill-pot') – of Harry Elwes, a well-known ale-drinker who was also the subject of a popular song called *The Brown Jug*, published in 1761. The familiar rotund figure, wearing a three-cornered hat and seated with a mug of ale, sold in large numbers, inspiring some 20 other humorous jug designs including the 'Thin Man' and the 'Squire'. The only female figure was 'Martha Gunn', a famous 19th century bathing belle who achieved notoriety by ducking the Prince Regent (later George IV) in the sea at Brighton.

The earliest English Toby jugs were a speciality of the two Ralph

△ STAFFORDSHIRE 'THIN MAN' *carefully painted with a brightly coloured costume and an expressive, detailed face. 1840; 12in high.* **£120 – £150**

◁ SAILOR TOBY *made in Staffordshire and identifiable by his blue-striped stockings. Standard transfer prints have been used on his hat and coat. Mid 19th century; 7½ in high.* **£250 – £300**

△ STAFFORDSHIRE TOBY *with a lift-off hat. He probably represents 'John Bull', who symbolizes England. The careful colouring is quite unlike the haphazard splashing of 18th century pieces. 1880; 10in high.* **£300 – £500**

▷ BONE CHINA TOBY *wearing a rather badly painted pink coat. The piece is unmarked, and could be the product of any one of around 25 Stoke-on-Trent factories. 1930s; 7in high.* **£30 – £50**

Woods (father and son), the famous Staffordshire potters. Their jugs are thinly potted and coloured in a sub-dued palette of browns, blues, greys and pale yellow, but the hats form-ing the lids are often missing.

Toby jugs were popular throughout the late 18th and 19th centuries, and were made by numerous factories. Reproductions of classic Toby jug designs, identifiable by their much brighter colouring, were made in the late 19th century by both English and Continental makers.

In the 20th century, 'character jugs' by makers such as Doulton have enjoyed a considerable following. Jugs from the Allied Generals series (made during World War I), for example, fetch around £150 to £250 each.

△ PARIAN TOBY JUG *This well-coloured example is unusual in that it is made from parian, a type of hard paste porcelain developed in the 1840s. 1850 – 70; 4in high.* **£30 – £40**

△ JAPANESE CHARACTER JUGS *(side view, right), loosely based on a Royal Doulton original. Brightly coloured export ware was made in occupied Japan after World War II. 1945; 3in high.* Each **£30 – £40**

CONTINENTAL TOBY JUGS

◁ FRENCH TOBY *made by the Sarreguemines factory in Staffordshire style. 1880; 8½ in high.* **£70 – £100**

▽ GERMAN TOBY *made of porcelain (not earthenware) and painted in bright colours, unlike his English counterparts. 1890; 7in high.* **£30 – £50**

When the British ceramics industry went into decline in the late 19th century, Continental manufacturers began to copy British designs. They even made reproductions of the traditional Staffordshire Toby jug in both pottery and hard-paste porcelain. These were often left unmarked and exported to be sold as the genuine article. Samson of Paris made good copies of 18th century English Tobys in pottery, and these are now worth around £200, as opposed to £1,800 for an original.

△ TOWN CRIER TOBY *This amusing and colourful German piece of unusual form illustrates the wide variety of Tobys available. 1890; 8½ in high.* **£30 – £50**

EWERS & BASINS

Many houses in this country did not have indoor bathrooms until the turn of the century, some not until after World War II. Before that time, washing in the morning was not something to look forward to. Water was left overnight in a ewer in the bedroom to be poured into a matching basin for washing. Anyone living in a house with servants (and every middle-class home had one) was

▽ **GATER, HALL & CO. EWER AND BASIN** *transfer printed in underglaze blue with sprays of flowers and with gilt line borders. 1914; 14in high.* **£40 – £60**

luckier: warm water was brought from the kitchen in the ewer.

The simplest bedroom sets included a ewer, basin and covered dish for soap; the more elaborate had, in addition, a toothbrush holder, sponge bowl, chamber pot (to be kept in the bedside cabinet) and slop bucket. Most of the sets available today consist solely of ewer and basin: the

smaller and more delicate bowls and dishes have often been broken.

The earliest sets to be found today are Chinese Canton wares dating from the early 19th century, and a ewer and basin might realize £1,000 to £1,500 at auction. A fine mid 18th century Sèvres ewer and basin made a record price for European ceramics of £143,000 eight years

▽ **STAFFORDSHIRE EWER AND BASIN** *with transfer-printed swan decoration. Colour printing was often more expensive than hand painting, which could be done by children. 1890; 15in high.* **£150 – £200**

ago. Most examples on the market, however, are of humbler origin.

Bedroom sets were produced by most Stoke-on-Trent factories and many elsewhere. The majority were made of earthenware and decorated with transfer-printed flowers, although some were hand painted. The value is affected by the quality of the piece, its condition, the factory (Doulton sets are worth double those of other factories) and by how attractive it is. These sets were made in their millions and large numbers have survived, providing buyers with a wide range from which to choose.

UNIQUE POTTERY OWL BEDROOM SET

This studio pottery set was made at the Wrecclesham Pottery, Farnham by Henry Corrigan, who worked there from 1914 to 1980. It is a one-off, produced by the potter as a wedding gift for his brother and is a fine example of a complete set, probably because it was rarely used. The soft, porous body makes it impractical, and the sharp, stylized owls' beaks would be easily chipped. This set was made in 1930, the large bowl is 16 inches in diameter, and the complete set is worth £300 to £400.

◁ **BELLEEK EWER AND BASIN** *Belleek is a sought after factory, but its earthenwares such as this ewer and basin are less popular than its parian porcelain. If the set were decorated and/or coloured, it would be worth more than double its present value; if it did not have the factory's mark, it would be worth less than half. 1870; jug 10in.* **£100 – £150**

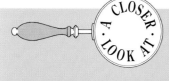 **A SUNDERLAND SET**

The pink lustre borders on this basin and ewer are typical of Sunderland pieces, although the technique was also used in Staffordshire. Dating these articles can be difficult, since they were made in the county for 50 years, from about 1800, were reproduced in the 1920s, and are in production again today. The clues are the quality of the printing, the lustre, and the body. This set dates from 1840, the bowl is 12 inches wide and the jug 9 inches high. It is worth £250 to £350.

'Watery' theme poem on lip of ewer.

Designs and text were transfer-printed.

Bridge over the Wear, detail from basin.

ART DECO TEA SERVICES

Fortunately for collectors, the tradition of keeping a teaset for best and using it only on formal occasions has ensured that there are many services around today, often in excellent condition.

In the 1930s, tea services were especially popular as wedding gifts. Most of the designs of the period were based on the rococo and neo-classical themes that had been popular since the 18th century, and the Art Deco style was considered a more daring alternative.

Art Deco took inspiration from modern architecture, the angular lines of cubism and industrial designs. Other influences included Art Nouveau, the functional forms of the Arts and Crafts movement, the Glasgow school and the Bauhaus movement. Classical forms and Japanese designs were also influential. Art Deco reached the peak of its development at the Paris Exhibition of 1925: the 'Exposition Internationale des Arts Décoratifs et Industriels Modernes', where the style was first exhibited.

Art Deco designs were characterized by clean, elegant lines and angular patterns, with stark black and white or brilliant colouring. A bonus was that pieces could be mass produced easily at affordable prices. Some factories applied designs by a combination of printing and painting, while others used lithographic transfer. In the latter process a design on paper is wrapped around an object so that when fired the pattern is transferred on to the surface.

Art Deco had largely declined in popularity by the outbreak of World

△ **BREAKFAST SERVICE** *for four people, complete with creamer and sugar bowl. Although typically Art Deco in shape and decoration, this service is relatively inexpensive. The value of such sets is, however, increasing steadily. 1930; teapot 4in high.* The set **£125 – £150**

War II, but contemporary taste has made it fashionable again. Some of the most valuable Art Deco tea services today are those designed by Clarice Cliff in the 1930s, particularly her 'Bizarre' and 'Fantasque' ranges. The brightly coloured designs of Cliff and her contemporary Susie Cooper are so sought after that sets are frequently split up and pieces sold individually.

Art Deco teasets decorated with flowers, however, are not particularly valuable, even though they were popular during the '30s. Clarice Cliff's crocus pattern sets, for example, are worth only a few pounds.

◁ **CLARICE CLIFF TEA SERVICE** *Part of a service in an unusual pattern from Cliff's 'Bizarre' range. The teapot is chipped and thus worth only £50. A complete tea service for six would fetch £1,000. 1930s; teapot 5in high.* **£150 – £200**

◁ **CLARICE CLIFF SUGAR BOWL AND JUG** *The great advantage of Clarice Cliff pieces to the collector is that they are invariably marked. The term 'Patina' (below) refers to the grainy texture, and 'Bizarre' is the name of the series. There is also a factory mark and a stamped patent number. 1930; 3in high. Each* **£30 – £40**

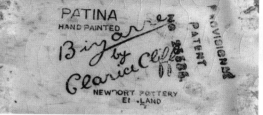

▽ **NORITAKE PORCELAIN** *An unusually good service for two by the Japanese factory, possibly based on a design by Frank Lloyd Wright. 1930s; plate 5in. The set* **£100 – £150**

▷ **SHELLEY BONE CHINA** *Part of a 6-setting service (lacking the teapot), by the Staffordshire firm, Shelley (mark below). The shape and pattern epitomize Art Deco design. Green and black was a popular colour combination. 1932; plate 6in. The set* **£500 – £600**

The earliest drinking glasses that are available in any great number are soda glasses, made in Italy in the 16th century. The most interesting English drinking glasses, however, in terms of collectability, are 18th century examples. Although generally large and heavy, glasses from this period varied considerably in design. Later examples, which were far more standardized, were smaller and lighter as glassmakers became increasingly adept at their craft.

Large-bowled, short-stemmed rummers, used for ale and cider, were introduced towards the end of the 18th century. Some were made to order and decorated with initials, coats-of-arms or significant dates, while others commemorated political, royal, military or other events.

A large number of the most popular rummers were plain – their appeal was in their moulded fluting or shape (most glasses were hand-blown until the late 19th century, after which they started to be moulded). Although a few glasses were enamelled, most decoration was wheel-engraved. Engravings of hops and barley were a favourite illustration, and the romantically-styled Jacobite glasses bearing emblems in support of the 'Young Pretender' Bonnie Prince Charlie were particularly popular.

▽ **VINE TENDRIL WINE GLASS** *from the Richardson factory in Stourbridge. The vine reflects the function of the glass and both the motifs on the bowl and the glass 'tendril' around the stem are gilded. 1840s; 7in.* **£500**

△ **PAIR OF VICTORIAN RUMMERS** *engraved with the Sunderland Bridge over the River Wear. Although the bridge was opened in 1796, its fame as the longest cast iron bridge in Britain ensured its popularity as a motif well into the 19th century. 1840; 6in high.* The pair **£400 – £500**

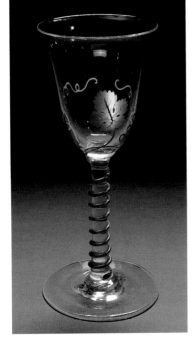

▽ **GEORGIAN DWARF ALE GLASS** *with folded foot, gadrooned baluster stem and gadrooning at the base of the bowl. Ale was more potent then, and taken in modest quantities. 1730s; 3in high.* **£200 – £300**

◁ **ALE GLASS,** *poorly engraved with hops and barley. These are typical bowl motifs of the time and reflect the type of drink the glass was designed for. 1770; 5in high.* **£90**

BOWL SHAPES

Early English drinking glasses had bowls of every shape and size, but by the end of the 18th century these had become standardized. Engraving on bowls was introduced in the 1730s. Vines were found on wine glasses and hops and barley on ale glasses.

  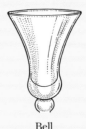  

Bucket Conical Bell Trumpet Cup

GADROONING Convex vertical line ornamentation, seen on furniture and silver as well as glass.

KNOP A ball or rounded projection in the stem of a glass.

PONTIL ROD The iron rod on which blown glass is formed. As the glass cools it is removed from the rod, leaving behind a tiny amount of residue known as the pontil mark (the pontil is sometimes called the 'punty').

POTASH GLASS Made in Europe, this refers to glass in which potash has been added to the mixture. It tends to harden fast and is ideal for engraving.

ROMER (ROEMER) This vessel, a forerunner of the rummer, is a goblet dating from the 15th century. It was made in Germany and the Low Countries (the Netherlands).

SODA GLASS This term describes glass that has had soda added to its original mixture, making it more malleable and easier to work. Venetian makers in the 15th, 16th and 17th centuries were noted for their soda glass.

▽ **CUT-GLASS GOBLET AND TANKARD**
Well cut with polished details, these two pieces were probably made in Stourbridge. 1930s; goblet 6½ in high, tankard 4½ in high. **Each £30 – £50**

◁ **RUMMER WITH LEMON SQUEEZER BASE** *engraved with a sailing ship and message of friendship. This type of base is rarer than the circular foot and is found mostly on better quality glasses. Late 1700s; 5in high.* **£350 – £500**

▽ **PRESENTATION GLASS RUMMER** *inscribed, 'Isabella Spence, a present from Isabella Closeton, her niece 1857'. A ship, 'The Atlas', is also engraved on the glass. 1857; 6in high.* **£180 – £200**

KNOPS AND FEET

The stems of most glasses had rounded projections or bulges known as knops. As glasses gradually became lighter, so knops became less prominent. Feet were either conical or domed.

Conical foot

Domed foot

Ball knop

Multiple knop

True baluster

Bladed knop

Mushroom knop

RUBY &
CRANBERRY GLASS

Although coloured glass had been produced at least since medieval times, notably for church use, translucent ruby red glass was unknown until the late 17th century, at which time manufacturers developed the colour using gold chloride as a tinting agent. Engraved and coloured glassware became popular on the Continent in the 18th century, but it was judged too flamboyant for the conservative English tastes of the time. From the 1850s, however, the Victorian relish for extravagant decoration created a demand for coloured glass goblets, bowls and vases. Particularly popular were ruby and cranberry glass (an American term for pale ruby glass).

The best ruby glass came from Bohemia, where craftsmen had perfected methods of

engraving glassware, usually with city views or landscapes. There too the techniques of flashing and casing glass (see 'Useful Terms') were

developed, and from the 1830s most of the decorative glass imported into England was of Bohemian origin. From about 1850, however, English factories at Stourbridge in the West Midlands, and French factories at Baccarat and St Louis started to produce high quality cut glass.

◁ **BACCARAT WASHSTAND SET** *of good quality, complete with soap and powder boxes. The ruby glass overlay has been cut away in fan shapes to reveal the clear glass beneath. 1880; jug 12in high.* **£500 – £800**

◁ **RUBY GLASS SET** *comprising a liqueur decanter, a vase with cover and a spirit decanter. The ear of corn design, faceted with windows, shows clear glass beneath. 1910 – 20; vase 19in high.* **£300 – £400**

▽ **CRUET SET** *on a silver-plated stand. The decoration on the glass is similar to that on the set on the left. 1910 – 20; 13in high.* **£300 – £400**

▷ **BOHEMIAN 'CASED' LUSTRE** *One of a pair, this ruby red lustre would have been displayed on a mantelpiece, the glass reflecting the light attractively. It is cased with opaque white panels painted with female portraits and bouquets of flowers. The panels have gilt borders. Pairs of lustres in red (or sometimes green) glass were very popular during the second half of the 19th century. They were a common feature of highly decorated Victorian interiors. 1860; 11in high.* **£600 – £900**

◁ **BOHEMIAN VASE WITH COVER** *The engraving on this vase – deer in woodland scenery, a common motif of Bohemian glass – is superbly executed. It gives the illusion of raised cameo rather than incised intaglio. 1850; 18in high.* **£2,000 – £3,000**

USEFUL TERMS

CASING A technique where clear or coloured glass is fused on to the inner surface of glass of another colour. The coloured outer 'case' is then partially cut away to reveal the clear or coloured glass beneath.

FLASHING Similar to casing, but clear or coloured glass is dipped into molten glass of another colour. The coloured outer surface is usually thinner than in cased glass.

LALIQUE

René Lalique (1860 – 1945) was one of the most remarkable and gifted commercial designers of the 20th century. Although best known today for the glassware that still bears his name, Lalique's first claim to fame was as France's premier jeweller. It was the popularity of his inventive and superbly crafted Art Nouveau jewellery in gold, silver and enamel that made Lalique's reputation in Paris at the turn of the century.

Lalique first began to explore the potential of glass as a decorative medium around 1904. His interest was further stimulated by an invitation to design embossed gilt paper labels for François Coty's perfume bottles. Lalique eventually designed not only the labels but also the bottles themselves, including their decorative stoppers. Coty was captivated by Lalique's designs and when they were put into production, increased sales reflected their popularity with Coty's clients.

Although Lalique's early pieces were made at the St Denis glassworks of the firm Legras et Cie, he established his own glassworks at Combs la Ville in 1908 (he had in fact set up an 'experimental' factory at Clairfontaine earlier, in 1902). Ten years later he opened a new, larger factory at Wingen-sur-Moder in the Alsace-Lorraine region, and by 1925 he was widely hailed as France's foremost glassmaker. The great majority of Lalique's creations were mass produced and employed mechanized techniques by which glass was machine-moulded

△ 'ROSCOFF' OPALESCENT FISH MOTIF DISH *Lalique incorporated fish into several of his designs for vases and tableware. This example features bubbles and fish heads radiating outward to the rim, which displays a fine, blue-tinged internal opalescence. 1930; 14in wide.* **£700 – £800**

with the aid of compressed air injection. His few handmade pieces were essentially 'one-offs', and are extremely rare and expensive today.

The versatility of Lalique's designs combined with the range of products made Lalique's output truly exceptional. The factory produced vases, light fittings, clock cases, tableware, car mascots and even church fittings, which can be seen in the church of St Matthew's Millbrook in Jersey.

◁ 'TELLINE' PERFUME BOTTLE *in clear and frosted glass, with a brownish 'Sienna' stain. Examples in blue or green are rarer. 1930; 4in high.* **£400 – £500**

△ 'MOINEAU' OPALESCENT CENDRIER *One of a range of ashtrays with central animal, floral or figure subjects. Opalescent pieces are unusual. 1930s; 4in high.* **£200 – £300**

▷ **SHALLOW PUNCH CUP** *with an unusual butterfly wing handle which has a frosted surface. The glass in this piece is relatively thick compared to the fragile, thin-walled wine glasses and decanters for which Lalique is better known. 1930s; 2½ in high.* **£60 – £80**

◁ **'COQUILLE' (SHELLWORK) BOWL,** *possibly Lalique's most successful design. The outside of this opalescent bowl features four scallop shells moulded in relief. 1930s; 8in wide.* **£300**

Although pieces in one solid colour are generally the most desirable, glass with an internal opalescence that catches the light is considered the most beautiful. The appearance of this glass was much imitated by Lalique's competitors such as Sabino and Verlys, but they never achieved its high standard. The Lalique factory ceased production of this distinctive opalescent glass in 1939, concentrating instead on clear and frosted glass.

Almost every piece of Lalique glass is signed 'R Lalique' or 'Lalique' (the 'R' was dropped after the master's death in 1945). There are at least 20 variations of his signature, including engraved, stencilled and moulded versions. Contrary to popular belief, Lalique was not responsible for signing each piece personally – production during his lifetime was estimated at over eight million pieces.

◁ **'MALESHERBES' JADE GREEN VASE** *in a design of overlapping leaves, enhanced by white staining. It is 'triple cased', that is, it is comprised of three layers of glass. 1932; 9in high.* **£2,000 – £2,500**

▷ **'COQ ET PLUMES' VASE** *The continuous frieze in low relief shows long-tailed cockerels set against tall feathers. 1930; 6½ in high.* **£400 – £600**

LALIQUE OR SABINO?

The clear and frosted glass figurine 'Suzanne' (near right) by Lalique eclipses the inferior copy (far right) from Marius Sabino's glassworks. The Lalique piece has a rare bronze illuminated base and represents the peak of the glassmaker's skill; the moulding of the opalescent Sabino figure is poor in comparison – notably the facial details. The hands of such figures are easily damaged and should always be checked for repairs.

The Lalique piece is valued at between £6,000 and £7,000, while the Sabino figure is worth £1,000 to £1,500. Sabino's solid colour pieces are of higher quality.

David Battie is a Sotheby's director and an expert on ceramics and Oriental works of art.

POTTERY, PORCELAIN & GLASS

Ceramics and glass probably have a wider range of appeal than any other works of art, and most households possess at least one or two interesting items.

That this category is so popular is demonstrated by the number of experts needed to service the pottery and glass queues at the Roadshows – twice as many are required as for any other subject. Added to that is the fact that delightful pieces, many of them bargains, can be had very cheaply indeed: for instance, you can pick up a 200-year-old plate for just 50p if you don't mind a tiny hairline crack. At the other extreme are incredibly expensive items, such as the Chinese pottery horse made during the Tang Dynasty (618 – 906) that sold recently for over £3,000,000.

Ceramics and glass are also desirable because of their relatively small size: you can keep adding to your collection without too much risk of running out of space.

The wide range of materials, styles, factories, countries and painters involved in the manufacture of pottery, porcelain and glass give the collector a huge choice of areas in which to specialize. Since many categories overlap, if interest in one area flags temporarily, there might be a strong market in another. Furthermore, ceramics are often colourful, dramatic and of practical use, factors that have attracted a particular group of ceramics hunters who are categorized as decorators, rather than collectors.

A decorator could be someone simply trying to find, for example, a large jardinière for their house, or a professional decorator looking for a group of Art Deco figures to adorn a celebrity's drawing room. For the decorator, the most important factors are not the date of the piece, the factory of origin or even its condition, but the general colour scheme and the overall visual impact it makes.

◁ GLASS BUST OF NAPOLEON III
by the French glassmaking company St Louis (famous for its paperweights). 1873; 8in high. £200 – £300

POINTS TO WATCH FOR

1 When buying an item, always assume that it has something wrong with it and that the person selling it knows something adverse about it but is not telling.

2 Check that the material, style, coloration, painting, modelling and gilding are consistent with the period in which the item is meant to have been made.

3 If the item you wish to buy bears a mark, is it the one you would expect to find on a piece of this date?

4 Does the seller answer your questions openly and reasonably, or is there a hint of evasion? If so, be wary about purchasing items from that particular shop.

5 If a small amount of damage is pointed out to you, check the piece carefully for further damage.

6 Prices on tickets are sometimes open to negotiation. Do not be afraid to ask for a discount.

7 If the price seems exceptionally cheap, ask yourself whether you have found a bargain or are being 'had'.

8 Always enquire as to whether a piece has been restored. If 'yes', ask the dealer to what extent; if 'no' or 'don't know', ask whether you can test it with a pin (which will glide over ordinary glaze and catch on softer restoration work). If the dealer refuses, take your custom elsewhere.

9 If buying at an auction that is not held at one of the major sale rooms, or at which you are given a guarantee (the policy will be set out in the Conditions of Sale), speak to the cataloguer and ask the questions in point 8.

10 Make sure that the seller gives you a full receipt, including date, attribution and condition report.

◁ COALPORT VASE *with raised paste gilding and painted panels. (The lid is damaged.) 1890s; 14in high.* £300 – £400

Most ceramics and glass were originally made for a practical purpose, and there is no reason why a careful owner should not continue to use them in the same way. In many instances the price of an antique example will be less than a modern piece serving the same function. How much more memorable to hold a dinner party at which your guests dine from century-old plates and sip wine – served in elegant Georgian glasses – poured from a Victorian decanter.

Whatever the reason for your interest in pottery, porcelain and glass – whether you are a dedicated collector with a large thematic collection or a decorator searching for a few outstanding pieces – I cannot think of a more fascinating or rewarding subject.

Places of Interest

Broadfield
  House Glass
  Museum,
  Kingswinford, West
  Midlands *19th and
  20th century glass*
Burrell Collection,
  Pollok Country Park,
  Glasgow *World famous
  collection including
  ceramics and stained glass*
City Museum & Art
  Gallery, Hanley, Stoke-on-
  Trent, Staffs *The largest
  collections of English pottery
  and porcelain in the world*
Minton Museum, London Rd,
  Stoke-on-Trent, Staffs
  *All aspects of the
  company's artistry*
Victoria & Albert Museum,
  Cromwell Rd, London SW7
  *Fine collections of ceramics
  and glass*

Care & Repair

1 All glasses and antique ceramics should be hand-washed – never put them in a dishwasher.

2 If using a plate or dish for cheese or any other fatty food, wash it immediately. Oils are difficult or impossible to remove once they have soaked into the body.

3 Always dry earthenware as soon as possible after washing; if left wet it may absorb moisture and become discoloured.

4 Use a shower attachment when washing flower-encrusted pieces and other delicate items, then leave them to dry. If you dry such pieces with a tea towel you run the risk of snagging and breaking them.

5 Earthenwares and ceramics with a crazed glaze – such as bone china and some soft paste porcelain – are water permeable; hard paste porcelain is not.

6 A dash of ammonia in the washing-up water will bring a sparkle to glass.

7 Don't warm plates and tureens in the oven, even at the coolest setting, since they may craze. Heat them by placing in hot water for a minute or two, then dry carefully.

8 Never use stick-on plate hangers for delft or majolica; they may remove the glaze.

9 Good pieces of pottery, porcelain or glass should only be repaired or restored by professionals.

10 If you don't want to sell a piece, don't have it restored or repaired if the damage does not offend.

△ **Staffordshire Teapot and Stand,** *transfer printed and hand coloured. 1890s; 7in high.* **£60 – £90**

▽ **Cut-Glass Scent Bottle,** *probably made in France and originally sold complete with scent. 1930s; 4½ in high.* **£40 – £60**

Fakes, Forgeries & Reproductions

There are probably more fakes, forgeries and reproductions of ceramics than of any other material: a fake is a genuine piece that has been altered, a forgery is an attempt to deceive, while reproductions are honest re-creations of earlier objects.

Many early deceptions – such as Worcester and Derby pieces with fake Meissen marks – are now accepted and even sought after by collectors. Problems arise when reproductions are removed from their original environment and become forgeries as a result of the way they are sold. A prime example is the large numbers of Korean copies of Chinese *famille-rose* and Canton porcelain that were imported as decorative items but are currently appearing at some small auctions and in some antique shops.

Every so often a very clever deception briefly fools the ceramics market. The best measures a collector can take when buying a piece is to question the seller closely and thoroughly examine the item of interest.

CLOCKS & WATCHES

BY SIMON BULL

My first stop on the '92 Roadshow was Queensferry in North Wales, and this delightful location produced the greatest 'if only...' of the year. Although clocks, watches and instruments from all periods and countries turn up Roadshows, my passion for over 20 years has been the 16th and 17th centuries.

As one might imagine, surviving examples from this period are particularly rare. It came as a surprise, therefore, when an English 'Monstrance' clock (a clock on a stand) – of a type that I was not aware even existed – appeared at our very first location.

'If only...' it had been in perfect condition, but in reality the original movement and dial had been replaced in about 1760, some 100 years after this extraordinary miniature clock had been made. A clock that could have fetched anything up to £40,000, therefore, was reduced to a fascinating fragment with a collector's value of only around £3,000.

At Stratford-upon-Avon, time ran out before we could film an exceptionally rare singing bird music box (the bird was covered with real hummingbird feathers). Made by the French firm Bontemps around 1880, it had a partly gilded and engraved case with an enamelled scene of a

young couple on the lid over the bird. The piece had been protected since the day it was made by a fitted velvet box, which was still intact. But it had been so well protected that the bird could manage no more than a gentle wheeze, and the owner had not heard it in full song for decades.

Fortunately, being armed with a small collection of watchmaker's tools, I was able to open the case and make a few minor adjustments: then, with a little gentle prompting, the bird revived. The quality of the song was clear and sharp (the music box having been used so infrequently over the years), demonstrating just how well such pieces functioned when originally made.

Another item that escaped the cameras at Stratford was a parasol. This is not an item that would ordinarily turn up at the clocks and watches table, but in this exceptional instance the ivory handle terminated in a chased gold finial, inset with a Swiss watch movement. Virtually all such pieces are of late 19th century origin, but examples in gold are by far the rarest and this parasol watch would have certainly fetched over £1,000.

Before we left Stratford, on a day that proved to be enormously rewarding, there arrived what appeared to be a good 18th century ebonized 'bracket' clock by Samuel Norton of London. The

◁ **EBONIZED BRACKET CLOCK** *The automaton scene in the arch enhances its value. 1740.* **£4,500 – £5,000**

▽ **MUSIC BOX** *from the Stratford Roadshow. Late 19th century; 4in long.* **£1,000**

◁ **BRACKET CLOCK** *by Samuel Norton. 21in high; 1760.* **£100** case and dial plate were indeed of the correct period, but the movement had been replaced at the end of the 19th century, most probably because the original wore out. Its value was therefore much reduced to around £100. An opportunity to film a fairly similar clock arose during our visit to Enniskillen in Northern Ireland. Although the clock was discovered in Ireland, it was in fact signed by Thomas Jackson of London and boasted many features of Dutch workmanship. Its standard mid 18th century design was augmented by an automaton scene in the arch, which increased its value to the region of £5,000.

My final Roadshow location was Orkney, where I was shown a possibly unique German ship's chronometer. It had clearly been saved from one of the German naval ships scuttled in Scapa Flow, Orkney's great natural harbour, during World War I. Signed 'Kittel of Altona', the movement incorporated certain characteristics that I had never seen before, and the chronometer featured a unique balance designed to compensate for mid-range temperature variations at sea. With such a fascinating history, and given its importance from a technical standpoint, it would almost certainly fetch over £5,000.

▷ **MONSTRANCE CLOCK** *made of engraved brass with tortoiseshell veneer base. 1660; 11in high.* **£3,000**

◁ **CHRONOMETER,** *rescued from a German ship during World War I. 1890; 7in wide.* **£5,000 – £10,000**

▽ **PARASOL WATCH** *with ivory handle. A very rare example of its type. 1880 – 90; 3ft long.* **£1,000**

FRENCH MANTEL CLOCKS

During the 18th century France led the world in the field of decorative arts, including the production of clocks and watches. The most talented craftsmen and designers were attracted to the court of Louis XIV, and the best makers continued to serve under Louis XV and Louis XVI, and during the Empire period of Napoleon I.

Clocks at this time were considered to be the most important decorative feature of any room, and great attention was paid to their style and construction. Appearance was so important, in fact, that craftsmen were generally more concerned with the ornate design of the cases than the complexity of the internal movements, which are often inferior to those of modern-day clocks.

Most French mantel clocks in Britain today are not genuine 18th century pieces but copies made during the Victorian era. In the 19th century the Industrial Revolution led to the rise of a large and prosperous middle class with a greater demand for luxury items. This was coupled with technical advances in all the skills needed to produce mantel clocks. The styles of 18th century clocks were revived, but

they were often modified to reduce production costs and to suit the smaller rooms of the average home. Victorian copies are, therefore, generally smaller than their original counterparts. Although many copies are beautifully made and finished, they usually lack artistic flair and clarity of design, and the overall effect is sometimes rather fussy. However, the mass-produced movements found in 19th century mantel clocks are exceptionally reliable and frequently continue to function long after many 18th century examples have stopped working.

French mantel clocks vary considerably in quality of workmanship, and it is principally this factor, together with condition, that determines their value.

EXPERT'S CHOICE

△ GILT BRASS MANTEL CLOCK *The case includes stylistic elements from the reigns of both Louis XV and Louis XVI, resulting in a hybrid shape that never actually existed in the 18th century but which is typical of Victorian taste. The elaborate scrolls, flowers and asymmetrical curves are features of rococo decoration. The dial, a 'cartouche' dial, was popular in France from 1685 to 1750 and was revived in the 19th century. 1875; 15in high.* **£600**

◁ FRENCH ART NOUVEAU MANTEL CLOCK SET *The bombé (bulging) clock case is accompanied by a pair of matching decorative vases. They are pierced all over and therefore unsuitable for holding fresh-cut flowers, but vases of this type were sometimes filled with scented petals. This set was originally silvered, but the plating has rubbed off over the years, fortunately without damaging the detailing of the figures. 1890; clock 15in high.* The set **£400**

A VICTORIAN MANTEL SET

The 'clock set' was an innovation of the Victorian period. Although 18th century clocks were sometimes accompanied by matching candelabra or vases, they were seldom conceived as a set to be grouped together. During the 19th century, when many revived styles were reproduced on a smaller scale, it became possible to produce a 'set' designed to fit on a mantelpiece.

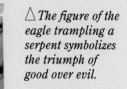

△ The figure of the eagle trampling a serpent symbolizes the triumph of good over evil.

▽ Known in France as a 'spagnolette' and in England as a 'sunburst', this was the most popular design of pendulum bob in 18th century France.

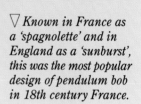

This veined marble and gilt brass clock set, made in 1880, includes a 21-inch-high clock and two matching candelabra. The detail (left) shows a pillar mount in the form of an Egyptian maiden. The set is worth £2,000, but the overall quality of the finish is average.

◁ A view of the movement showing the bell and the pendulum suspension behind. In all 18th and early 19th century clocks the pendulum was suspended on a silk thread. The system visible here has a 'feather' spring, invented by A. Brocot in around 1830.

135

ORMOLU CLOCK STYLES

'Ormolu' is the French word used to describe the gilt finish on bronze or brass. French clocks, furniture mounts and many *objets d'art* from the 18th and 19th centuries are described as 'ormolu-mounted'.

Egyptian style, late 18th C

Rococo style, mid 18th C

Louis XV ormolu and marble, 18th C

Louis XV style, 19th C

Empire style, late 19th C

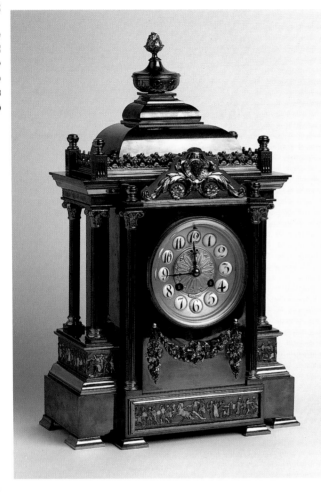

△ **MANTEL CLOCK,** *which appears to be made of marble but is in fact steel with gilt decoration. It was produced for export to Great Britain, and although the movement is signed 'Marti à Paris', the dial is by John Bennett. The clock is in excellent condition, and its protective glass dome (not shown) is intact. 1880; 17in high.* **£400**

FAMOUS CLOCKMAKERS

The ten makers whose names appear most frequently on standard Paris-made movements are listed below, with their dates of working and, where appropriate, trademarks. (If a movement is unsigned, this does not necessarily indicate that it is of inferior quality.)

H. MARK (1820 – 60); LE ROY ET FILS (1830 – 90); A. BROCOT (1840 – 65); V. A. P. (1840 onward); VINCENTI ET CIE (1850 – 70); C. A. RICHARD ET CIE (1850 – 1900), trademark – RC and a staff entwined with two snakes; JAPY FRERES (1850 onward); MARTI ET CIE (1860 – 1900); DUVERDREY ET BLONQUEL (1870 onward), trademark – a lion; S. MARTI (1900 onward).

△ **PORTICO CLOCK,** *examined by Richard Price. It has a striking movement signed 'Rollin à Paris'. The pine case is veneered in coromandel wood, and the bezel, bases and capitals are of fire-gilt brass. 1860; 2ft high.* **£600**

◁ **BLUE GLASS PORTICO CLOCK** *with gridiron pendulum. The base and columns of this exceptionally rare French clock are made of ribbed blue glass, with ormolu mounts. This type of work is sometimes described as 'Palais-Royal' after the area of Paris where it was usually sold. 1840; 2ft high.* **£5,000**

BEZEL A grooved ring which secures the protective glass of a clock face.

BOMBE Convex or bulging shape, used to describe clock cases in this style.

CARTOUCHE A dial on which the numerals have been painted on lozenge-shaped enamel plaques set in a decorated brass plate.

FIRE-GILDING or **MERCURY-GILDING** A technique for gilding metal. Pure gold is amalgamated with mercury, then coated on the desired surface and heated gently over charcoal. The mercury evaporates, leaving the gold bonded to the surface.

GRIDIRON A type of pendulum invented by John Harrison. Alternating steel and brass rods are combined to form a pendulum which remains of constant length despite temperature changes. (Brass expands more slowly than steel.)

PORTICO CLOCK A clock with four columns supporting a raised section called an entablature.

BRONZE CLOCKS

During the 19th century casting techniques were developed to the point where bronzes of high quality could be produced in great numbers. As a result, some of the most impressive Victorian clock cases are composed of sculptured bronze figures, animals or objects, with the clock movement incorporated in the overall design. Favourite subjects include figures from Ancient Greek and Roman mythology, such as the gods Apollo and Cupid and the goddesses Venus and Diana (together with related animals or objects) and characters from popular literary works. Bronze clocks are often very heavy, requiring a marble base to support their weight.

◁ **FRENCH LOUIS XVI MANTEL CLOCK** *signed 'Piolaine à Paris'. The cases of clocks of this type are usually made of brass or marble, but white porcelain, decorated with flowers was used for this very rare example. The free-standing figures and additional mounts are of gilt brass. The bezel of the glass covering for the dial is missing. 1780; 14in high.* **£4,000**

▷ **FRENCH ORMOLU AND BRONZE CLOCK** *by Julien Le Roy of Paris. One of the most important French clockmakers of the 18th century, Julien Le Roy held the position of clockmaker to King Louis XV. The solid and uncluttered design of the case is typical of the transitional period between Louis XV and Louis XVI. 1775; 11in high.* **£3,000**

◁ **BRONZE AND MARBLE MANTEL CLOCK** *The fine reclining figure on this decorative piece, next to an urn full of scrolls, represents 'Learning' or 'Philosophy'. The white enamel dial is signed 'Marshall, Paris'. 1870; 18in high.* **£600**

ENGLISH WALL CLOCKS

The first English wall clocks (as distinct from wall-hanging lantern clocks) appeared in the second half of the 17th century. Modelled on Dutch timepieces, these clocks were introduced as a result of the strong links between England and Holland, which culminated in the accession of the Dutch prince William of Orange to the English throne in 1688.

The earliest English wall clocks resembled the hood of a grandfather clock and ran for 30 hours. With short pendulums and weights that hung below the case, they also incorporated a verge escapement. The invention of the anchor escapement around 1670, however, led to the introduction of a case to prevent the pendulum being accidentally stopped or knocked out of beat.

There are several obvious advantages in using wall clocks in public buildings rather than any other timepieces: since they are secured to the wall, there is no reason why the dial should not be large enough to be clearly visible at a distance. In addition, only the height of the room limits the height at which the clock can be mounted, and with no base or plinth in contact with the floor, wall clocks cannot be knocked by passers-by. From around 1720, eight-day wall clocks started to become a standard fixture in inns and coffee houses (where much business was conducted) and were soon being sited in various public buildings and institutions.

Sometimes called 'Act of Parliament clocks' (incorrectly, since they existed at least 50 years before the Act), 18th century wall clocks were often very grand, with dials up to 3 feet in diameter, gold-leaf numerals and chinoiserie lacquerwork cases. The misnomer refers to Prime Minister William

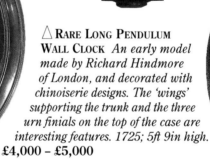

△ **RARE LONG PENDULUM WALL CLOCK** *An early model made by Richard Hindmore of London, and decorated with chinoiserie designs. The 'wings' supporting the trunk and the three urn finials on the top of the case are interesting features. 1725; 5ft 9in high.* **£4,000 – £5,000**

◁ **MAHOGANY 'TEARDROP'-SHAPED WALL CLOCK** *This unusual timepiece, signed 'Jno (John) Nevill of Norwich', has large Arabic numerals, typical of the 18th century. 1790; 4ft 2in high.* **£3,500**

▷ **MAHOGANY 'DROP DIAL' OR 'TRUNK' CLOCK,** *so-called because of the small trunk below the dial where the pendulum is housed. The dial is engraved and silvered. 1780; 2ft 2in high.* **£3,500**

WALL CLOCK SHAPES

The earliest wall clocks had long pendulums, identical to those in grandfather clocks, and were weight driven. Spring-driven wall clocks with short pendulums beating half-seconds date from the mid 18th century.

'Act of Parliament'

'Longcase' or 'Teardrop'

'Tavern'

'Drop dial'

'Standard dial'

Pitt's 1797 Act of Parliament imposing a tax of five shillings per annum on all clocks. Although this legislation was highly unpopular, and in fact shortlived, many individuals did dispose of their timepieces. In response, a number of innkeepers took the opportunity of installing a large wall clock on their premises in the hope of attracting more business. This tradition survived the repeal of the legislation in 1798, although these clocks (which are also referred to as 'tavern clocks', for obvious reasons) tended to have less ornate mahogany cases.

The survival of the English wall clock throughout the Victorian era was secured by two major factors: the spread of the railways and the expansion of the Empire. Every station waiting room had a simple, circular clock with a white, painted dial or a plain mahogany-cased 'drop dial'. The initials of the railway company (GWR, LNER and so on) were often painted on the dial, and examples could still be seen in stations in rural areas until quite recently.

Every government office in the control of the British Empire had a wall-mounted timepiece, as did the gentlemen's clubs to which every 19th century imperial official belonged. Elaborately carved and decorated, these mahogany wall clocks were once a familiar sight behind the porter's desk.

Wall clocks are still used in many public buildings and offices. However, the introduction of the electrically powered quartz clock and the digital dial have ensured that today's wall clocks bear little resemblance to their predecessors.

▽ **CLASSIC MAHOGANY WALL CLOCK** *without a pendulum, signed 'Penney of Cambridge'. The movement has a gut line linking the fusee to the spring barrel, an indicator of high quality. 1875; 15in wide.* **£400**

◁ **INLAID AND LACQUERED 'DROP DIAL' WALL CLOCK** *The elaborate decoration of this clock, which incorporates mother-of-pearl inlay, makes it equally valuable as an item of furniture or a timepiece. It is in very good condition. 1860; 2ft high.* **£400 – £600**

▽ **MAHOGANY 'DROP DIAL' WALL CLOCK** *with a good-quality fusee movement (below right) that strikes the hours on a bell. (After about 1870, strikes on gongs rather than bells started to become more common.) The original signature 'Thomas of Lincoln' appears on the painted dial. 1870; 16in wide.* **£1,250**

△ **WALNUT-VENEERED STRIKING WALL CLOCK** *with elaborate carved decoration, typical of good quality mid Victorian clocks from makers in the north of England. 1850; 15in high.* **£550**

AMERICAN SHELF CLOCKS

Most of the American shelf clocks in Britain today are of the mass-produced variety. Exported from the USA by the thousand at the end of the last century, these clocks were retailed in Britain (and elsewhere) at exceedingly low prices. High-quality mass-produced American clocks, on the other hand, were reserved for the home market, and consequently few reached our shores.

Perfect or well-preserved examples of the cheaply mass-produced clocks are now much sought after, particularly by American dealers. Certain details mark out some clocks as more distinguished than others, but good general condition is the most important factor.

Distinctive features of American clocks include the various shapes of case – notably 'gothic' or arched – the glazed, and often decorated, doors, transfer-printed panels below the dial, and an overall sturdiness of construction. Makers' names are usually marked on the dial, and cases sometimes contain trade or instruction labels (which increases value).

For clocks to fetch the highest prices veneer work should be intact – preferably with the original finish – since repairs and revarnishing can prove expensive. Dials, usually hand painted on tin and featuring some light floral decoration, should also be well-preserved. As a general rule, clocks that run for eight days are more desirable than those which run for only 30 hours.

▷ **MAHOGANY MANTEL CLOCK**
This veneered 'eight-day' clock with an arched top is signed by the Boston maker, W. H. Young (detail below). The design, usually referred to as the mantel 'regulator', after the name of its distinctive pendulum (which could be adjusted by hand), was popular during the 19th century. It has fine carving below the dial. 1850; 19in high. **£800**

◁ **'STEEPLE' OR 'GOTHIC' SHELF CLOCK** *A cheaply made version of a popular design, this clock has a stamped dial and undecorated glass door. The veneers on the clock case are thin and not particularly attractive. The overall condition of the clock is also poor. 1885; 19in high.* **£20**

FAMOUS AMERICAN CLOCKMAKERS

The most famous makers settled on the East coast of America, mainly in and around New England.

ELI TERRY Windsor, Conn., 1792; in Plymouth, Conn., 1794 – 1860s. Pioneered new methods of mass production, initially of wooden movements.
SETH THOMAS Plymouth, Conn., 1813; company became The General Time Corporation in 1949.
CHAUNCEY JEROME Plymouth, Conn., 1818; moved to Bristol and New Haven, Conn. Exported clocks to Britain after 1842.
NEW HAVEN CLOCK CO. Conn., 1853; produced clocks from 1856. 3 million timepieces manufactured in 1950.
ANSONIA CLOCK CO. Ansonia, Conn., 1858; also in Brooklyn, New York, 1879 – 1930.
E. N. WELCH & CO. Forestville, Conn., 1864 – 1903.
CHELSEA CLOCK CO. Chelsea, Mass., 1897 – 1904.

◁ 'Repeater' Alarm Clock *by Seth Thomas. Robust and practical-looking, this clock is unusual in that it runs for eight days and the alarm automatically resets for the same time each day. The original instruction label (below) is inside the back door. 1890; 9in high.* **£100 – £200**

▽ Veneered Shelf Clock *by the Ansonia Clock Co. The veneer is local spruce wood, stained and polished to look like mahogany. The print on the door below the dial is probably a replacement since it does not cover the glass. 1885; 12in high.* **£50**

▽ Shelf Clock *by the New Haven Clock Co. The wooden mouldings were stamped out on a steam press and applied individually to the case, producing finer decoration than the 'gingerbread' method (below left). 1895; 22in high.* **£175**

◁ 'Gingerbread' Shelf Clock *by the New Haven Clock Co. (detail above). The raised pattern was formed by steaming the wood then pressing it into a mould, in much the same way as gingerbread was traditionally made. 1900; 22in high.* **£125**

BLACK FOREST MANTEL CLOCKS

The Black Forest region in south west Germany is largely associated with cuckoo clocks, but in fact this area became a centre for dozens of clock- and watch-making companies and many other types of clock were also made here.

Clock-making began in this region in the 17th century. Farming was the traditional occupation, but it was supplemented in winter by wood-carving. This proved to be a useful skill in the early years of the clock-making industry when virtually all clock cases were made of wood. By the 1720s clock-making had become an established cottage industry and the century that followed is considered to be the peak period for handmade clocks. Competition from the USA in the 1850s, however, brought about the decline of the small workshop and the establishment of large factories.

Bracket and mantel clocks were not made in substantial numbers until 1870 because the technology required to mass produce springs did not yet exist. By the end of the 19th century, however, around eight and a half million clocks per year were being produced in this region, and the majority of those that have survived today date from the 1870s until the Depression in the 1930s.

Since Germany and the USA were competing for the same European markets, their clocks can be difficult to tell apart if unsigned. In German clocks, cases are stained rather than veneered; there may be directional arrows by the winding hole, and a brass hook with a pin secures the door.

◁ **'FAUX MARBRE' (FAKE MARBLE) MANTEL CLOCK** *The plinth and central section of this wooden clock have been lacquered in black to simulate marble. The remaining surfaces have been painted to give the effect of inlaid striated (with bands of colour) marble. It was made by the Hamburg American Clock Company of Württemberg for export to England, where slate and marble clocks were particularly popular in the late 19th century. 1890; 12in high.* **£80**

△ **'STEEPLE' PATTERN MANTEL CLOCK** *with an alarm function. The 'R=A' marked on the adjustable 'gridiron' pendulum stands for 'Retard/Advance'. There is a tiny nut below the 'R=A' dial: when it is turned to the left (toward the R) the clock runs more slowly; when it is turned to the right (toward the A) it runs more quickly. 1900; 17in high.* **£50**

MAKERS' TRADEMARKS

Trademarks can be found stamped on the back of the movement or on a trade label pasted inside the case.

Gustav Becker

Hausuhrenfabrik Winterhalder

Junghans

D.R.G.M.
Deutsches Reichs Gebrauchs Musterschutz (post-1918 patent mark)

Hamburg American Clock Company

RARE CLOCK

Dating from about 1860, this 12-inch-high picture clock is of above average quality and is a considerable rarity. The movement, signed by Sattele Eisenbach, a well-known maker, runs for 8 days rather than the usual 30 hours. The glazed and gilt frame serves as a 'front door', and the leopard's eyes move back and forth in time with the pendulum's swings. The clock was valued at £2,000.

◁ 'FOUR GLASS' CLOCK, so-called because all four sides are glass. The design was first popularized in France but, as with many decorative features, it was successfully copied by Black Forest makers. The lion and the base appear to be made of gilt brass, but were in fact cast in spelter (an alloy of zinc and tin which has been specially treated to look like bronze). 1895; 16in high. £100

▷ 30-HOUR STRIKING CLOCK in Art Deco style. Made of oak, this is a typical example of the type of Black Forest clocks that were made for export to England. It is marked behind the pendulum with the crossed arrows trademark of the Hamburg American Clock Company. In contrast to the case, the dial features 18th century-style stamped gilt floral spandrels in the corners. 1920; 12in high. £50

▽ FRUITWOOD MANTEL CLOCK with an unusual alarm that activates a music box (inset) containing interchangeable cylinders which play different tunes. The case features roof tile decoration. 1895; 10in high. £150

▷ ARCHITECTURAL-STYLE MANTEL CLOCK by the Hamburg American Clock Company. Although this is a German company, they probably chose an 'American'-sounding name to improve their sales potential in England, where the market for mass-produced clocks was dominated by the USA. The trade label in the back (right) is still intact and the steel spiral striking 'gong', complete with hammer, can also be seen. 1900; 20in high. £100

ENGLISH VERGE WATCHES

◁ **GOLD HUNTER-CASED VERGE WATCH** *by Jno (John) Bailey. In such watches the intricate engraving on the backplate is concealed from the casual observer. Hunter-cased watches of this date are quite rare. 1820; 2in wide.* **£450**

The verge watch takes its name from the 'verge' escapement which was the first mechanical controller of clocks and watches. Dating from the 13th century, records show that it remained the only practical escapement for the next 400 years until 1690 when the anchor escapement was developed.

An escapement is the part of a clock or watch mechanism that allows the power stored by the spring to escape at regular intervals, so causing the train of wheels and cogs connected to the hands to turn. The escapement is thus responsible for a watch showing the correct time.

The first watches, which more closely resembled small portable clocks, appeared in the early 1500s, following the invention of the coiled-up spring (mainspring). Before that, the motive force for most timepieces

was provided by weights. These early examples were poor time-keepers and even if a watch lost or gained as much as half an hour a day it was considered accurate.

Devices such as the fusee (a cone-shaped object attached by a cord to the spring barrel to equalize the tension of the spring) helped to regulate the force of the mainspring, but it was not until the invention of the balance spring – usually known as the 'hairspring' because of its similarity to a coiled hair – and the minute hand in 1680 that any sort of accuracy could be guaranteed.

Watches could now be relied upon

▽ **FINE EARLY VERGE WATCH** *by the notable English maker, Peter Garon. The dial is made of engraved and chased silver with a gilt centre. 1690; 2¼ in wide.* **£1,500**

as timekeepers, and by about 1800 some 7,000 workers were employed in the watchmaking trade in Clerkenwell, London, manufacturing around 120,000 watches a year. Many other watchmaking communities existed around the country, most producing the reliable English verge watch. The watch-making industry continued to expand rapidly and thrive throughout the 18th century.

Certainly more accurate escapements were developed during the 18th century, but the verge remained

USEFUL TERMS

HUNTER-CASED Watch with a cover over the dial to protect the dial and glass – supposedly developed for use when hunting. The French term for such cases is 'savonette' meaning envelope.

HALF-HUNTER-CASED Similar to a 'hunter', but with a window in the centre allowing the hands to be seen at all times. On later examples the numerals were often engraved or enamelled around the window.

PAIR-CASED Watch with two cases, one inside the other, for extra protection from dust. Large 19th century English watches of this type were known as 'turnips' or 'farmers' verges'.

PENDANT AND BOW Terms used to describe the 'handle' and 'ring' by which a watch could be supported or attached to a chain.

the most popular for general use until about 1850. Its long survival is due to a number of factors, but most notably to its robust construction and reliability. Furthermore it would keep going even if roughly handled, it could be repaired by most watch-makers and it lasted for generations.

When buying a watch of this type it is important to check that it works properly and is in good condition. Repairs, including minor ones, can be prohibitively expensive, particularly if parts for the movement have to be specially made. Inspect cases for damage, and check that opening buttons (if present) work.

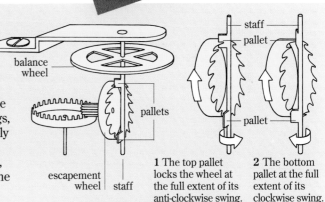

△ **SILVER PAIR-CASED VERGE WATCH** *This type of watch, known as a farmer's verge, was introduced around 1800 and remained popular for the next 60 years. Watch papers were often placed in the backs of such watches over the years by individual repairers. 1825; 2¼ in wide.* **£120**

▽ **UNUSUAL SINGLE-CASED SILVER VERGE WATCH** *with half-hunter window in the cover. An additional small chapter ring in the centre is visible when the watch is closed. 1820; 2in wide.* **£120**

▷ **SILVER PAIR-CASED VERGE WATCH** *with classic Roman and Arabic chapters and 'beetle-and-poker' pattern hands. A clock-repairer's watch paper has been placed inside the case. 1770; 1¾ in wide.* **£250**

VERGE ESCAPEMENTS

The balance wheel swings alternately clockwise and anti-clockwise rotating the staff of a verge escapement. As it does so, the upper and lower pallets, or flags, attached to the staff alternately lock the escapement wheel. This allows the wheel to turn, regulating the movement of the spring-driven watch train.

balance wheel

pallets

escapement wheel | staff

staff
pallet
pallet

1 The top pallet locks the wheel at the full extent of its anti-clockwise swing.

2 The bottom pallet at the full extent of its clockwise swing.

▷ **CLASSIC SILVER PAIR-CASED VERGE WATCH** *This example has a rather unusual feature – it has letters in place of the more usual twelve numerals on the dial. The letters spell out the owner's name, Thomas Harris, and the watch is undoubtedly a one-off made to special order. 1810; 2¼ in wide.* **£200**

ENAMELLED WATCHES

Although painting in enamel was first developed in France around 1625, the greatest number of outstanding enamel watch cases was made in Switzerland (primarily Geneva) in the early 19th century.

Painting a picture in enamel is extremely difficult. The artist applies the enamel mixture (of very finely ground glass and colour pigments bound together by oil of lavender) to the white surface or 'ground' of a watch, box or plaque. The item is then fired in a kiln at a high temperature, and the coloured enamel liquefies and is fixed. Some enamels change colour when they are fired, however, and fix at different temperatures. This means that the picture must be built up in stages, with the enamel colours requiring the highest temperatures being applied first. The firing process is carried out several times, and each time there is a risk of complete failure.

India and China were prime destinations for enamelled watches. Frequently decorated with portraits of emperors or maharajahs, they were shipped to the East (along with other cargo) to be presented to the ruler of the country in an attempt to win favour and goodwill, thereby

▽ **BLUE ENAMELLED WATCH** (front and back view). This Swiss gold enamelled watch is signed 'Le Comte, Genève'. The dial features typical Swiss engraving. The back has been engine-turned (a process which requires a special lathe), creating a spiral pattern. This has been enamelled in a translucent blue. It is centred with rose diamonds. 1875; 1½ in across. **£450**

▽ **SWISS ENAMELLED GOLD WATCHES** (front and back views).
1a & **1b** Made for the French market, this piece is signed 'Berthoud à Paris'. 1780; 2in across. **£2,000**
2a & **2b** Hunter (enclosed) watch with a lakeside view. 1870; 1½ in across. **£750**

1a

2a

1b

2b

1a

2a

SWISS ENAMELLED GOLD WATCHES
(*front views left, back views below*).
1a & **1b** *A repeating watch (at the press of a button it restrikes the preceding hour) of unusually small size. It is wound by a crown (not a key), which is usually a sign of a watch made at a later date. The split pearls (natural pearls split in half) indicate that it was probably made for export to China, where such decoration was very popular. Repeating watches of such a small size are rare, and this factor increases its value considerably. 1890; 1½ in across.* **£3,000**
2a & **2b** *A smaller watch with split pearls, also made for the Chinese market. The tiny rose diamonds set in the lady's bow and the frill in the front of her dress are interesting details. 1890; 1¼ in across.* **£750**

encouraging future trading links.

Swiss watches are often decorated with lakeside scenes because Lake Geneva was of course a major inspiration for craftsmen. A considerable number of watches were also commissioned by princes and other members of the European nobility. These frequently bear a miniature portrait of the owner, creating a truly personalized watch.

▽ FOB WATCH WITH ENAMELLED
BOATING SCENE (*3a* & *3b*) *Although this Geneva-made gold watch was manufactured at a comparatively late date, the enamel painting is of a very high standard. The delightful opalescent effect gives the impression of a dawn sky. 1900; 1¾ in across.* **£600**

1b

2b

3a

3b

Simon Bull, a regular contributor to arts and antiques publications, is an expert in antiquarian horology, and a consultant for Habsburg Auctioneers.

COLLECTOR'S · CHECKLIST ·

CLOCKS & WATCHES

△ **FRENCH LYRE-SHAPED CLOCK**
This 8-day mantel timepiece features a red marble and ormolu lyre-shaped case backed by a velour-covered mount. 1900; 16in high. **£400**

Although one of the undoubted joys of owning a collection of time-pieces is being able to sit in a room and listen to the sound of several different clocks ticking away at the same time, collectors are equally fascinated by the craftsmanship that goes into the making of a clock. The skills of a cabinet-maker are required for the case, an horologist for the movement, an engraver for the decoration, and, often, a gilder for the fine finishing touches.

Almost any longcase clock is now something of a prized possession, and the days when certain types could be bought for as little as £50 are long gone. Today, anything costing less than £500 is truly a bargain, unless it is in appalling condition, or it was made at a very late date. The heyday of the English longcase clock was the 100 years between 1670 and 1770, but they were still being made in the traditional manner almost a century later. By the 1870s, however, competition from America and

Germany, both of which were producing cheaper mantel clocks, had virtually killed the British industry. (Incidentally, tens of thousands of these clocks, built to last for only a few years, have survived; part of their appeal is that many have skeleton movements, and it is not beyond the skills of the amateur to effect a simple cleaning job.)

Small floor-standing clocks were produced in Germany until well into this century, but these are of interest mainly for their complex striking mechanisms, or Westminster chimes.

It is never advisable to run any clock for long periods when the movement is dirty. Longcase clocks, however, are forgiving, and a properly adjusted longcase movement is a sturdy mechanism that will run for years, even if somewhat neglected.

Black marble or slate mantel clocks, which were almost unsaleable 20 years ago, can still be found for under £100, and often represent very good value for money. The

POINTS TO WATCH FOR

1 It is important to establish that the movement and case of a mantel clock belong together. View unexplained screw-holes in the case or movement with suspicion.

2 With longcase clocks check that the dial fits correctly into the case aperture, and that the seat board has not been altered.

3 An original signature is important, particularly if it is a well known name. (It is easy to change these on painted dials.)

4 Original painted dials show signs of 'crazing' and deterioration, even if they have been cleaned and professionally restored.

5 Hands are often replaced due to damage, but if they are in the correct style and of the right quality, this does not detract from the value.

6 Check the running time of a clock; those that run for only 30 hours are generally less valuable than those that run for a full week.

7 Make sure that both wrist and pocket watches are at least in working order: repairs can be prohibitively expensive.

8 Check that 'gold' pocket-watch cases really are gold; some American makers made excellent quality cases in rolled gold.

9 Cases in 18ct gold are more valuable than those in 9ct, unless the movement has collector's interest; 14ct gold was often used in watch cases made by American manufacturers.

10 Always have a waterproof wristwatch resealed by a watchmaker if you buy it second hand. (It may well have been opened for inspection.)

▽ **COCKTAIL WATCH,** *with diamonds mounted in platinum. The bracelet is made from 9ct white gold. 1935; face ¾ in long.* **£350**

best examples have French movements striking the hours and half hours and, despite the clocks' sombre appearance, the movements are often very fine. If a movement is in good condition or you can get a reasonable quote for cleaning, a little home 'surgery' can often refresh the case.

If you prefer to collect pocket watches, the possibilities are almost unlimited. Swiss and American makers produced superb quality timepieces by the million, and many have been handed down through successive generations. Although examples in gold have a higher intrinsic value, watches in silver or rolled gold can be found very cheaply, considering the level of craftsmanship involved. Supply at present outstrips demand, but beware: if the movement is not in general good order, repairs can be expensive.

▷ **FLICK CLOCK,** *made in Germany by Junghans. These clocks are also referred to as 'Ticket' or 'Plato' clocks. Similar clocks were made in the United States under the name 'Ever-Ready Plato Clock'. 1905; 5in.* **£250 – £300**

NEW COLLECTABLES

Since the Swiss firm ETA launched the 'Swatch' on an unsuspecting public in 1984, nearly 100 million of their plastic watches have been sold world-wide. Despite costing only £20 for the basic models, and having been conceived originally as 'throwaway' items (the case is sealed and although Swatches are reliable, they cannot be repaired), collecting them has developed to the point that it is now an international phenomenon.

The launch of a new model is greeted by long queues outside the shops. Until the market is saturated, these models change hands at two or three times the cost price.

Swatch collecting is better compared to stamp collecting than to acquiring classic wrist or pocket watches. They can be grouped by year of production, model range or type, with prices varying from little more than the original cost up to £20,000 for the rarest Kiki Picasso model, of which only 140 were made. Bear in mind that unless the model is extremely rare, watches must be in pristine condition to have any value.

CARE & REPAIR

1 To improve wooden clock cases that are dull, use a good wax polish; if this is unsuccessful, use a proprietary surface cleaner. To remove very stubborn surface grime, the cleaner may be used with 0000 grade wire wool.

2 Wood, marble or stone clock cases that have come apart should be reassembled with water-soluble adhesive. (Never use impact or contact adhesives, which are impossible to remove.)

3 Clean marble clock cases by wiping gently with a cloth dampened with water and a mild solution of washing-up liquid. Remove grease with cottonwool soaked in benzine, and wipe the surface dry immediately.

4 To improve dulled black marble, apply several thin coats of black shoe polish.

5 Be careful when attempting to clean metal cases. Brass may be cleaned with non-abrasive metal polish, but gilded metals need specialist treatment. Bronze should not be polished, just dusted occasionally.

6 Never oil a dirty clock. If you are planning to clean the movement yourself, make sure it is completely unwound before dismantling it. Wash out thoroughly using benzine, then clean the pivot holes with sharpened matchsticks. When re-assembling, put a drop of light oil (sewing-machine oil) on each pivot and on the pallets of the escapement. Do not oil the wheels.

7 Don't open the backs of watches with a knife. Repairs to both wristwatches and pocket watches should always be left to specialists.

△ **SILVER PAIR-CASED POCKET WATCH,** *with an Ormskirk escapement and signed James Gregory, Ormskirk no 2. The term 'pair-cased' refers to the fact that there are two cases: an inner and an outer. The dial is decorated with a frigate and the name Thomas Baldwin. 1793; 2¼ in across.* **£900 – £1,200**

PLACES OF INTEREST

Fairfax House (York Civic Trust), Castlegate, York *Outstanding collection of 18th century clocks*
Museum of the History of Science, Broad St, Oxford *Clocks, watches and early scientific instruments*
Science Museum, Exhibition Rd, London SW7 *Clocks and watches through the ages*
Syon House, Brentford, Middlesex *Fine collection of clocks*
Victoria & Albert Museum, Cromwell Rd, London SW1 *Collection of clocks and watches*

SILVER, GOLD & JEWELLERY

BY IAN PICKFORD

After a fascinating start at the Alexandra Palace Roadshow, where I met the neighbour of the woman who had played the piano on the very first programme transmitted from 'Ally Pally' in 1936, each successive venue seemed to produce more and more interesting silver.

Although the most important piece of silver – a 17th century Danish tankard – was seen at Hemel Hempstead, the most remarkable location for me was Yeovilton. Indeed, in all the years I have been with the Roadshow there has not been another to match it. Yet although it was wonderful to see so many magnificent items, it was also very frustrating that owing to lack of time I reluctantly had to pass over pieces that I would ordinarily have been more than delighted to record for the programme.

Among these were a set of four George III candlesticks, a Russian enamel salt in the shape of a throne and a fine George I silver tankard. Most remarkable of all, however, were two charming

17th century Dutch silver marriage caskets, one with an extraordinary history. Many years ago it had been given to the owner's small daughter to play with. She subsequently lost it in her sand-pit, but it was rediscovered years later when the sand-pit was cleared.

Since I had to pass on so many beautiful items over the course of the series, it was essential that what I eventually recorded was very special indeed. The first piece that I chose was a William IV epergne. It was in mint condition with all its fittings intact: these converted the arms from dish-holders to candleholders.

Tea caddies will always remind me of Yeovilton. Two important finds there were a remarkable cased set and a superb single chinoiserie example. The cased set, comprising a pair of caddies and a sugar bowl, was remarkable not for its style, maker or the fact that it was complete (many such sets on the market are in fine condition);

◁ **SILVER EPERGNE,** *the branches of which can support either candleholders or glass dish-holders. 1835; 18in high.* **£5,000 – £6,000**

▽ **BASTING SPOON** *Hanoverian with rat tail design; shows original family crest. 1718; 13in long.* **£700**

what was significant about this particular set was its history. Each one of its owners is recorded, from 1750 to the present day, and a painting of the family that originally owned it also survives.

Hemel Hempstead was a particularly memorable show. It produced the most important piece in the entire Roadshow series, the silver peg tankard presented to Sir Philip Meadows by the King of Denmark. Since I am a spoon enthusiast, however, I was much taken with the splendid George I basting spoon which is still being used by later generations of the family whose crest was engraved upon it almost 300 years ago.

I generally see very little Old Sheffield Plate at Roadshows, but a remarkable Old Sheffield Plate telescopic candelabra was brought to me at the Hemel show. Quite a few telescopic candlesticks can be found today, but telescopic candelabra are very rare indeed. This example was all the more remarkable for its unusual decoration of naval cartouches around the base.

△ **TEA CADDIES AND SUGAR BOWL** *complete with shagreen case and a portrait of the original family of owners. 1750; 7in high.* **£8,000 – £10,000**

Few pieces of gold, apart from jewellery, turn up at Roadshows. Rochdale, however, produced what Ian Harris described as 'the biggest, best and most wonderful rattle' he had ever seen. In 18-carat gold, it was rare and wonderful indeed.

Although the medieval spoon that I have always hoped for didn't turn up during this series, the magnificent items that were brought along week after week more than compensated.

▽ **GOLD RATTLE** *with bells, whistle and coral teether 1860; 7in long.* **£7,000 – £10,000**

▷ **TELESCOPIC CANDELABRA** *made from Old Sheffield Plate, with two telescopic sections. 1800; 21in high.* **£700 – £900**

FLATWARE

Dining traditions in England changed radically during the late 17th century. Until this date it was customary for guests to take along their own spoons and knives to a banquet (the use of forks was rare, and even considered 'foppish'). Charles II's return from exile in France, however, and his accession to the throne in 1660, led to the introduction of dining customs from the Continent which included that of using a fork. Setting a table with matching spoons and forks became common practice, knives in a similar pattern were added, and thus developed the flatware service.

▽ **FORK STYLES** *from the early 18th to the mid 19th century. Dognose (1) and Hanoverian (2) had only three prongs. Around 1760 four prongs (3–14) were introduced. Three other important stylistic groups are also shown below: Old English and its variants (3–7), Fiddle Pattern and its variants (8–11) and the King's group. The latter group includes Hour Glass (12), King's (13) and Queen's (14) patterns.*

FLATWARE TERMS

The projections at the junction of the bowl and the handle of a spoon are called the 'shoulders'. The upper part of the back of the bowl of the spoon is known as the 'heel'.

shoulders

heel

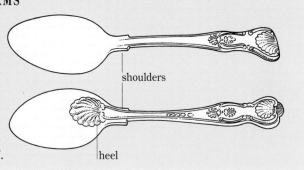

USEFUL TERMS

SERVICE A set comprising 12 table-spoons, 12 forks, 12 dessert spoons and 12 dessert forks.

PART SERVICE Any set containing fewer pieces than the above.

STRAIGHT SERVICE A set in which all the pieces are of the same date, maker and style.

MIXED, OR HARLEQUIN, SERVICE A set with mixed dates and/or mixed makers.

HAND-FORGED Spoons or forks made by the traditional method of hammering a thick rod of silver. High-quality pieces were made in this way, usually in London.

MACHINE-MADE Pieces stamped out from blanks, dating mainly from the mid 19th century onward. Most of this type of flatware was made in Sheffield and Birmingham.

RAT TAIL A decorative rib pattern on spoons at the junction of the handle and the back of the bowl. Assumed (incorrectly) to have been used to strengthen the 'join' – in fact there is no join.

REPRODUCTION KNIVES

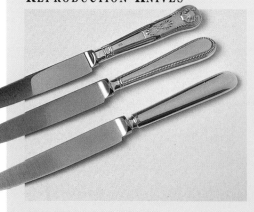

Knife handles in the 18th century were mostly made of thin sheet silver filled with pitch. Many were damaged or destroyed, however, because the pitch expanded when the knives were placed in hot water. Few original knives have survived in usable condition, but it is acceptable to mix reproduction knives (shown here) in a matching pattern with original flatware services of spoons and forks.

Trefid and Dognose

The earliest flatware pattern, Trefid, characterized by two decorative notches in the spread top of the handle, was introduced to England from France in the 1660s.

After about 1700 notches were no longer made at the top of the stem, and the Trefid pattern became Dognose (also known as Shield End or Wavy End). Dognose is the earliest pattern in which services can be found today, but they are extremely rare. Few pieces were made after 1720, but reproductions appeared in the late 19th century.

Hanoverian

The Hanoverian pattern, of which there are two main types, dominated flatware design in the early and mid 18th century. The first type, Hanoverian with rat tail, was made during the reign of George I (1714 – 27). The second, more common, type, without rat tail, dates from the George II (1727 – 60) period.

Forks at this time usually had three prongs – the fourth prong did not appear until around 1760. Some reproduction forks, made from the late 19th century onward, have had a rat tail design added to match the original rat tail pattern spoons.

A service in Hanoverian pattern is probably the earliest that most collectors could realistically consider buying. But collecting is expensive and often difficult, largely because forks in this pattern are hard to find and often faked. Fine late 19th and 20th century reproduction services are, however, widely available.

Spoon decoration

Until about 1760, spoons were set with the open bowl downwards in the French manner. This enabled the decoration on the backs of the spoons to be admired by diners. After about 1760 spoons were set open bowl upwards and fronts of handles were decorated instead.

Spoons with up-turned ends sat steadily on the table when placed face downwards. After about 1760 spoons were set with the open bowl upwards, and handle ends turned the other way.

Pre-1760 spoon, with handle turned up

Post-1760 spoon, with handle turned down

EARLY SPOONS

The earliest English spoons date from the 13th century. Apostle spoons, made in the late 15th century, remained popular until the mid 1600s when they were replaced by the Trefid pattern. Early Scots pattern spoon ends are similar to Trefids, but the former pattern dates from the 16th century.

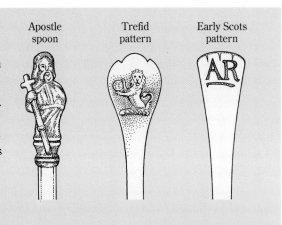

Apostle spoon · Trefid pattern · Early Scots pattern

△ **DOGNOSE PATTERN,** *named after the pointed shape of the end of the handle. This was the principal pattern of the Queen Anne period (1702 – 14). The matching fork has three prongs and the back of the bowl of the spoon should have a rat tail design. Straight services are found only from the late 19th century onward.*

▽ **HANOVERIAN PATTERN** *The top spoon is Hanoverian with a rat tail. Such pieces were placed, as here, with the open bowl face down on the table, so that the hallmark – and any added decoration – would be clearly visible. The handles of the spoon and fork set turn upwards. The fork is three-pronged, as was usual before 1760.*

Old English

First produced in about 1760, and made in its plain form ever since, Old English flatware differed from Hanoverian services in two important respects. Four-pronged forks were introduced and the ends of the spoon handles turned down (although fork handles continued to turn up for comfort). There seems to have been no real reason for this change, other than fashion.

A number of decorative variations were produced. The earliest is the Old English Feather Edge, made in the 1760s and '70s, and followed by Old English Bead in the 1780s, and both Old English Thread and Old English Bright-Cut in the 1790s.

Old English pieces seemingly dating from the late 1750s are likely to be modernized Hanoverian. Many spoons had their ends turned down in the late 18th century.

Fiddle

The Fiddle pattern was the most popular style of flatware in 18th century France. It was made occasionally in Britain during that time, but it did not become popular until early in the 19th century, after which it dominated flatware production.

The name derives from the violin-shaped handle, which spreads at the top and widens to form shoulders at the junction of bowl and stem. Variations developed quickly, the most popular being the Fiddle Thread and Shell. A fine version of this pattern, with a more elaborate 'shell', is referred to as Fiddle Husk.

Fiddle Pattern went out of style at the beginning of this century and remained unpopular until its revival in recent years.

△ OLD ENGLISH PATTERN (PLAIN), *made from around 1760 onward. The spoon turns down at the end, but the fork (now four-pronged) continues to turn upwards.*

△ OLD ENGLISH PATTERN VARIATIONS
1 *Old English Feather Edge.* 2 *Old English Bead.*
3 *Old English Thread.* 4 *Old English Bright-Cut.*
These four variants continued to be produced intermittently during the 19th century, and all are made today.

△ FIDDLE PATTERN *table and dessert spoons and forks, with teaspoon. The knives are modern reproductions of the Old English Pattern. It is standard practice to match Old English pattern knives with Fiddle pattern flatware, Old English Thread with Fiddle Thread, and so on.*

▷ FIDDLE PATTERN AND VARIATIONS
1 *Plain Fiddle Pattern (1800 – 1920).*
2 *Fiddle Thread (1810 onward).*
3 *Fiddle Thread and Shell (1815 onward).*
4 *Fiddle Husk (1820 onward).*
All exist in complete services, but the particularly fine Fiddle Husk is the most difficult to find.

Hourglass, King's and Queen's

The Hourglass pattern, popular in Britain from the early 19th century, was based on 18th century French designs. King's was essentially a development of the Fiddle Thread and Shell, giving a waist to the wide top of the handle, modifying the edge and adding decoration at the point where the handle begins to widen. Hourglass, which is often mistaken for King's, is characterized by an hourglass shape where the handle begins to widen.

As the 19th century progressed,

◁ **19TH CENTURY PATTERNS** *The best way to identify these patterns is to examine the large shell. On Hourglass and King's pieces (left and centre), it is concave, and on Queen's (right), it is convex. Also, an hourglass motif is used where the handle widens for Hourglass pattern, and a floral effect for King's.*

SILVER, GOLD & JEWELLERY

PLACE SETTINGS

The pieces shown left are (from left to right): table knife; cheese knife; table spoon; dessert spoon; teaspoon; table fork; dessert fork. Both settings below are acceptable, but may be changed depending on the food being served.

Traditional formal setting

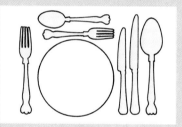

Alternative formal setting

patterns became more elaborate. Queen's pattern was a development of King's. The main differences are that in Queen's pattern the large shell at the top is convex instead of concave, and a flower head is added to the floral motif at the point where the handle widens at the top. King's, Queen's and Hourglass have been made continuously in Britain since their introduction, and they remain among the most popular designs.

Price guide

Flatware prices vary enormously, depending on the pattern and date of manufacture. A fine, straight 60-piece set of King's, Queen's, Hourglass or Fiddle Thread, for example, would cost around £5,000 for a late 19th or early 20th century service, and around £10,000 for an early 19th century service.

SINGLE OR DOUBLE STRUCK?

Flatware is generally stamped in a steel die to produce the characteristic raised decoration. If only the front is decorated (far right), the piece is 'single struck'; if front and back are both decorated (right), the piece is 'double struck' – double struck is usually considered more desirable. Scottish flatware is frequently decorated on the front only.

BUTTER KNIVES

First produced in the last years of the 18th century, butter knives soon superseded silver butter spades, which continued to be made in small numbers throughout the 19th century.

The earliest butter knives were individual pieces, not part of a service, generally with bone or ivory handles, the latter often stained green. By the early 19th century, however, they had become an integral part of the standard flatware service, and were handmade in all the main flatware patterns. Butter knives made during the 18th century and most of the 19th are about as large as a dessert spoon (nine inches long), while those made from the end of the 19th century are the size of a teaspoon or smaller.

Several regional variations developed in the early 19th century. Silver handles similar to those used for spoons were popular with London makers, while Birmingham craftsmen continued to use ivory and introduced handles made of mother-of-pearl. Another important innovation was the heavy, pitch-filled 'loaded' silver handle from Sheffield.

The most valuable butter knives have an unusual shape (anything other than a 'scimitar' blade is desirable), a celebrated maker (Paul Storr's work is much sought after), or an interesting engraving.

The knives illustrated on these pages are made of solid silver, unless otherwise stated.

1 2 3 4 5 6 7

◁ **IVORY, BONE AND HORN HANDLES**
1 *Bone handle. By Thomas Lawrence, Birmingham, 1834; 6in long.* **£40**
2 *Ivory handle. France, 1820.* **£30**
3 *Stained ivory handle. By Peter and Anne Bateman, London, 1796.* **£70**
4 *Stained ivory handle. By Thomas Shaw, Birmingham, 1826.* **£40**
5 *Stained ivory handle and silver-plated blade. 1800; 9in long.* **£20**
6 *Polished horn handle (possibly not original) and silver-gilt blade. Probably by Joseph Smith, London, 1809.* **£30**
7 *Bone handle. Joseph Taylor, Birmingham. 1813.* **£30**

▷ **VICTORIAN BUTTER KNIVES,** *all with the most popular blade-shape – the curved scimitar. 'Loaded' silver pieces (**2**), made from thin stamped-out sheet silver forming a hollow handle, were made weightier by being filled with pitch.*
1 *Mother-of-pearl handle. By Hilliard & Thomason, Birmingham, 1859.* **£40**
2 *Loaded silver handle. By Aaron Wadfield, Sheffield, 1845.* **£50**
3 *Engraved handle. Made in USA, 1860.* **£30**
4 *Rose pattern. By John Stone, Exeter, 1851.* **£50**
5 *Engraved twist handle. By Reid & Sons, Newcastle, 1869.* **£40**

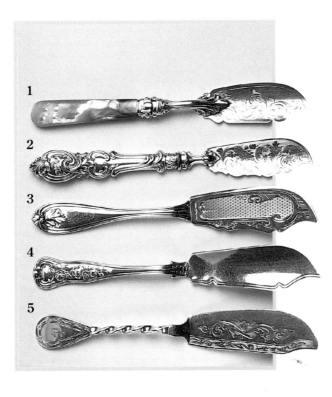

1 2 3 4 5

1 2

△ **FIDDLE PATTERN KNIVES**
1 *Milkmaid engraving. By Hyam Hyams, London, 1869.* **£50**
2 *Cow engraving. By Charles Boyton, London, 1871.* **£50**

NON-SILVER HANDLES AND UNUSUAL BLADES

A selection of early butter knives. At 7 – 9in long, they are larger than knives made toward the end of the 19th century.

1 Plain curved blade, large carved mother-of-pearl handle. By Thomas Shaw, Birmingham, 1833. **£50**

2 Agate handle. By John Tongue, Birmingham, 1843. **£70**

3 Engraved octagonal blade, bone handle. By 'JL', Birmingham, 1818. **£70**

4 Stained ivory handle. By John Daly, Dublin, 1795. **£90**

5 Scoop blade, bone handle. By Joseph Willmore, Birmingham, 1810. **£80**

6 Ivory handle. By Cattle & Barber, York, 1810. **£80**

7 Engraved blade, rectangular agate handle. By George Unite, Birmingham, 1836. **£70**

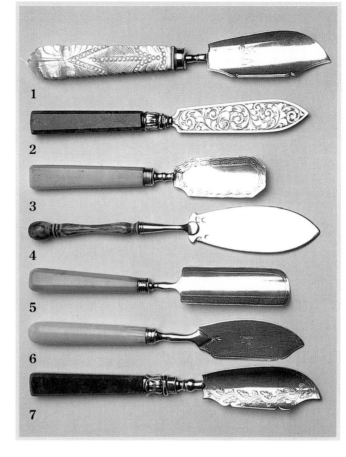

△ **1** Palm pattern. By George Adams of Chawner & Co., London, 1878. **£80**

2 Loaded silver handle. By Hilliard & Thomason, Birmingham, 1863. **£50**

3 Loaded silver handle, vine pattern. By Martin, Hall & Co., Sheffield, 1846. **£50**

▽ **1** By Francis Higgins, London, 1872. **£60**

2 & 3 Stag hunt pattern. By William Chawner, London, 1826 – 7. The pair **£200**

◁ **1** Loaded silver handle. By Martin, Hall & Co., Sheffield, 1857. **£50**

2 Bead-edged and cartouche handle. By James Dixon & Sons, Sheffield, 1871. **£40**

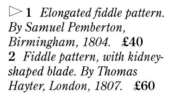

▷ **1** Elongated fiddle pattern. By Samuel Pemberton, Birmingham, 1804. **£40**

2 Fiddle pattern, with kidney-shaped blade. By Thomas Hayter, London, 1807. **£60**

▽ **1** Curved fiddle pattern, with initials. By Barber & Whitwell, York, 1812. **£60**

2 Fiddle pattern, with initials. Madras, India, 1830. **£40**

3 Fiddle and shell pattern with crest. Edinburgh, 1811. **£50**

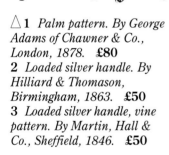

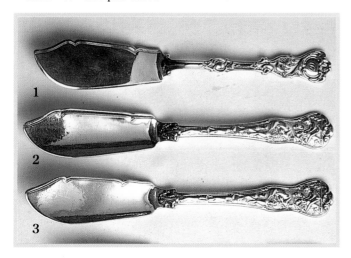

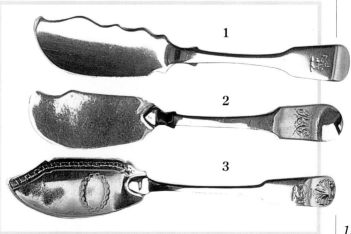

TEA ACCESSORIES

When tea first became popular in England at the end of the 17th century, it was such an expensive commodity that it was brewed only in small quantities. Most tea-making equipment from this time is, therefore, relatively small.

The name 'caddy' derives from the Malay 'kati', meaning a weight of just over 1lb. It seems likely that British traders in Malaya were sold a 'kati' of tea, and simply assumed that the weight was the name of the container. Early 18th century caddies had detachable sliding bases or tops to allow the subsequent insertion of a lead liner which helped to keep the leaves inside fresh. Few caddies today still have their original liners intact, but those that do tend to be in excellent condition.

Caddies were usually made in pairs – one for black tea and one for green – and came with a box or covered bowl for sugar. This set was kept in a wooden box, and sometimes also included teaspoons, sugar 'nippers' or 'nips' and a mote spoon (the forerunner of the caddy spoon).

In the second half of the 18th century tea became less expensive, and tea caddies increased in size accordingly. For no obvious reason, fewer caddies seem to have been made in the mid 19th century, but by the 1880s they were again being produced in very large numbers.

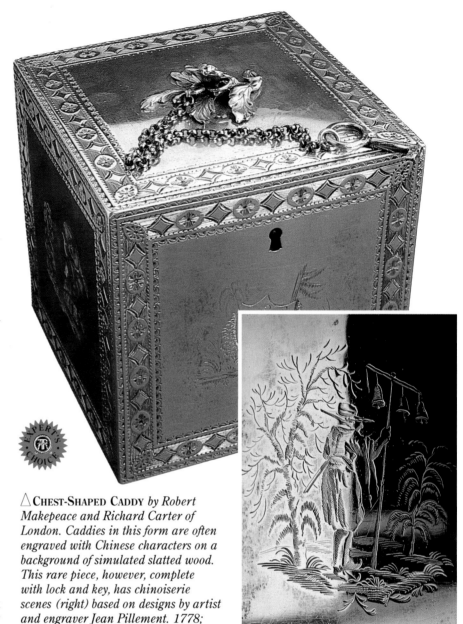

△ **CHEST-SHAPED CADDY** *by Robert Makepeace and Richard Carter of London. Caddies in this form are often engraved with Chinese characters on a background of simulated slatted wood. This rare piece, however, complete with lock and key, has chinoiserie scenes (right) based on designs by artist and engraver Jean Pillement. 1778; 3½ in high. Insurance value* **£15,000**

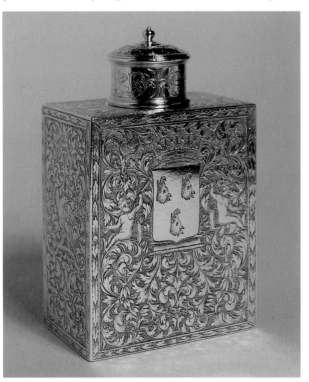

◁ **SILVER-GILT CADDY,** *by Isaac Liger of London, made for the 2nd Earl of Warrington, whose arms are engraved on the front. The lid would have been used as a measure for the tea. 1706; 4½ in high.* **£30,000**

▷ **ELECTROPLATED CADDY** *made by Martin Hall & Co. of Sheffield. The lid (reminiscent of early 18th century designs) and the neo-classical swags are beautifully engraved. It is rather rubbed, and would be worth more in better condition. 1880; 5in high.* **£30**

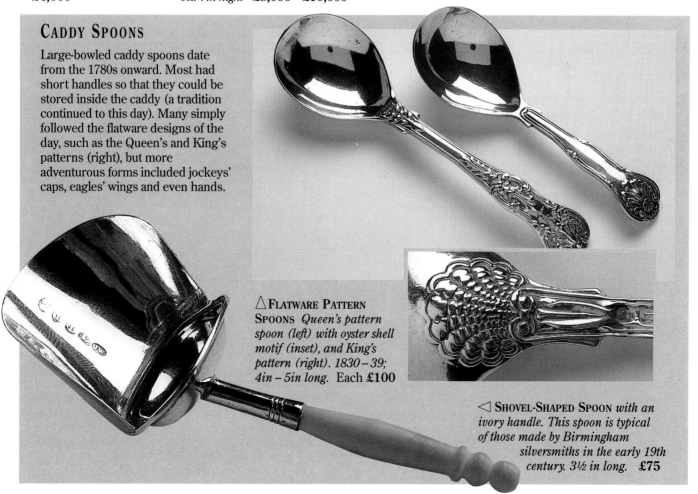

△ **ROCOCO-STYLE SUGAR CASKET** *This Dutch piece is somewhat unusual. Unlike most silver items, which are made from sheet silver, it was cast solid, making it much heavier. Sugar boxes and caskets are rare, and a fine piece such as this is especially desirable. 1764; 7in wide.* **£4,000**

▷ **SILVER CADDIES AND SUGAR BOWL** *made by Samuel Taylor of London, a specialist tea caddy maker. In superb condition and with fine rococo-style decoration (inset), the pieces come in their original silver-mounted shagreen box. Their fully documented history greatly increases the value. 1750; box 7in high.* **£8,000 – £10,000**

CADDY SPOONS

Large-bowled caddy spoons date from the 1780s onward. Most had short handles so that they could be stored inside the caddy (a tradition continued to this day). Many simply followed the flatware designs of the day, such as the Queen's and King's patterns (right), but more adventurous forms included jockeys' caps, eagles' wings and even hands.

△ **FLATWARE PATTERN SPOONS** *Queen's pattern spoon (left) with oyster shell motif (inset), and King's pattern (right). 1830 – 39; 4in – 5in long.* Each **£100**

◁ **SHOVEL-SHAPED SPOON** *with an ivory handle. This spoon is typical of those made by Birmingham silversmiths in the early 19th century. 3½ in long.* **£75**

Throughout history, stylists have looked to the past for inspiration, reviving formerly popular styles while at the same time inventing new ones. Stylists in the 19th century, however, as well as reviving past forms, deliberately mixed styles, developing a distinct and easily recognizable hybrid that marked the Victorian era. From about 1815 the Rococo was the major influence, but by the end of the 1820s other forms had also been resurrected.

In spite of this free use of past designs and styles, they were seldom directly copied in the 19th century. The most popular of the revival styles, the Rococo, offers a good illustration of this principle of finding inspiration in earlier

designs. The original mid 18th century Rococo style, which initially developed in France but soon spread throughout Europe, was strongly influenced by marine forms, with decoration consisting of shells, coral, waves, seaweed and similar motifs. The scrollwork engraving, too, was influenced by the sea, as

one C- or S-scroll led the eye easily on to the next, in the same way that one wave flows into another.

In the 1750s and '60s the style evolved and flowers, which had been only a minor detail early on, became increasingly popular. Equally important to the overall design of the best-quality pieces, however, were areas

◁ **BENONI STEPHENS TEA/COFFEE SERVICE** *This is a complete four-piece service to which the owners have added a kettle and stand made in 1839 (with a naturalistic flower and leaf decoration, inset), also by Benoni Stephens. Both the tea and the coffee pots also have flower-motif decorative knops. 1835; kettle 18in, teapot 7in high.* **£8,000**

▷ **ELECTROPLATED TEAPOT** *Part of a three-piece set including a milk jug and sugar bowl, this teapot is a true mixture of styles. The stylized floral pattern on the lower body is pure Rococo, while the knop and feet are more naturalistic. The plain panels are classical in origin. 1860; teapot 6in high.* **The set £120**

△ **COMPOSITE SILVER SET** *This fine quality teaset is an excellent example of mixed design: the shape is late 18th century but the engraved decoration is rococo revival. Teapot 1872, 5in high; bowl and jug 1881.* **£500 – £800**

SPOUT DECORATION

Rococo revival spouts are a mix of previous styles.

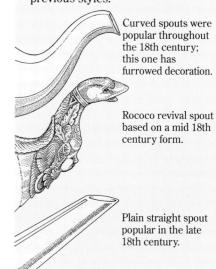

Curved spouts were popular throughout the 18th century; this one has furrowed decoration.

Rococo revival spout based on a mid 18th century form.

Plain straight spout popular in the late 18th century.

△ **ELECTROPLATED NATURALISTIC SERVICE** *Naturalism is found in many forms in Victorian silver; the design of this five-piece set with coffee pot and water jug is based on an artichoke. 1860; teapot 4in high.* **£150**

▽ **JAPANESE STYLING** *The engraved panels of this silver teaset reflect the 19th century vogue for oriental design. The unusual decoration increases the value by at least £500. 1879; teapot 5in high.* **£1,000 – £1,500**

left completely unadorned to provide a contrast to all the decoration.

Rococo revival pieces from the 19th century lack fluidity of design. They seldom incorporate marine forms, but instead are a riot of scroll-work and floral ornamentation, mixed with surviving elements of Regency Classicism. A teapot, for example, might have a Classical oil lamp-shaped body, but be decorated with rococo revival scrolls and flow-ers. Typical also of rococo revival pieces is their almost total lack of plain surfaces. It is as though in the 19th century every possible surface had to be filled with some device or motif. The result, generally, is a smothering of decorative effects.

There are, perhaps, more varia-tions of the Rococo, in combination with other styles, in tea and coffee services than in any other objects. This is not surprising: the wealth created through the Industrial Revolution made it the ambition of every Victorian of a certain stature and class to be able to serve tea using a silver teaset. Along with the canteen of flatware, the silver teaset became an essential wedding gift. For those who could not afford 'real'

SILVER AND ITS LOOKALIKES

SILVER (All periods)
Objects made entirely of sterling silver (925 parts per 1,000) or Britannia silver (958.4 parts per 1,000).

OLD SHEFFIELD PLATE (1760 – 1850)
Sterling silver fused to a copper ingot then rolled into a sheet from which objects are made.

ELECTROPLATE (1840 – present)
ON NICKEL – EPNS (1840 – present)
Nickel objects, covered in silver by an electrolytic process.
ON COPPER (1840 – present)
As above, on copper objects. Often used to simulate Old Sheffield Plate.
ON BRITANNIA METAL – EPBM (1850 – 1920) As above, on Britannia metal objects (this is an alloy of 80% tin, with copper and antimony added for strength).

◁ **IRISH TEASET** *A copy of a mid 19th century rococo revival set, complete with spouted jug for hot water or coffee, by makers and retailers West and Son of Dublin. The decoration covers most of the surface and each piece stands on four shell feet. 1915; teapot 6in high.* The set **£1,500**

Female figure on handle

A CLOSER LOOK AT

A ROCOCO REVIVAL TEAPOT

This silver teapot is typical of the rococo revival, in particular in the scrollwork around the plain oval cartouche, which does not 'flow': the eye is not led easily from one scroll to the next. The caryatid, or reclining female figure, on the handle is reflected in the casting of the spout.

Floral knop

Oval cartouche, engraved with owner's initials

Shell motif on feet

ROCOCO REVIVAL DECORATIVE MOTIFS

This detail of the foot of a kettle stand (right) is a good example of the variety of decoration found in rococo revival pieces. Typically, almost no areas are left undecorated – even the background is textured (this was usually achieved by hammering the inside of the object to produce a raised surface pattern on the outside). There is an abundance of scrollwork, which leads the eye into floral swags around the base of the stand. In contrast to many revival pieces, here the shell and scroll decoration is formally arranged and comparatively restrained. (Although these are common Rococo motifs, they are used less often in revival pieces, where scrolls and flowers predominate.)

▽ **PRESENTATION TEA/ COFFEE SERVICE** *This mid 19th century rococo revival service is in very good condition: like many presentation pieces it was probably for display rather than use. The exterior is chased – that is, hammered to create a raised surface pattern – and the interiors of the sugar bowl and the milk/cream jug have been gilded. 1850; teapot 8in high.* **£2,500**

The mask on this cast spout (left) reflects the design of the caryatid on the handle. Typically, the C-scrolls go nowhere. The hallmarks (below) are for West and Son, the maker, Dublin and 1915.

silver, manufacturers worked to perfect electroplating processes, which enabled the production of cheaper alternatives of an increasingly acceptable quality.

The great majority of 19th century silver teasets comprised a teapot, sugar bowl, milk or cream jug and a hot water jug which could also be used for coffee. Small-size sets, known as 'bachelor' or 'spinster' teasets and usually consisting of three pieces only – teapot, milk jug and sugar bowl – were made for use at breakfast. Most sets, however, were fairly large, and teapots with a capacity of two pints were usual. After about 1820, spirit-burning kettles, often with elaborate stands, became popular again, having gone out of fashion in the second half of the 18th century, when silver urns became the most common method of heating water. A tray could also be added to a set.

Today, as well as complete sets, it is possible to find composite sets, so called because the teapot was made at a different date from the milk jug and sugar bowl.

SILVER TRAYS

The distinguishing feature of a tray as opposed to a salver or waiter is its handles. Today, silver trays are usually associated with tea and coffee services, but this has not always been the case. Some mid 18th century 'trays', for example, were in fact used first and foremost as soup tureen stands.

There are four principal tray shapes – oblong, shaped oblong, oval and shaped oval. The earliest examples are generally oval trays dating from the late 18th century. These are often decorated with bright-cut engraved motifs, in which the designs are cut to reflect the light. Simple oblong forms began to appear in the early 19th century, and from the mid 19th century onward all four shapes were made; the most common being shaped oval and shaped oblong. Trays dating from this period were often large and heavy enough to be used as stands; this has led to doubts as to whether they were intended to be carried at all.

Gallery trays, which were used for drinks, were particularly popular during the late Victorian and Edwardian periods, and they are in plentiful supply today. Many thousands were made in electroplate (copper or nickel coated with a thin layer of silver). Electroplated copper trays are often mistaken for Old Sheffield Plate (silver fused with copper and worked as one metal), which is more valuable.

When examining a tray, check the handles, which take a lot of strain, particularly where they join the body. Splits or repaired splits reduce the value considerably, as do any signs of an inscription which has been filled in or removed from the centre of the tray. (Most trays were originally engraved in this way.)

△ ELECTROPLATED OVAL TRAY *which is actually a meat dish with handles. The broad rim within the gadroon edge indicates its intended use. Similar silver trays were made by adding handles to earlier pieces. These had to be resubmitted to the Assay Office, and should have later hallmarks on the handles. 1900; 21in wide.* **£150**

▽ SHAPED OBLONG TRAY, *typical of those produced at the beginning of this century, and often accompanied by a teaset. These trays were very popular as presentation pieces. They are frequently found with quite lengthy inscriptions (though not in this case) which, unless they incorporate a coat-of-arms, reduce the value. 1910; 23in wide.* **£1,000**

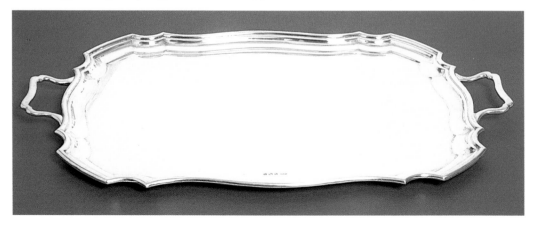

▽ **OVAL SILVER TRAY** *The shape was first introduced in the late 18th century. This piece has a delightful 'rayed' effect issuing from the central oval cartouche, and features handles which 'flow' attractively from the main body. 1870 – 80; 23½ in wide.* **£2,200**

△ **GALLERY TRAY,** *so named after the pierced, usually vertical borders. Silver examples are generally of fine quality and decorated with neo-classical designs, but most gallery trays, including this one, are electroplated. Those with a nickel base (EPNS), as here, are generally well made, but copper versions are of poorer quality. 1910; 14½ in wide.* **£90**

EXPERT'S CHOICE

A CLOSER LOOK AT

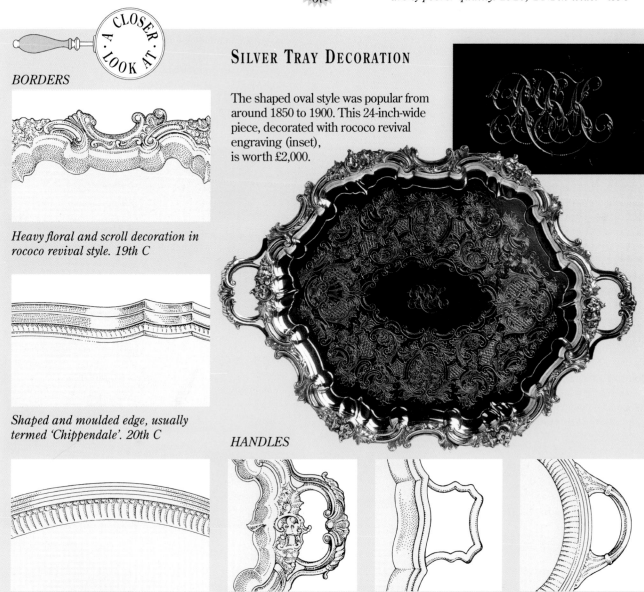

SILVER TRAY DECORATION

The shaped oval style was popular from around 1850 to 1900. This 24-inch-wide piece, decorated with rococo revival engraving (inset), is worth £2,000.

BORDERS

Heavy floral and scroll decoration in rococo revival style. 19th C

Shaped and moulded edge, usually termed 'Chippendale'. 20th C

Thread, or reeded edge with a 'lobe'-style decorated border within. Late 19th C

HANDLES

Scroll (bifurcated ends) and shellwork handle. Mid 19th C

Shaped and moulded scroll handle. Early 20th C

Thread (or reed) and acanthus leafwork handle. Late 18th C

EXOTIC SILVER

Because of its intrinsic value, silver has long been used to create a wide range of exotic objects, from the functional to the purely eye-catching.

Many of these objects fall into the category of presentation pieces. These were often engraved with personal inscriptions for the recipient, especially from the mid 19th century onward. Certain pieces were also modelled for special occasions. For example, rosebowls in the form of gondolas were appropriate wedding presents because of their romantic association with Venice.

Impressive-looking inkstands were commonplace on writing desks, and although the majority were usually just larger versions of the standard models of the day, exotic examples can also be found. Architectural forms in silver, such as castles and churches, were popular, and replicas of particular buildings were sometimes presented to their architect or owner.

Table centrepieces in silver, known as epergnes, became popular in the early 18th century. They were

△ **GONDOLA ROSEBOWL** *by the German manufacturer Württembergische Metallenwaren Fabrik, best known for their Art Nouveau and classical designs. Made using the electroplate technique, it still has the original glass liner and gilt metal grill, and it is in excellent condition. 1900; 16in long.* **£400 – £500**

△ **ELEPHANT AND CASTLE ORNAMENT** *made in Japan. This extraordinary elephant is bronze, while the rest of the piece is silver, set with exquisite 'shibayama' panels (ivory inlaid with mother-of-pearl). Two dragons climb the sides of this superbly-finished piece and the domed cover has an eagle finial. 1900; 14in high.* **£10,000 – £15,000**

◁ **ORNATE SILVER CASKET** *probably made in Europe using the electrotyping technique. Such caskets were lined inside with velvet, or sandalwood if designed for cigars, to cover the roughly finished interior. Mid 19th century; 9in long.* **£150 – £200**

△ **MOSQUE INKSTAND** *made by Elkington & Company and hallmarked in London, with two inkwells, a stamp box and a depression for pens at the front. The engraving on the buildings is excellent. A presentation piece, it also bears an inscription. 1898; 12in long.* **£4,000**

generally used for serving sweet-meats, fruit and savoury titbits. A basic epergne consists of three or more dishes supported on a decorative frame, while more elaborate versions can hold as many as ten baskets and dishes, towering high above the table

Presentation snuff boxes, which were bestowed on kings, princes and dignitaries, can be found from the 18th century onward. In the 19th century these developed into the more flamboyant 'freedom' caskets, many of which still contain elaborate freedom or presentation scrolls awarded to those granted the Freedom of a City. Original scrolls add to the value of these pieces as does any enamel work in good condition, such as an armorial crest.

Elaborate jewel caskets started to appear in the mid 19th century, and remained popular into the 20th century. Many of these were made by electrotyping: this process involved taking a mould from a model and then depositing layer upon layer of copper on the inside of the mould. When complete, the final piece was coated in silver. Copper was the first base metal used, but it was later replaced by nickel.

Animals have always been favourite subjects for more exotic pieces of silver: 16th and 17th century drinking cups, particularly from Germany, survive in the form of stags, bears and cockerels, for example. These animal groups can be an acquired taste, but it is rare to find an example that is lacking in character or interest.

△ 'CAMEL' CENTREPIECE *made using the electroplate process. Each piece is marked with a design registration -mark. Originally this would have had one large and three smaller glass dishes for holding fruit, nuts or even flowers. The missing dishes greatly affect the value; if they were present the piece would be worth three times as much. 1865; 23in high.* **£300**

△ VICTORIAN CENTREPIECE *with its original cut and frosted glass dish on a stem of fruiting vines. This piece was made in London and is a fine example of the Victorians' love of ornamentation. It was obviously intended to hold fruit and could well have been part of a 3-piece set consisting of another identical piece and a larger one with branches. 1869; 19in high.* **£2,000**

AN EPERGNE

Popular as centrepieces after about 1720, the earliest epergnes took the form of a central tureen with a large dish above and lower branches that held smaller dishes. The branches of this 18-inch high example support candleholders, but these can be removed and replaced with glass dishes. Made in 1835 by Robinson, Edkins & Aston of Birmingham, it is in mint condition with all its glass intact, and is worth £5,000 to £6,000.

△ *The detailing on this fine piece is superb.*

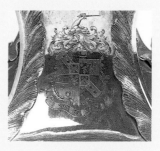

△ *The engraving shows the family coat-of-arms.*

The custom of a groom presenting his bride with the gift of a toilet set or dressing table set, often in a wooden case, was introduced in the late 17th century and continued into the Edwardian era. The material, composition and decoration of such sets varied, but the finest were made from silver or, sometimes, gold.

The contents of an 18th century dressing table set included a mirror on an easel frame; a casket to hold hair combs (often mistaken for jewellery boxes); a pair of candlesticks with snuffers and a tray; various-sized pots – often glass with silver lids – for face creams and powders; clothes and hair brushes; ivory or tortoiseshell combs with silver mounts, and a pincushion. A small ewer and basin, with salvers, also frequently formed part of the set. Although individual pieces exist, today it is rare to find a complete set from the 18th century.

Most dressing table silver on the market dates from after the intro-duction of powered presses in the 1840s. As such, the pieces are mostly mass produced, with die-stamped decoration, although many were accurate copies of 17th and 18th

△ COMPLETE DRESSING TABLE SET *Since they have a long association with weddings, it is appropriate to find a dressing table set decorated with the romantic figures of a lady and gentleman (left), surrounded by scrolls and swags in a particularly elaborate design. Today the mirror is the most saleable part of the set; the brushes need rebristling, which can be costly. 1900; mirror 12in long.* **£700 – £1,000**

◁ VICTORIAN COMB BOX *with a contemporary inscription, July 3rd 1881. The condition is poor: over-polishing has resulted in a series of holes in the lid. Although this kind of damage can be repaired, an example in good condition can be bought for £150 – £200, which is probably less than the cost of repair. 1881; 5in across.* **£50**

▽ **EDWARDIAN HAND MIRROR** *decorated with the scrolling flowers and foliage typical of the period 1890 – 1910, the highpoint of Art Nouveau. This piece is in good condition: points to check for are that the mirror glass itself is undamaged; that there are no holes in the decoration, and that there are no splits or creases where the handle joins the body. 1906; 11in long.* **£140**

◁ **CIRCULAR TRINKET BOX** *made in Birmingham. Many of these boxes were velvet lined and fitted with slots to hold rings. 1930; 3½ in across.* **£120**

▽ **ENAMEL-TOPPED BOX** *for trinkets or rings, with a silver base. The cabriole legs were an Edwardian innovation. 1911; 5in across.* **£50 – £60**

century designs. The contents of dressing table sets also changed by the mid 19th century. Once dressing tables started to be produced with integral mirrors, manufacturers made hand mirrors to include in the set. Women took to wearing elbow-length gloves, and high, buttoned boots, so glove stretchers, shoe horns and button hooks became essential items; improved plumbing and lighting made ewers, basins and candlesticks obsolete, and the advent of the machine age enabled the first production of metal nail files and nail scissors.

Although complete Victorian or Edwardian dressing table sets can be found today, many have been split up and pieces sold individually. Some of these items – button hooks, for example – have now become collectable in their own right.

▽ **TRINKET BOX** *with stamped rococo-style swags and scrollwork decoration, and a gilded interior. The matted background emphasizes the decoration, but needs extra care in polishing since a residue of polish will clog the surface. 1895; 3½ in across.* **£50 – £60**

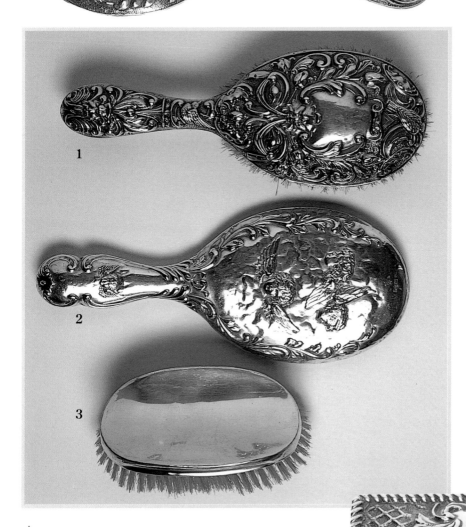

△ **MIRROR AND BRUSHES** *Both the 1920s brush* (**1**) *and turn-of-the-century example* (**3**) *retain their original bristles. The hand mirror* (**2**) *is decorated in one of the most popular styles – cherubs' faces peering through banks of clouds, based on the paintings of 18th century Swiss artist Angelica Kauffman. The appeal of this image was clearly its overwhelming sentimentality.* **1** *1920; 10in.* **£60 – £80** **2** *1910; 10½ in.* **£150 – £200** **3** *1900; 5in.* **£150 – £200**

INSECT BROOCHES

Given the inherent loathing that many people have for 'creepy crawlies', it is quite surprising that insect-style jewellery has been so popular through the ages.

Novelty jewellery abounded during the 19th century, when even the housefly caught in a spider's web was considered an acceptable subject. In the late 19th and early 20th centuries, spiders were fashionable models – their small bodies and spread-eagled legs providing an ideal basic shape for brooches.

With the opening of the Suez Canal in 1867 and the discovery of Tutankhamen's tomb in 1922, the distinctive scarab (sacred beetle) jewellery of the Ancient Egyptians became popular. Beetles in porcelain and stone, for example, were mounted on coloured wings (a symbol of the sun god, Ra) and worn as brooches.

After butterflies, bees and lizards were the most popular subjects for novelty brooches. In the 19th century, bees were reproduced naturalistically, using diamonds and other gemstones mounted in silver on a gold base. (Their 20th century counterparts tend to have more durable platinum mounts.) Lizards were set with diamonds, emeralds or green garnets running in a line down their backs. Brooches of this type have been widely copied since, in paste or marcasite set in silver.

◁ BEE BROOCH *set with diamonds and emeralds. It has ruby eyes and a gold and silver mount. The value of such pieces depends primarily on the workmanship. 1860; 1½ in wide. Insurance value* **£6,750 – £7,000**

△ SAPPHIRE AND PEARL FLIES *set in gold, on graduated chains. Surprisingly, perhaps, the fly was a popular motif on Victorian brooches. 1890; 1½ in wide.* **£250 – £350**

◁ BAR BROOCH *featuring a fly set with a half pearl and pink tourmaline and a spider on a chain. In 9ct gold, it was hallmarked in Chester. 1900; 8in wide.* **£80 – £120**

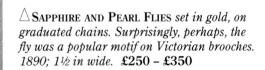

▽ **FLORENTINE PLAQUE BROOCH** *made from 'pietra dura' (stones composed mainly of silicates) in a 15ct gold mount. Some plaques were cut in Derbyshire, but the finest were made by Florentine stonecutters and mounted in England. 1850; 1in wide.*
£400 – £600

△ **SCARAB BROOCH** *mounted in 15ct gold openwork wings with serpent shoulders. Sarah Bernhardt's performance as Cleopatra in the 1880s caused a resurgence in the popularity of scarab jewellery, which had begun with the opening of the Suez Canal in 1867. 1870 – 80; 2in wide.* £300 – £400

BUTTERFLY BROOCHES

The most fashionable subject for insect brooches is the butterfly, followed closely by any insect with wings that are bigger than its body. A large expanse of wing gives a jeweller ample scope to emulate the brilliance and coloration of the real creature, using a variety of gemstones and coloured enamels.

△ **GOLD BROOCH** *studded with rose diamonds, sapphires, rubies and pearls. It has a detachable mount. 1860; 1½ in wide.* £700 – £1,000

◁ **SILVER BUTTERFLY,** *which would have been engraved before the application of the blue enamel. 1920 – 25; 2½ in wide.* £60 – £80

△ **VICTORIAN BUTTERFLY** *set with diamonds, rubies, sapphires and a large emerald, which upsets the balance of the piece. 1880; 1in wide. Insurance value £2,400*

△ **GOLD BROOCH** *set with three rose-cut diamonds in an ivy leaf design within a wirework border. The hollow back holds a locket. 1880; 1in across.* **£200**

▷ **PORCELAIN PLAQUE** *set in a gilt metal brooch mount. This religious subject (landscapes are more popular) is transfer printed, others are hand painted. 1880 – 90; 1½ in across.* **£80 – £120**

The heavy appearance we tend to associate with Victorian furnishings also extended to fashion and jewellery. This is hardly surprising: Victorian women dressed in large crinoline dresses required substantial-looking jewellery to match.

Although Victorian brooches look weighty, many are in fact surprisingly light, since they were often made from hollowed-out metal in a thin gauge. (This also had the advantage of keeping costs down.) The hollow space at the back of the brooch could be used to hold a locket containing a photograph, miniature painting or lock of hair.

Victorian jewellery is generally very colourful, with bright enamels and multi-coloured gemstones among the most popular materials. Mounts also changed, with closed, pinched designs and foiled backs replaced by lighter, more open settings.

Although diamonds were popular with the Victorians, they were very crudely cut by today's standards. Much thicker and heavier, and with fewer facets, they appear cushion-shaped and can be distinguished by the black spot that appears in their centre when they are viewed from the top (this optical illusion occurs when the culet, or central point at the back of the stone, is cut off).

Diamonds draw a certain amount of colour from their surroundings, and for this reason gold, while used, was not the preferred setting material. Most 19th century gold and diamond brooches have silver fronts and claws to reduce this effect. (Platinum only started to replace gold and silver in popularity in this century.)

As in many other areas of design, Victorian jewellers drew their inspiration from diverse sources. The major archaeological discoveries of the 19th century, which included quantities of jewellery, were highly influential; decoration in particular was inspired by earlier styles. Wirework,

▽ **GOLD-MOUNTED SWALLOW BROOCH** *with a pearl head. Its rose-cut diamond wings are tipped with garnets and rubies. 1880 – 90; 1½ in across.* **£2,000 – £2,500**

▽ **GOLD WISHBONE BROOCH** *made in South Africa. The patriotic colours of the ruby, diamond and sapphire were intended to appeal to English troops. 1880; 1¼ in.* **£250**

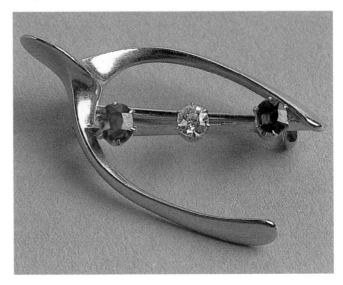

for example, which protects the edges and high spots on brooches was copied from the early Etruscans. Cameo-making, originally practised in Ancient Rome and Greece, underwent a strong revival. World events were also influential: the opening of the Suez Canal fuelled an interest in Egyptian styles in the 1870s, and increasing trade with the East inspired stylized Japanese and Chinese decoration during the 1880s.

At the end of the 19th century the graceful flowing lines of Art Nouveau styling came to dominate many areas of design. In jewellery, these styles persisted into the Edwardian era.

◁ **GOLD WREATH BROOCH** *set with half-pearls, a design that remained popular throughout the Edwardian era. This piece could only be worn on heavy or coarse fabrics: its broad flat pin would damage fine silks or linens, for example. 1890; 1in across.* **£120**

▽ **ROLLED GOLD SWIVEL BROOCH** *The engraved ribbons have the effect of making the rather flat frame of this Victorian brooch appear heavier. The classical-design shell cameo was made for export in Italy, and mounted in pinchbeck in this country. It swivels to reveal a hair locket in the back. 1860; 2½ in across.* **£150 – £200**

◁ **MOURNING BROOCH** *with applied decoration of a spray of hair held with a seed pearl clasp (seed pearls signify tears). The reverse is an open locket to hold a photograph or miniature. Mourning jewellery incorporating human hair was particularly popular with the Victorians. 1865; 2¼ in across.* **£120 – £180**

CAMEOS

The finest cameos are cut from hard stones such as agate, although the majority are made from shell. Less popular today are molten lava examples.

▽ **CHARMING ITALIAN CAMEO** *in a later gold mount. This is very finely carved. 1860 – 80; 1½ in across.* **£300 – £400**

◁ **ITALIAN BLUSH PINK SHELL CAMEO** *mounted in gold with a ropework border. 1880; 1½ in across.* **£150**

▽ **SHELL CAMEO** *While this cameo is of very good quality, the claw mount leaves its edges unprotected. 1880 – 90; 2in across.* **£200**

RINGS

◁ **DIAMOND AND ONYX RING** *Onyx is not one of the most valuable stones, but it can be used effectively, as in this Art Deco ring. 1920.*
£1,800 – £2,500

△ **BOAT-SHAPED SAPPHIRE AND DIAMOND CLUSTER** *in a platinum mount. Unlike gold, platinum does not affect the colour of the diamonds. 1915.*
£650 – £700

Although the Romans were the first people to offer rings specifically as engagement gifts, they have been exchanged as tokens of love and marriage for thousands of years, their circular shape symbolizing eternal fidelity.

Until the 15th century, gemstones were generally cut very simply and assumed second place to the decoration of the gold or silver in a ring. Not until jewellers developed the art of faceting, with rose-cut and its derivative, the brilliant-cut, did makers and buyers start to place primary emphasis on the stone.

Towards the end of the 18th century, rings became less ornate, with delicacy the keynote. By the end of the 19th century, however, large stones in impressive settings were fashionable once more. In the early years of this century, gold and silver were largely superseded by platinum, which is stronger and harder, and can be used for more delicate mounts.

△ **CROSSOVER RING** *with diamonds and rubies in a fine gold setting. Crossover rings have gone out of style, denying this pretty example a high market value. 1928.* **£200 – £300**

▷ **GOLD MOONSTONE RING** *Both the choice of stone, and its complementary gold setting are typical of the hand-crafted aesthetic of the Arts and Crafts movement. 1915 – 20.* **£100**

DIAMOND SHAPES

The six most popular shapes of diamond are usually brilliant-cut (that is, cut with 58 facets), to allow as much light as possible to reflect through the stone. The earlier rose-cut has either 24 or 36 facets. Shape does not affect the value of a diamond, but a good cut does.

Brilliant   Oval

Marquise   Heart

Emerald   Pear

△ **DIAMOND AND PEARL RING**
The central pearl of this ring has been cut in half so as not to stand too proud of its millegrain (beaded) platinum setting on a gold shank. 1910. **£250 – £350**

▽ **TARGET CLUSTER RING**
mounted in gold and silver and set with 24 brilliants (diamonds cut with 58 facets). The stones are pavé set, closely spaced so that little or none of the setting is visible. 1910. **£850 – £900**

◁ **HALF-HOOP OPAL AND DIAMOND RING** *Half-hoop rings have always been popular, and were especially fashionable at the end of the 19th and beginning of the 20th centuries. Though generally mounted on 15ct or (as here) 18ct gold hand-carved shanks, they were also widely copied in 9ct gold cast mounts. These should nevertheless bear a hallmark. This ring is complete with its Belfast retailer's box. 1911.* **£175**

MOURNING RINGS

Bought by the bereaved in memory of the dead, with money bequeathed for the purpose, mourning rings were popular from the 17th to 19th centuries. Made in gold, they were usually enamelled in black, or white for the unmarried. This unusual example, dated 1808, has turquoise blue enamelling, and is worth £150.

△ **OPAL RING** *with inset diamonds, in a sturdy 19th century gold mount. The ring has a rather heavy look, and the opals are a little too milky to have great commercial value. So-called black opals, which have visible touches of red, green and blue 'fire', are more highly prized. The value of rings of this type depends very much on the quality and desirability of the stones used rather than on the mounts. 1920.* **£300 – £350**

COSTUME JEWELLERY

Imitation jewellery has been produced for hundreds of years. Costume, or fashion, jewellery, which was not intended to look real, however, was an innovation of the 1920s and '30s. Its rise in popularity may have its origins in the changing social status of women after World War I. The typical 1920s 'flapper' was out for a good time, and a short skirt, bobbed hair and fun jewellery were all part of her image.

By making accessories an integral part of the overall look, the revolutionary Paris-based fashion designers Coco Chanel (1883 – 1971) and Elsa Schiaparelli (1896 – 1973) made mass-produced fashion jewellery acceptable in *haute couture*. Both had individual styles, but Chanel in particular mixed the exotic Romanoff jewels showered on her by her Russian lover, the Grand Duke Dimitri, with 'fakes' made to her own designs, saying that it was the look that mattered: the value of the jewels was unimportant.

The jewellery included in Chanel's first *haute couture* collection of 1924 showed clear Russian influences, featuring, among other pieces, long gilt and pearl chains and crosses. Her designs were bold, far more so than the precious jewellery being produced by the leading French jewellers, such

as Cartier and Van Cleef & Arpels.

The other major influence on 1920s design was the opening of the tomb of Tutankhamen in 1922, precipitating a rush of Egyptian-style jewellery.

The dominant style of the 1920s and early '30s, however, was Art Deco. The geometric outlines and bold use of strong colour contrasts were ideally suited to costume jewellery designs. Black and white, or black and crystal, pieces made from onyx and glass or rock crystal were very popular.

In the 1930s American manufacturers followed the French lead, with designers such as Trifari (the largest company), Corocraft and Miriam Haskell all producing good pieces.

△ **FOX-HEAD BUCKLE** *in celluloid, a hot-mouldable plastic developed by American John Wesley Hyatt as a substitute for ivory. 1940 – 45; 5in wide.* **£45**

Among the most sought-after pieces by Trifari are the 'jelly belly' range of animal brooches.

Miriam Haskell designed pearl and gilt jewellery and signed most of her pieces. Since the pearls were mounted by hand on fine gilt wire to the back plate, no two pieces are exactly alike. This, again, makes them desirable.

Costume jewellery production was badly affected by World War II, when many of the metals used were needed for the war effort. American makers

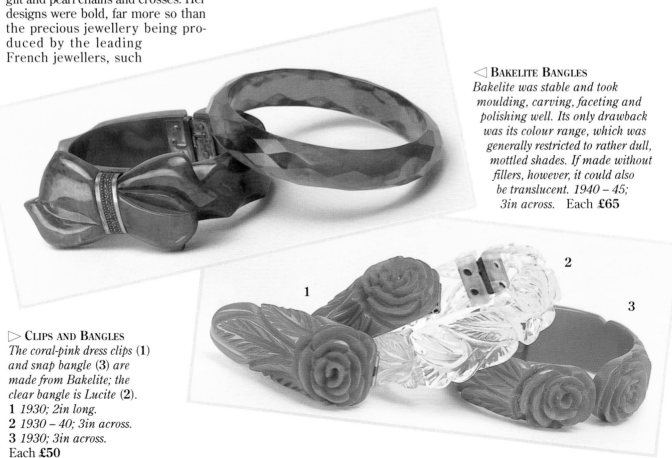

▷ **CLIPS AND BANGLES**
The coral-pink dress clips (1) and snap bangle (3) are made from Bakelite; the clear bangle is Lucite (2).
1 *1930; 2in long.*
2 *1930 – 40; 3in across.*
3 *1930; 3in across.*
Each **£50**

◁ **BAKELITE BANGLES**
Bakelite was stable and took moulding, carving, faceting and polishing well. Its only drawback was its colour range, which was generally restricted to rather dull, mottled shades. If made without fillers, however, it could also be translucent. 1940 – 45; 3in across. Each **£65**

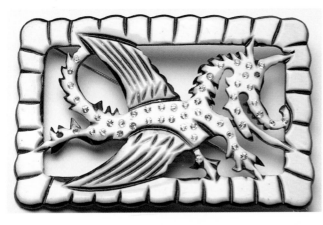

◁ DRAGON BUCKLE *in carved and pierced white Bakelite (to imitate ivory) and diamanté. Bakelite was a popular material, often used in Art Deco-style jewellery. 1940; 4½in wide.* **£45**

▷ WOODEN SAILOR BROOCH, *carved in America. Wood cannot be cast or moulded but it can be whittled quickly enough to make items such as this financially viable. Military subjects were popular in the 1940s. 1940 – 45; 4in high.* **£25 – £30**

◁ RED GLASS BEAD NECKLACE *interspersed with faceted cut-glass rondels. Glass beads of this size are heavy and need frequent re-stringing if worn often. 1940; 15in long.* **£30 – £40**

turned to sterling silver, usually gilded. This cost more but gave the jewels a higher 'perceived value'. Art Deco gave way to '40s or 'retro' style, in which smooth, untextured metal predominated. The rubies and diamonds, and red or two-coloured gold that became popular in precious jewellery design, were also reproduced in costume pieces.

Today, costume jewellery from the 1920s and '30s is quite rare. A great deal was lost during the war, or simply thrown away when it went out of fashion or was damaged.

When buying costume jewellery, only choose pieces in perfect condition, with 'gems' that glitter brightly, and gilding in good condition. Check the pins, catches or fastenings – they are not usually very sturdy and are difficult and costly to repair. Also, try to find named pieces: they are more expensive, but worth it. Among the names to look for are Eisenberg, Kramer, Pennino, Jomaz (Joseph Mazer) and Hattie Carnegie.

△ IMITATION LAPIS LAZULI EARRINGS, *in fact made of glass. Glass has been used in jewellery for thousands of years; it is relatively easy to colour and far more durable than modern plastics. 1920 – 30; 2in long.* **£15 – £20**

▽ EGYPTIAN-STYLE NECKLACE *made in gilt metal with inlaid rectangles of natural and black-dyed mother-of-pearl. A great deal of work has gone into this piece, since each section is sawn and fitted by hand. 1940; 14in long.* **£75**

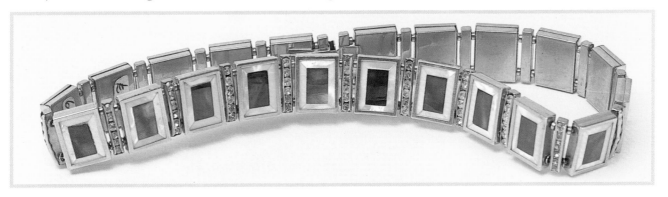

177

Ian Pickford is a lecturer and consultant, as well as the author of several reference works on silver and hallmarks.

COLLECTOR'S CHECKLIST

SILVER, GOLD & JEWELLERY

Collecting silver can be enormously rewarding, particularly if you collect only those pieces you really enjoy and learn as much as you can about your chosen field of collecting. By limiting your collection to items within a specific price range, you will be able to buy the finest pieces available, rather than possibly ending up with a collection of expensive but poor or second-rate examples.

It is always worth getting to know a dealer with a sound knowledge of your particular field. He or she will keep you informed of interesting pieces coming up for sale at auction, and may be able to bid for them on your behalf. If there is a particular piece which you would like to buy, do not ask more than one dealer to look out for it at the same time. Should such a piece come on to the market, you may find that several dealers are trying to acquire it for you, creating an artificially high price which you will have generated.

Do not be tempted to display your entire silver collection at one time. If you are burgled you will almost certainly lose the lot, and the task of starting from scratch may simply be too daunting.

The principle of buying the best you can afford applies equally to jewellery. Prices vary from just a few pounds for costume jewellery to many thousands of pounds for pieces set with precious stones. Designer jewellery, by Chanel or Dior, for example, can also be costly. Silver, however, is more modestly priced. Die-stamped brooches from the 1880s onward are a good choice, and there are plenty of these around. Art Deco jewellery is currently popular, as are 'fun' pieces from the 1940s and '50s.

△ **PORRINGER** *with porcupine knops, by A. E. Jones of Birmingham. 1911; 3in wide.* **£300 – £350**

POINTS TO WATCH FOR

1 The condition of silver is of paramount importance. Serious collectors should only acquire items in top condition, unless there is little or no chance of finding a better example.

2 Examine the colour or patina of silver in daylight: fine old silver has a deep grey-blue colour; bad surfaces are very white with a 'brushed' look; and any light brown stains which are not removable tarnish will reduce the value.

3 Most antique silver was originally engraved with a family crest or initials. When a family sold its silver, they often had this form of identification removed, so buyers should check for white areas or thin patches in the body where such engravings would usually be found.

4 A magnifying glass or 'loupe' is invaluable when examining items of jewellery close up. A loupe is like a magnifying glass, but smaller: the correct strength of magnification for inspecting gems is 'magnification x 10', so if buying, ask for this type.

5 Many gold items dating from the 19th century have a frosted finish. Do not polish such pieces, it will reduce their value.

6 Hold areas of chased decoration or repoussé work up to a strong light – holes or splits will show up very well. Also check any high points of decoration for wear.

▷ **DUTCH SIFTER SPOON** *for flour, with an attractive turned wooden handle. 1800; 8in long.* **£70 – £80**

7 Check engraving, particularly if it enhances the value of a piece. Crisp engraving on an otherwise worn item may well have been added later.

8 Examine all silverware for repairs, looking closely at vulnerable areas such as handles, feet and hinges. Brown stains here often indicate recent solder repairs. And remember, jewellery repairs can be very costly.

9 When buying a piece that you intend to use, first try it out – a dripping spout on a pot, or grape shears that do not cut properly, can be very irritating.

10 Fine pieces of silver may have badly or weakly struck maker's marks and hallmarks. These should not be seen as a reflection of the overall quality of a piece.

OLD = VALUABLE?

It is incorrect to assume that an old item of jewellery is more valuable than a modern one; the factors that affect price today are quality of workmanship, degree of rarity and the materials used.

Nor is it safe to assume that a piece of jewellery is very old simply because it has been in a family for generations – allowance must be made for overlapping generations and the date of acquisition.

In an age where craftsmanship is at a premium, quality of design and manufacture can far outweigh the precious materials used. Modern jewellers can buy nearly all the components of a brooch or ring, for example, ready for fitting together. However, a number of craftsmen still use the traditional – and time-consuming – methods that will ensure that a piece becomes collectable in the future.

CARE & REPAIR

1 Check the claws of antique jewellery periodically in case they need tightening or retipping. For repairs, always consult a reputable jeweller.

2 Hold silver in one hand and polish it, using a cotton cloth, with the other. Resting silver on a table causes stress.

3 Regularly used silver such as flatware requires little or no extra polishing. Hand wash it (never use a dishwasher) and dry immediately.

4 Never use commercial cleaners on soft gems such as pearls or shell cameos. They will scratch the surface.

5 Do not allow salt to come into contact with silver for any length of time, and always empty and rinse salt cellars after use. Keep silver away from sources of sulphur pollution, such as open coal fires and oil-fired boilers.

6 Keep each item of jewellery in its original box, fitted case or purse. Delicate items such as cameos and chains can be damaged if heaped together with hard stones.

7 To store silver, wrap it in acid-free tissue or pure cotton (or specially impregnated cotton bags that prevent tarnishing). Never wrap silver in newspaper, chamois leather, plastic bags or wool-based material.

◁ **PASSION FLOWER BROOCH** *made of simulated emeralds, amethysts, topaz and diamonds. 1760; 3in wide.* **£1,000**

GOLD & DIAMOND CARATS

A carat is the standard for measuring both gold and precious gemstones.

Gold used in jewellery contains a mixture of pure gold and alloys, and the amount of pure gold in an item establishes its quality. A carat is a 24th part of the item being measured, thus 9ct is $\frac{9}{24}$ pure gold to $\frac{15}{24}$ alloy, and 18ct is 18 parts gold to 6 parts alloy.

Diamonds and other gems are weighed in carats. One carat is equal to 200 milligrams. Diamonds weighing less than one carat are called 'pointers'. One carat is made up of 100 points, thus a diamond of 60 'points' is $\frac{60}{100}$ of a carat.

▷ **ART DECO CLIP** *with a central opal set with diamonds in a platinum setting 1910; 1½ in long.* **£2,500**

PLACES OF INTEREST

British Museum, London WC1 *Jewellery and metalwork*
Sheffield City Museum, *Cutlery and Old Sheffield Plate*

GOLD STANDARDS & MARKS

The earliest recorded attempt to regulate the standard of gold in England was in 1238. In 1300 a statute was passed decreeing that all silver and gold must meet a certain standard. In the case of gold this was the Paris standard of 19.2 carats. By 1480 the standard was reduced to 18ct gold, and in 1854 a statute was passed allowing the use of 9ct, 12ct and 15ct as alternatives to 18ct and 22ct gold. Although this statute is strictly enforced today, most 19th century gold items do not bear assay marks: also confusing are the many convincing gold simulations on the market such as rolled gold, gilt metal and pinchbeck (copper-zinc).

Foreign assay marks on 20th century items are generally not acceptable by British standards and most pieces must be resubmitted for assay before being sold.

Gold, like silver, bears the following marks: maker's mark, standard mark, assay office mark and a date letter. (Scottish assay offices use their own town marks.)

	Until 1974		1975 to present		SCOTTISH MARKS	
22ct	👑	**22**		👑 **916**		
18ct	👑	**18**	or **18**	👑 **750**	Edinburgh	
14ct	**14**	**585**		👑 **585**		
9ct	**8**	**375**		👑 **375**	Glasgow	

ARMS & MILITARIA

BY BILL HARRIMAN

There is always a buzz of excitement on the evening before the first recording of a new series of the *Antiques Roadshow*, as the experts and production staff gather for dinner. It is somewhat similar to starting a new term at school, complete with all the anxieties and expectations associated with such an event.

I have long given up predicting what will turn up on the day. When I first started at the Roadshow I looked for regional variations, but experience has proved that these do not exist. For instance, my Scottish trips have yielded only one Highlander's dirk, albeit a very fine specimen. With hindsight, the idea of regional variation now seems faintly naive. After all, the UK is a small island with good communications and in so diverse a field as arms and militaria there is no real reason why any particular type of artefact should be concentrated in any one area.

Our last programme came from Rochdale, with its superb Victorian gothic-style Town Hall. Here, I was brought my favourite item of the series, a very fine quality English flintlock sporting gun by Ryan of Birmingham. A great deal of snobbery has always existed about Birmingham-made guns, which are supposedly less good than their London counterparts. This is illustrated by the fact that many Birmingham makers sold their products through retail outlets in London in order to charge higher prices. The elegant gun opposite, which has survived in good condition, equals without doubt those made in the capital.

Early in the series we visited Farnham, and I was delighted to see two very handsome watercolour and gouache studies of British military subjects. These would have been used as original artwork for postcards. The first one featured the drums and drum-major of an English Line Infantry Regiment (c. 1905) and was signed 'Ebberson'. The second painting, which was far finer, depicted the regimental mascots and Orderly of the Middlesex Regiment. The detailing was exceptional, even down to a small boy and his father watching from the barrack gate.

A superb collection of Royal Marine Light Infantry items also turned up at Farnham. It included a scarlet tunic for a colour sergeant, his sash, medals, swagger-stick and personal records. Effectively documenting one man's career, and providing the 'human dimension' that is so appealing to collectors, such groups are always more valuable than an amalgam of single items.

I have always had a passing interest in the '45 Rebellion and Bonnie Prince Charlie because I

△ 'MASCOTS OF THE MIDDLESEX REGIMENT' *(pictured right with Bill Harriman and owner). The painting is from a set by Ebberson. 1905; 11in wide.* **£400**

△ **FLINTLOCK SPORTING GUN** *1825; 4ft 2in.* **£1,000**

was born in Derby, which was the southernmost extent of his 'invasion' of England, and one of my ancestors served in Lord Mark Kerr's Dragoons which fought at Culloden against the Jacobites in 1746. Consequently, at York I was fascinated to handle a fine silver-hilted smallsword inscribed 'Carried for his Prince by Patrick Fea of Airie 1746'. Although its condition was not very good, this piece absolutely 'radiated' a turbulent and romantic period of British history, although it is unlikely that Fea would have run on to the Hanoverian bayonets carrying such a flimsy weapon. It was more likely to have been worn as a male fashion accessory than a fighting sword.

An item that really caught my eye at the Queensferry Roadshow was a World War II German naval officer's dirk, which had been surrendered in Liverpool by a U-Boat captain. It was in exceptional condition and still retained its suspension straps.

Overall, the '92 series was most enjoyable. And my favourite venue? It has to be the Fleet Air Arm Museum at Yeovilton. The setting was truly amazing, and the sight of Hugh Scully being squeezed into the cockpit of a Sopwith Pup will remain with me for ever!

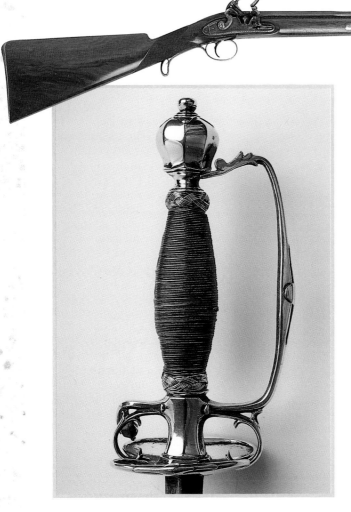

◁ **SILVER-HILTED SMALLSWORD** *1730; 3ft long.* **£400**

△ **NAZI NAVAL OFFICER'S DIRK** *from a captured U-Boat officer. 14in.* **£300**

◁ **ROYAL MARINE INFANTRY** *full dress tunic and personal effects. 1910.* **£400**

SWORDS

The technique of smelting iron was developed around 1200BC, and enabled the production of the first effective fighting weapons. Until then, swords had been made with bronze blades, but iron and steel proved far superior. Both metals had several advantages over bronze: longer weapons could be made, and they could be worked to provide a blade with a sharp cutting edge and flexible core that would not shatter on impact.

As swords evolved they became increasingly specialized to meet the needs of the user. The Spanish short-sword developed by the Romans, for example, was an effective close-quarter weapon around which much of the Roman military doctrine was based. In every development of the sword, the hilt was improved to give greater protection to the user's hand, with as little extra weight gain as possible.

The increasing popularity of the bayonet from about 1700 spelled the end of the sword as the infantry-man's secondary weapon (after the flintlock musket). The Cavalry retained the sword as its primary arm, however, and the last pattern (or design) of British Cavalry sword was adopted as late as 1908, when air power was in its infancy.

Sabres developed from Indian or Persian swords and spread eastward with invading armies. Their curved blades made them easy to use, and they eventually became a Cavalry weapon, although they proved more effective for cutting than thrusting.

Swords have much to recommend them as collectables, their immense variety of style and steely elegance making them a popular choice with collectors of militaria. There are, however, many copies on the market, which have been artificially aged to appear genuine. In addition, the Victorians made good copies of medieval and renaissance swords, which they used for interior decoration. These are eminently collectable in their own right, but can sometimes be offered as genuine. If you are in any doubt, get a second opinion before buying.

◁ **SPANISH SWORD** *This type of hilt, used 1550 to 1820, is called a 'bilboe' (a corruption of Bilbao where the design originates). 1770; 3ft 4in long.* **£150**

△ **INDIAN ARMY SABRE** *with scabbard, probably issued to the Mountain Artillery. The design of the blade, which was made in Sheffield, dates from 1796. An original scabbard, as here, always increases the value of a piece considerably. 1915; 3ft long.* **£150**

▷ **SILVER-HILTED SMALLSWORD** *Although smallswords could be used if the need arose, they were primarily fashion accessories. The guard of the solid-silver hilt (below) bears an inscription from the 1745 Jacobite rebellion: 'Carried for his Prince by Patrick Fea of Airie 1746'. Such a provenance adds greatly both to the historical interest and the value of a weapon, giving the 'human dimension' collectors seek. The blade is damaged; if it were not, the sword would be worth in the region of £1,000. 1730; 3ft long.* **£400**

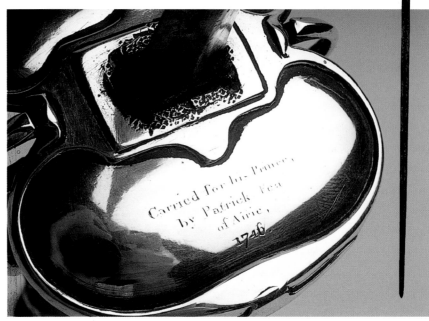

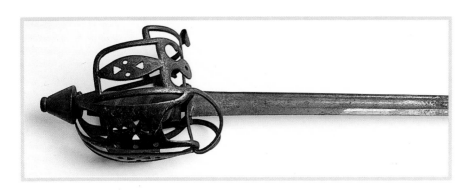

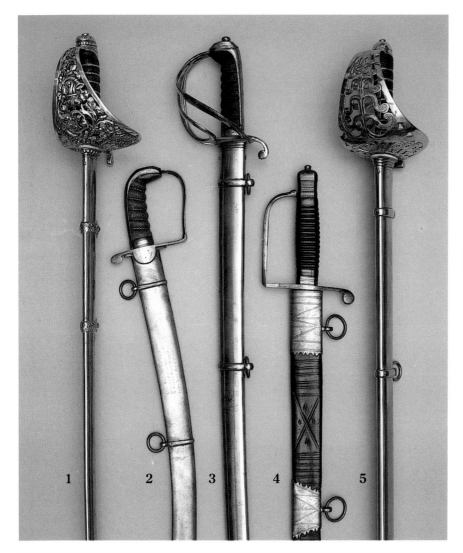

◁ **SCOTTISH BASKET-HILTED BACKSWORD** *This typically Scottish sword was probably made for use by a Highland Militia Regiment and is of very basic (or 'munitions') quality. Nevertheless the guard would have offered excellent protection for the user's hand. 1750; 3ft 9in long.* **£300**

HILT DEVELOPMENT

Hilts evolved from a simple bulb with a bar over the knuckles to the all-encompassing hand guard.

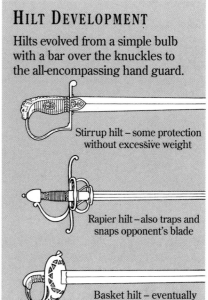

Stirrup hilt – some protection without excessive weight

Rapier hilt – also traps and snaps opponent's blade

Basket hilt – eventually became solid guard

◁ **BRITISH OFFICERS' SWORDS** *for Infantry (1) and Cavalry (2–5), all in good condition, with original scabbards.*
1 *1822; 2ft 11in long.* **£825**
2 *1770; 2ft 10in long.* **£390**
3 *1821; 2ft 11in long.* **£260**
4 *1796; 2ft 10in long.* **£375**
5 *1878; 2ft 8in long.* **£2,500**

▽ **PAIR OF CHINESE SHORTSWORDS** *These two swords fit into the same scabbard, which is covered with dyed and polished sharkskin (called shagreen), also used to cover sword grips. The set may have been captured by a soldier in the T'ai P'ing Campaign of the 1860s. 1850; 23in long.* **£75 – £100**

1   2   3   4   5

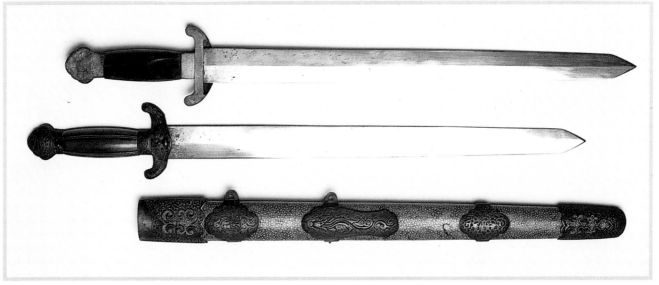

ARMS & MILITARIA

183

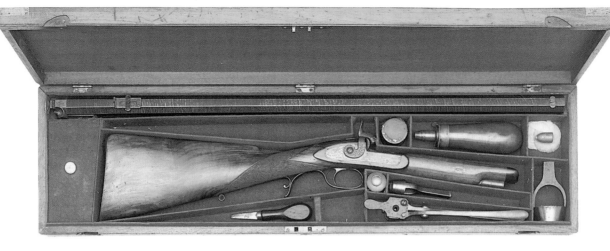

The earliest firearms were ignited by a length of smouldering cord (the match) which the firer blew on to keep alight. This created smoke which game could sense long before the hunter came into range. The invention of the wheel-lock in the 16th century helped to solve this problem. In a wheel-lock mechanism, the wheel is turned against a spring, and released by the trigger to produce sparks that ignite the powder in the pan. This meant that the gun could be wound and primed, ready for any game that might appear.

At around the same time, it was discovered that twisted grooves cut along a barrel's interior gave a spin to the bullet, making its trajectory far more accurate. This was known as rifling and, when combined with the wheel-lock around 1550, it produced

▽ **RARE GERMAN 22-BORE PERCUSSION GUN-RIFLE** signed 'Stoermer, Herzberg'. *The two pairs of interchangeable barrels mean it could be used as a shotgun or rifle, depending on the game being hunted. 1830; 3ft 9in.* **£2,400**

the first viable sporting weapon. The wheel-lock was expensive and complicated to make, however, which restricted its use to the nobility.

By about 1630 the flintlock, in which a flint strikes sparks from a metal plate to ignite the powder charge, was becoming more common, finding favour with sportsmen for its simplicity and quick action.

To shoot flying birds, the sportsman has to be able to aim and fire quickly, with only his shoulder on which to rest the gun. This required a well-balanced gun (which is not so important when shooting deer, for example, when the sportsman can line up his target). Here, English makers from the late 18th to the mid 19th centuries excelled. The names John and Joseph Manton, John Twigg, James Purdey and Henry Nock are synonymous with fine sporting guns.

The flintlock, however, was prone to misfire in damp weather and its flash often made birds swoop away. In response, Alexander Forsyth developed the percussion system, which uses a disposable metal cap

△ **12-BORE PERCUSSION DEER-STALKING RIFLE** signed 'H. Clive' and cased with accessories. *The coming of the railways opened places like Scotland to English hunters. Increasingly, guns were cased for protection. 1845; 3ft 9in.* **£900 – £1,000**

▷ **ELEGANT FLINTLOCK SPORTING GUN** signed 'William Ryan & Son, Birmingham'. *There is a certain snob value about London-made guns, but this good piece proves that gunmakers in Birmingham were just as capable of producing fine work. 1825; 4ft 2in.* **£1,250**

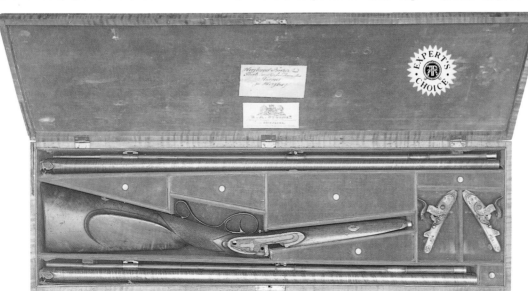

△ **12-Bore Double-Barrelled Shotgun** *made in Birmingham, but retailed by Banks of Chippenham, a ship's chandler rather than a gunsmith. Of poor quality, it would probably have been used by a gamekeeper, not a sportsman. 1880; 3ft 11in.* **£50**

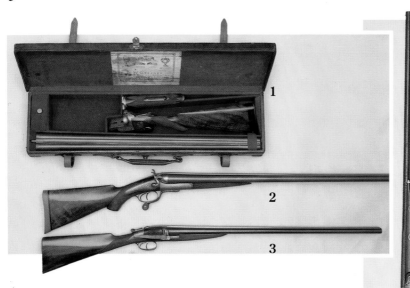

△ **Double-Barrelled Guns** *for coastal wildfowling (1 – 2), made in London and Liverpool, and a Gye & Moncrieff patent design (3). 1880s.* **1** *3ft 11in* **£1,000;** **2** *4ft 8in* **£800;** **3** *4ft* **£450**

▽ **Percussion Guns and Rifles** *The English guns (1, 2, 3, 5) are by Moore & Woodward, Rigby, Blanch, and Nock. The Belgian gun (4) is by Lassence-Rong; the Swiss gun (6) is by Paul. 1840.* **1** *3ft 6in* **£800;** **2** *3ft 10in* **£1,800;** **3** *3ft 10in* **£425;** **4** *3ft 10in* **£650;** **5** *3ft 9in* **£500;** **6** *3ft 11in* **£950**

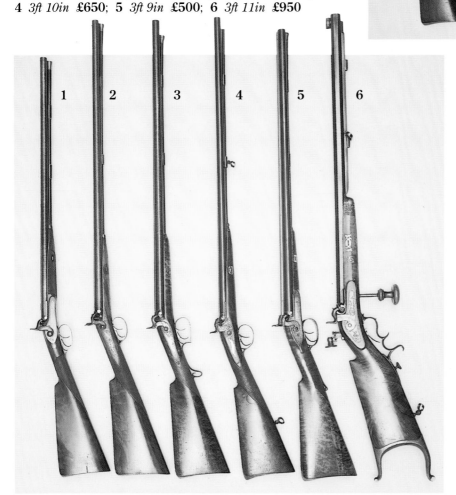

△ **Five Sporting Guns** *The percussion guns (1 – 3) are by three of the most important English makers: Ezekiel Baker, Joseph Manton and Durs Egg (actually John Egg using his famous father's name). The English flintlock (4) is by Heathcote; the Austrian flintlock (5) is for shooting fowl. 1760 – 1860.* **1** *4ft 1in* **£450;** **2** *4ft* **£700;** **3** *3ft 8in* **£825;** **4** *4ft 1in* **£1,250;** **5** *4ft 3in* **£650**

containing solid explosive. This was weatherproof, and from around 1820 was the favourite method of ignition.

Percussion caps paved the way for breechloading guns which gave sportsmen a much greater rate of fire as powder, shot wadding and cap were combined in a single weatherproof cartridge. Since this was slipped into the breech, rather than rammed down from the muzzle, it was safe to use and easy to load and unload.

There is little difference between sporting guns made today and those made 100 years ago. Such guns are prized for their simple elegance, perfect balance and exquisite craftsmanship, and English gunmakers are still the leaders in the field.

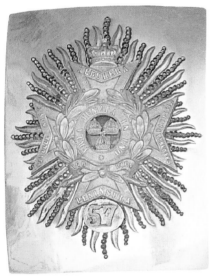

UNIFORM ACCESSORIES

Metal helmet badges and other accessories associated with military uniforms have been used for purposes of identification, decoration and fastening since the end of the 17th century. It was at this date that the regular or 'standing' armies of Europe were raised, and soldiers' uniforms, complete with accoutrements, were first produced in large numbers.

Military accessories date from before the introduction of uniforms, however. In medieval times, soldiers wore their own clothing on campaign and showed their allegiance to their leader by wearing his badge on their coats. These were usually derived from the nobleman's coat of arms. For example, Richard III's men took a white boar as their symbol.

The badge system was outlawed by Henry VIII in an effort to emphasize the national character of his army and prevent civil war. Henceforth soldiers were only permitted to wear the red cross of St George. The first uniform coats also appeared during the reign of Henry VIII. When England invaded France in 1544, records state that soldiers of the 'Vaward' (forward division of the army) were identified by coats of 'blew clothe garded [trimmed] red'; those of the 'Battell' (main division of the army) wore red and yellow, while those of the 'Rearward' (rear guard) wore blue and yellow. The first British soldiers to wear red uniform coats were Oliver Cromwell's 'New Model Army', raised in 1644, and red remained the dominant colour for British Army uniforms for the next 250 years.

The tradition of associating

△ SILVER LACE 'WING' EPAULETTES, *or shoulder badges, for an officer of the Light Infantry Company of the 5th Royal Lancashire Militia. They bear the hunting, or bugle-horn, emblem that has long been associated with the Light Infantry. 1840s; 7in wide.* **£250**

▽ OFFICERS' SHOULDER BELT PLATES *of The 57th (West Middlesex) Regiment of Foot. The 57th gained its nickname – 'The Die-Hards' – for its fortitude during the Battle of Albuhera in 1811; it suffered 75% casualties. 1835; 3in high.* **£300 – £350**

▷ **1** OFFICER'S GILT SHAKO PLATE *of the 2nd West India Regiment. A shako is a tall felt or leather hat, standard army issue by 1800. 1869; 4in high.* **£125**
2 OFFICER'S COPPER SHAKO PLATE *of the Royal Honduras Militia. 1811 – 20; 4in high.* **£140**
3 OFFICER'S SILVER BELT BADGE *of the 1st Warwickshire Rifle Volunteers. 1863; 4in high.* **£100**

1 2 3

▽ **19TH CENTURY OFFICERS' INSIGNIA** *including two helmet plates of The 20th (East Devonshire) Regiment (3 & 5) dating from 1844 and 1878. In 1881 the 20th became The Devonshire Regiment, and Exeter Castle was added to the badge (6 & 8). (All badges shown are 3 to 4 inches high.)*

1 *Gilt star shako plate of the Royal Bucks Militia, 1829 – 44.* **£370**

2 *Gilt helmet plate of the Lanarkshire Yeomanry, 1857.* **£320**

3 *Gilt shako plate of The 20th (East Devonshire) Regiment, 1844.* **£460**

4 *Gilt helmet plate of The 11th (North Devon) Regiment, 1878.* **£140**

5 *Gilt helmet plate of The 20th (East Devonshire) Regiment, with a silver-plated sphinx at the foot, 1878.* **£130**

6 *Silver-plated helmet plate of the 3rd Volunteer Battalion, The Devonshire Regiment, 1880s.* **£170**

7 *Frosted gilt shoulder belt plate of The 20th (East Devonshire) Regiment, pre-1855.* **£160**

8 *Gilt helmet plate of The Devonshire Regiment, 1880s.* **£180**

9 *Frosted gilt shoulder belt plate of The 88th (Connaught Rangers) Regiment, with green enamel centre, pre-1855.* **£310**

regiments with particular counties was introduced in 1881; before this regiments were simply given a number. The regimental emblem formed the helmet plate, or cap badge, and was often repeated on epaulettes, shoulder belt plates (worn from the late 18th century until 1855) and the waist belt plates that replaced them, and buttons.

Accessories worn by officers were always of much higher quality than those issued to lower ranks. Officers' badges are generally gilt or silver and sometimes enamelled, while lower ranking badges were made of brass. Furthermore, while accessories such as pouches, belts and epaulettes made for officers often incorporated gold or silver wire woven into lace or braids, those for private soldiers were less well made and far more utilitarian.

Military accessories are a popular and diverse field for collectors, suitable for both the beginner on a small budget and the enthusiast interested in a particular regiment or campaign.

◁ **BELT PLATE** *for a cavalry officer of a Dragoon Guard Regiment. Gilt and silver-plated, it bears the royal cipher and motto flanked by oak leaves and acorns. 1860; 4in wide.* **£100**

◁ **GILT AND SILVER BELT PLATE** *for an Indian Army officer of the 6th Regiment. The star below the emblem is silver plate. Indian Army militaria is always sought after, which accounts for the high value of this piece. Mid 19th century; 4in wide.* **£310**

△ **SHOULDER BELT OVAL** *of the Chiswick Armed Association, mounted with a watercolour of a private soldier. Volunteer corps were formed by patriotic citizens for home defence during the Napoleonic emergency. 1802 – 10; 19in high.* **£270**

Bill Harriman is a consultant on firearms and a restorer of antique weapons.

COLLECTOR'S CHECKLIST

ARMS & MILITARIA

The diverse field of 'Arms and Militaria' is more susceptible to faking than any other category of antiques. Anyone starting a collection should be acutely aware of this problem and try to gain as much experience as possible of handling or viewing genuine pieces.

Although the sheer range of arms and militaria can be bewildering at first, for your collection to have a substantial resale value, it is best to specialize at an early stage. Try to resist the temptation to amass an eclectic collection of pieces, as a thematic rather than a miscellaneous collection invariably fetches a higher price. In addition, it is always worth buying at the top end of the market if you can afford it, since five first-rate examples represent a better

△ RIBAND, BADGE, STAR AND COLLAR *of the Knight Grand Cross of the Order of St Michael and St George. 19th century; badge 3in wide.* **£3,000**

investment than 10 mediocre pieces.

Once you have decided on a theme for your collection, don't start buying immediately. Instead, spend some time acquiring a good library and visit national collections to get a 'feel' for the subject.

It is also a good idea to meet fellow collectors by joining a specialist society. Only make purchases when this groundwork has been done, preferably from a reputable dealer who should provide written particulars for every piece you buy, in case you should ever need verification. Auctions are the next step, but you should carefully examine any piece you are interested in before bidding, as fakes abound. Once your collection has begun to grow, it is important to have it insured, recording each item with written descriptions as well as photographs.

In general, it is only worth purchasing firearms which are worth at least £100 each. The resale value of any firearm will be drastically reduced if it has been 'refinished' – either by tampering with or replacing the moving parts or by overcleaning and polishing the metal until it becomes very shiny. A genuine old patination is

POINTS TO WATCH FOR

1 Until proven otherwise, assume that a firearm is loaded and never point a gun at anyone.

2 Metal that has been artificially aged with chemicals often has an acidic, vinegary odour.

3 When buying helmet plates, cap badges and buttons, make sure that you are acquiring an antique piece rather than a modern 'restrike' from an old mould.

4 In the 1820s, '30s and '40s old flintlock guns were frequently converted to percussion cap ignition, and many of these have recently been reconverted to the flintlock mechanism. Check the locks of such weapons carefully for new castings of original parts; they may look fresh and unpitted considering their supposed age.

5 Beware of 'composite' swords comprising mismatched blades and hilts. They can often be identified by new hammer marks on the pommels and an uneven joint between hilt and blade. In addition, the blade should align with the hilt in a straight line, and a good quality sword has a balanced feel.

6 Large numbers of replicas of rare swords and bayonets have been made in India in recent years. These can be identified by their crude etching, modern leather grips and poorly tempered blades.

7 Third Reich daggers are perhaps the most faked items of all in this field. Faking began immediately after World War II, using old stock from arms factories.

8 Many cutlery cases have been adapted to house pistol sets. They are usually shallower and less sturdy than the genuine articles.

9 Beware of accurate photocopies or laser prints of old trade labels.

10 Always be suspicious of rare pieces that appear to be in very good condition for their age.

△ HOLSTER PISTOL *issued to cavalry of the Honourable East India Company. The H.E.I.C. lion crest can be seen on the lockplate. 1840; 15in long.* **£400**

much sought after by collectors.

The standard of faked firearms can be very high – good enough to fool even experienced collectors – but one of the giveaway signs on some modern replicas is a visible dip along the length of the barrel or frame. This may signify that the modern proof marks (indented stamps, including a date mark) have been filed down to disguise the weapon's true age.

Fake swords are generally easier to spot than fake firearms, since the overall workmanship is often crude. In addition, swords without scabbards are always cheaper than mint examples, and fairly good pieces can be bought for around £100.

CARE & REPAIR

1 Never clean steel with emery paper; use fine steel wool soaked in a light oil, such as sewing machine oil.

2 Clean gunstocks with fine steel wool soaked in methylated spirits, and finish with boiled linseed oil.

3 Prevent the rusting and corrosion of metal parts by coating with light oil or vaseline.

4 Never use commercial metal polish on nickel-silver or brass, since the abrasive powder looks unsightly if caught in the grooves of a piece. A saturated solution of table salt in vinegar is a much better cleaning agent.

5 Never 'snap' or 'dry-fire' (fire without any powder) the action of a flintlock or percussion weapon, as this mechanism is easily broken.

6 Uniform fabrics and paper ephemera fade easily and should not be exposed to sunlight.

7 Leather benefits from periodic applications of hide food. Finish off with a gentle application of boot polish using a soft cloth.

8 Many specialist stockists of arms and militaria sell cheap and accurate replacement gun parts. While these should not be passed off as the original fittings, they can enhance the appearance and value of a piece.

◁ **WORLD WAR I MILITARY MEMORABILIA** *from a collection formed by the present owner's great-grandfather, who was a sergeant. 1914 – 18; photograph 7in high.* The collection **£75**

◁ **IMPERIAL GERMAN PIPE BOWL** *commemorating Reservist Infantry Regiment No. 173. It was mass produced and then marked individually with the name of a soldier. 1909 – 11; 6in long.* **£125**

CONDITION & QUALITY

The two words most widely misused and least understood in the Arms and Militaria field are 'condition' and 'quality'.

Condition refers to the state of preservation of an artefact, while the quality is a combination of the standard of materials used and the skill of the craftsmen who used them. Thus, it is perfectly possible to have a poor quality item in fine condition and vice versa.

PLACES OF INTEREST

Imperial War Museum, London SE1 *Displays of 20th century warfare*
Royal Armouries, HM Tower of London *Arms & armour*
Scottish United Services Museum, Edinburgh Castle *History of Scottish armed forces*

THE STATE OF THE MARKET

In recent years, the cheaper end (under £50) and the quality section (£2,000 or more) of the Arms and Militaria market has remained stable, while the range in between has suffered sudden fluctuations. This is due not solely to economic factors but also to restrictive legislation.

The Firearms (Amendment) Act of 1988 caused a great deal of uncertainty among collectors, who feared that it would soon be illegal to sell even antique firearms. Further legislation has banned the sale of weapons such as knuckleduster knives, swordsticks and blowpipes made after 1900. In order to possess most cartridge-loading guns, you need a Firearms Certificate – specialist dealers can advise collectors about individual weapons.

◁ **'GUN MONEY' COIN,** *so-called because when James II came to Ireland he had to have his cannons melted down in order to make coins to pay his troops. 1689; 1½ in wide.* **£30**

PICTURE ACKNOWLEDGEMENTS

We wish to thank the following individuals and organizations for loaning photographs for use in this book.

b = bottom; c = centre; l = left; r = right; t = top

David Battie: 96 tl, tr, c, b; 97 t, c, bl, br; 100 cl; 101 t;103 tr, b; 105 tr; 108 t, c, b; 109 t, c; 115 tl, tr, c, bl.
Bridgeman Art Library: 40 bl; 99 bl; 111 tr; 158 bl. Christie's Colour Library: 19 tl; 20 t; 136 b; 137 t, c.
© DACS 1992: 128 t, bl, br; 129 tl, tr, cl, cr, bl. Angelo Hornak Library: 124 bl.
Robert Opie Collection: 74 c; 75 tl, c. Strike One (Islington) Ltd: 139 t, bl, br.
Wallis & Wallis: 183 c; 184 t, b; 185 cl, cr, b; 186 t, cl, cr, b; 187 t, cl, cr, b.